Everyman, I will go with thee,
and be thy guide

Edmund Spenser

SHORTER POEMS
A SELECTION

Edited by
JOHN LEE
University of Bristol

EVERYMAN
J. M. DENT · LONDON
CHARLES E. TUTTLE
VERMONT

Introduction, notes and other critical material copyright
© J. M. Dent 1988

This edition first published in Everyman Paperbacks
in 1998

J. M. Dent
Orion Publishing Group
Orion House, 5 Upper St Martin's Lane,
London WC2H 9EA
and
Charles E. Tuttle Co., Inc.
28 South Main Street,
Rutland, Vermont 05701, USA

Typeset in Sabon by SetSystems Ltd, Saffron Walden, Essex
Printed in Great Britain by
The Guernsey Press Co. Ltd, Guernsey, C.I.

British Library Cataloguing-in-Publication Data
is available upon request.

ISBN 0 460 87683 X

To my father, Dr V. J. Lee

ACKNOWLEDGEMENTS

This Everyman edition of Spenser's shorter poems is indebted to the work of previous editors, and in particular the editors of the Johns Hopkins Variorum edition. Where the Everyman edition draws on the work of more recent editors, I have tried to acknowledge the debt. Thanks are also owed to the knowledge and kindness of colleagues and friends: Pippa Bagguley, Richard Beard, Myrna Blumberg, George Donaldson, Helen Lucas, John Lyon, Andrew Marland and Mike Pincombe.

CONTENTS

NOTE ON THE AUTHOR AND EDITOR

EDMUND SPENSER was born during the years 1552–4, probably in London. His father may have been a clothier; the family were of modest means, and Spenser went as a poor scholar first to Merchant Taylors' School and then, in 1569, to Pembroke Hall, Cambridge. This year saw the publication of some verse translations.

After university, Spenser became the secretary in turn to Bishop Young, the Earl of Leicester and, in 1580, to Lord Grey, Lord Governor of Ireland. Ireland became his home, and after Grey left he continued to serve the English Government in various capacities, which from 1586 on involved him in the colonization of his 3,000-acre estate in Munster.

His poetry is intimately bound up with his politics and social aspirations. His importance as a poet was assured with his ground-breaking *The Shepherds' Calendar* (1579). Travelling to London and the court with Sir Walter Ralegh in 1589, he won the Queen's favour with *The Faerie Queene*. *Complaints* (which included the Ovidian *Muiopotmos*) was published in the wake of this public success.

Colin Clout's Come Home Again, an ambivalent account of the journey to London, followed in 1595. *Amoretti and Epithalamion*, in part a celebration of his second marriage (to Elizabeth Boyle), was published in the same year. 1596 saw the next three books of *The Faerie Queen*, and also *Prothalamion*, a betrothal poem.

In 1598 his estate was overrun in one of the frequent Irish rebellions. He took refuge in Cork. As Sheriff of the city, he took a letter detailing what had happened to the Privy Council in London. About a month later he died in Westminster, on 13 January. He was buried in the Abbey at the expense of the Earl of Essex.

JOHN LEE is a Lecturer in English Literature at the University of Bristol. His publications include articles on Greek tragedy, Tudor and modern poetry, and critical theory.

CHRONOLOGY OF SPENSER'S LIFE

Year	Life
1552/4	Born, probably in London; father probably a clothier, family of modest means
1561(?)	At Merchant Taylors' School, London
1569	Contributes verse translations to van der Noodt's *A Theatre for Worldings*; enters Pembroke Hall, Cambridge, as a poor scholar
1570	Friendship with Gabriel Harvey
1573	Graduates BA, 11th out of 120
1576	Graduates MA, 66th out of 70
1577	Perhaps in Ireland at beginning of July
1578	Secretary to John Young, Bishop of Rochester, in Kent In London by December
1579	At Leicester House in October; acquainted with Philip Sidney and John Dyer Marries, probably to Machabyas Chylde on 27 October; two children: Sylvanus and Katherine *The Shepherds' Calendar* entered for publication on 5 December in the Stationers' Register

CHRONOLOGY OF HIS TIMES

Year	Literary Context (England)	Historical Context
1553		Mary I's accession
1557	Richard Tottel, *Miscellany*	
1558		Elizabeth I's accession
1559	*A Mirror for Magistrates*	
1563	Barnabe Googe, *Eclogues, Epitaphs and Sonnets*	
1565–7	Arthur Golding, Ovid's *Metamorphoses*, trans.	
1569		The Red Lion built in London (first purpose-built English playhouse)
1570		Elizabeth excommunicated by the Pope
1572		St Bartholomew's Day Massacre
1573	George Gascoigne, *A Hundred Sundry Flowers*	
1575	Thomas Churchyard, *The First Part of Churchyard's Chips*	
1577		Grindal, Archbishop of Canterbury, suspended from office
1579		Jesuits begin coming to England
1579 & 1581		Elizabeth considers marrying the Duc d'Alençon, a moderate French Catholic

Year   *Life*

1580   Secretary to Lord Grey, Lord Governor of Ireland at £20 a year[1];
            arrives Ireland in August
            Almost certainly witnesses siege of Smerwick in October and
            November; this ends with massacre of 600 Italian and Spanish
            soldiers
            Spenser-Harvey correspondence published in December
1581   Appointed Clerk of Faculties in Irish Court of Chancery (sells
            post in 1588)
            Second edn of *The Shepherds' Calendar*
1582   Leases New Abbey, Co. Kildare for £3 a year
            Lord Grey leaves Ireland; Spenser's secretaryship ends

1583   Appointed Commissioner for Musters in Co. Kildare for two
            years
1584   Probably serving as secretary to Lodowick Bryskett, Clerk of
            Munster, at £7 10s. a year
1586   Involved in Munster plantation
            Third edn of *The Shepherds' Calendar* pubd
1587   Serving as Bryskett's deputy

1588   Friendship with Ralegh

1589   In possession of Kilcolman, a 3,000-acre estate in Munster; £20
            a year rent; establishes colony of six householders; legal disputes
            with Lord Roche
            At end of year travels to England with Ralegh; private audience
            with Queen Elizabeth
1590   *The Faerie Queene*, Books 1–3 pubd

1591   Granted pension of £50 a year by Elizabeth
            Complaints (including *Muiopotmos*, *Daphnaida* and 4th edn of
            The Shepherds' Calendar pubd
            Probably returns to Ireland

1. A schoolmaster earned around £20 a year at the turn of the century.

Year	Literary Context (England)	Historical Context
1579–83		Desmond rebellion in Ireland
1580	Philip Sidney, *Astrophel and Stella* (pubd 1591) and *Apology for Poetry* (pubd 1595)	
1582		Plague devastates Cork; famine in Munster
1582–92	Sir Walter Ralegh's poems written	
1584		Sir Walter Ralegh founds first English colony in America
1586		Sir Philip Sidney dies
1587	Christopher Marlowe, *1 Tamburlaine*	Mary Queen of Scots executed
1588	William Byrd, *Psalms, Sonnets and Songs*	Spanish Armada defeated Leicester dies
1589	George Puttenham, *The Art of English Poetry* Thomas Kyd, *Spanish Tragedy*	Civil War in France
1590	William Shakespeare, *Two Gentlemen of Verona*	
1591	Sir John Harington, Ariosto's *Orlando Furioso*, trans.	Proclamation against Jesuits
1592	Samuel Daniel, *Delia*	June: plague closes London theatres for two years
1593	William Shakespeare, *Venus and Adonis* Christopher Marlowe, *Hero and Leander* Michael Drayton, *Idea*	

Year   *Life*

1594   Appointed Queen's Justice for County Cork
        Marries Elizabeth Boyle on 11 June; one son, Peregrine

1597   *The Faerie Queene*, Books 4–6, *Prothalamion, Four Hymns* and
        second edn of *The Faerie Queene* pubd

1598   *A View of the Present State of Ireland* registered for publication
        in April (pubd 1633)
        Rebellion in Ireland breaks out in June; Kilcolman burnt on 15
        October; Spenser and family take refuge in Cork
        As Sheriff of Cork, delivers letter and *A Brief Note of Ireland* to
        Privy Council in London, probably on 24 December; paid £8
1599   Dies 13 January, and buried on 16 January in Westminster
        Abbey at Essex's expense

1609   Folio of *The Faerie Queene*
1611   Folio of *Works*

1617   Second Folio of *Works*
1620   Memorial to Spenser erected in Westminster Abbey by Ann
        Clifford

1679   Third Folio of *Works*

Year	Literary Context (England)	Historical Context
1594	William Shakespeare, *The Rape of Lucrece*	
1595	John Donne's poetry in circulation	Riots in London
1596		James VI of Scotland (and later James I of England) asks that Spenser be punished for the depiction of his mother, Mary, in *The Faerie Queene*, Book 5 Essex storms Cadiz
1597	John Dowland, *First Book of Songs* Francis Bacon, *Essays*	
1598	Ben Jonson, *Every Man in his Humour*	
1599		Essex fails in Ireland
1600	*England's Helicon* (anthology)	
1601	Samuel Daniel, *Works*	Essex rebels and is executed
1602		Tyrone defeated in Ireland
1603		James I's accession; Sir Walter Ralegh found guilty of treason and imprisoned
1604		Peace with Spain
1605		Gunpowder plot
1616	Ben Jonson, Folio *Works*	
1623	William Shakespeare, Folio *Plays*	

INTRODUCTION

'Small good to one who had by Mulla's stream/Fondled the maidens with the breasts of cream.'[1]

In this way a twenty-year-old John Keats characterized the lack of attractions of his own poetry. What interest could the reader find in Keats's poetry, he asks, knowing Spenser's? For the maidens are Spenser's, found by one of the rivers that run through his shorter poems.

To Keats, as to most of his Romantic contemporaries, Spenser was above all a sensuous poet, the creator of a timeless, dream-like otherworld, of such imaginative abundance in its language and imagery that its experience was akin to an erotic pleasure. This Spenser is seen most clearly in this edition in *Muiopotmos: Or, the Fate of the Butterfly* (1591). The poem is a delicate and dazzling achievement. The tone is light, shifting and playful. It begins in high epic style, with the narrator calling on the Muse of tragedy, Melpomene, for the inspiration to tell the sad story of Clarion. Yet once Clarion is known to be a butterfly, the tone is revealed as that of mock-epic. But not consistently or for long; the poem does not survive on the comedy and lessons of proportion that are the staple of mock-epic. Though a butterfly, Spenser's Clarion *is* princely, the reader following him as he ranges through the skies, 'lord of all the works of nature' he surveys, 'feeding upon their pleasures bounteously'. There is grandeur of imaginative vision here that approaches the sublime, and it is tempting to see Clarion as the imagination itself, playfully ranging from heaven to earth and flower to flower, feeding on one pleasure after another. The poem is, it turns out, a celebration of the variety of the beauties of life. 'What more felicity can fall to creature,' the narrator asks, 'Than to enjoy delight with liberty?' Keats made the question the epigraph to his first (1817) volume of poetry.

Yet delight and liberty, it seems, cannot last; the poem is also a recognition of, and lament for, mutability. Within the garden of delights lurks a spider, Aragnoll, who traps and kills the innocent Clarion. Spenser's world is mythical and unreal, but it is not unrealistic. Spenser, as a mythmaker – following the Roman poet Ovid, who is perhaps the strongest single influence on this poem – understands myth to be a particular form of the enduring human attempt to make sense of the world. The critic Harold Bloom, invoking William Blake as a comparison, suggests that *Muiopotmos* be read as both a song of innocence and a song of experience.[2] Bloom's is a productive comparison, in its stress on the inclusiveness and complexity of Spenser's vision.

Keats's characterization of Spenser tends to omit Spenser's songs of experience; understandably so, as he – and most other Romantic writers – sought to show what particular qualities they valued in Spenser's poetry. The Romantic Spenser is, then, the sensuous Spenser. But Spenser is yet more sensuous, or perhaps sensual, than the Romantic period is usually willing to allow.[3] Keats's 'maidens with the breasts of cream' remembers a line from Spenser's *Epithalamion* (1595): 'Her breast like to a bowl of cream uncrudded.' In omitting the rare word 'uncrudded' (uncurdled), Keats omits both the intense physicality and the related pressure of time which are present in Spenser's poem; Spenser's celebration of the woman's beauty contains, and is motivated by, the recognition that her breast, in colour and texture, will curdle. This mixture of rich fantasy and desolating actuality – a sort of Elizabethan magic realism – creates an imaginative world far stranger for the reader than that suggested by Keats's homogeneous faery-land image of nymphs and rivers. That sense of strangeness may increase when it is realized that *Epithalamion* celebrates Spenser's marriage, in 1594, to his second wife, Elizabeth Boyle. The world of Spenser's poetry is constantly both shifting away from, and becoming part of, the everyday world.

One of the best known of such shifts comes in *Prothalamion* (1596), where the swans of the poem's first seven stanzas disappear to reappear as the brides of the final, tenth stanza (*birds* becoming *brides*). The swans, as much as the brides, are Elizabeth and Katherine Somerset, whose betrothal to Henry Guildford and William Petre the poem celebrates. Yet they are also angels, gliding down the 'silver streaming Thames', figures of the ideal world of God's unending love into which marriage, in Christian belief, offers mortal humankind an entry.

Such statements run the risk of banality: swans do not become angels, in any meaningful sense, simply by being described in terms of them, any more than the ideal world can be invoked simply by being named. In part the achievement of this transformation is, again, a question of the control of imagery and the richness of the language; but just as important is Spenser's musicality, his control of the sounds and rhythms of language. *Prothalamion*'s swans become angels, part of an ideal world, to the extent that their description, their embodiment in the language of the verse, is ideally harmonious – what the reader is willing to accept as sounding in some way angelic, beyond the range of everyday talking voices.

Spenser achieves this magnificently, both in general and especially in *Prothalamion*. Keats, a little further on in the poem with which we began, remembered how he learnt the 'sweets of song'; he names as his first teacher Spenser, whose vowels 'elope with ease,/And float along like birds o'er summer seas'. Coleridge, who prided himself on the sharpness of his poet's ear, found Spenser's control of metre and rhythm to be so subtle that it was 'painful' to unpick; *Prothalamion*'s 'swan-like movement' he thought 'exquisite'.[4] From vowels to words, on to lines, and up to stanzas, Spenser's melodies rarely falter or grate, and it is in his control of complex stanzas – *Prothalamion*'s movement is built up through 10 stanzas of 18 lines – that he is so distinctively excellent. Analysis of such musicality is difficult: large-scale features may be noted, such as the way in which he uses grammatical units sometimes to support and sometimes to counterpoint metrical units; or his remarkable facility with rhyme. However, the most convincing argument for Spenser's success in this area is the almost continuous praise of Spenser from subsequent poets.[5]

Such musicality is a matter of sense, as well as of sound. Reading *Prothalamion* aloud, the ear's attention is drawn to the refrain: 'Sweet Thames run softly till I end my song.' The line chimes out sweetly, its own rhythms running softly to the end of each stanza. As it recurs, its sound becomes a two-fold signal: like a rhyme, it directs the reader to look backwards and compare the stanza that is coming to a close with the preceding stanza; while at the same time it announces that a new stanza is about to begin. A refrain, the poem makes clear, is a kind of poetic New Year's Day, ringing out the old and ringing in the new.

The danger is that the line itself will become simply a pleasant structural signal, no more than a peal of bells; for repetition may just as easily hollow meaning out of a line as add significance to it. By placing the river in the refrain, Spenser avoids this danger. A river has a similar two-fold quality to a refrain. It has both cyclic and linear aspects, being constantly present and yet always flowing away; 'you can never,' said the Greek philosopher Heracleitus, 'step into the same river twice'.[6] It seems both a part of an ideal world, in which nothing changes, and of the actual world, where nothing remains the same. By placing the river in the refrain, the refrain's repetition becomes expressive of this two-fold aspect of the river's nature; while the river's two-fold nature gives meaning to the repetition. So the river, in its lyrical recurrence, is both the unchanging river of an ideal world in which white swans glide effortlessly to their destined marriages, and also the unstoppable river of time. The sound develops the sense, and the sense enriches the sound.

Moreover, the refrain continues to gather new meanings as it recurs. For this river is the Thames, a river that, as it runs through the London of the poem, becomes charged with the mercantile, nationalist and imperial aspirations of Elizabethan London and England, which themselves long for the trick of sustainable glory, the trick that had so memorably eluded Rome and Troy. So the refrain flows ever stronger and wider through the poem; and in ending the poem, it knows it cannot close it. This is apt both for a *Prothalamion* – a pre-wedding song which looks forward to a marriage to come – and for the imperial concerns which are by now bound up with the river Thames. It is this 'undersong', as Spenser terms it, that will flow out of the poem and down to the present century, flowing through Alexander Pope's 'Windsor Forest' (1713), under Conrad's sombre meditations on empire in *Heart of Darkness* (1902), and – emerging in direct quotation – into 'The Fire Sermon' of T. S. Eliot's *The Waste Land* (1922). This endurance and resonance, this ability to command attention and structure the thought of others through centuries, is a form of power; Spenser's poetry, through its complex and thoughtful musicality, has, at its height, this force.

'For why a God's name may not we, as else [also] the Greeks, have the kingdom of our own language?'

With this rather impatient question, Spenser the Elizabethan and national poet comes into sight. Spenser's question is specifically addressed to the rather recondite issue of whether quantitative verse is possible in English.[8] That issue, in turn, arises from the larger, now forgotten question of whether English is as capable a literary medium as Latin or Greek.⁹ Could a literature in English ever equal the achievements of Greece and Rome? Spenser believed it could, and, though his attempts at quantitative verse were lack-lustre, he had good reason for his confidence; for, with his first collection of verse, Spenser had given English poets, if not the kingdom of their own language, at least the keys to one of its gates.

The publication in 1579 of *The Shepherds' Calendar* marks the beginning of the great age of Elizabethan poetry. It contains, as its subtitle announces, 'twelve eclogues proportionable to the twelve months'. Only about half the volume is made up of poetry; the rest consists of critical commentary by one EK. (EK may be Spenser, or his friend Gabriel Harvey, a Fellow of Cambridge University; or possibly it might be another Cambridge Fellow, Edmunde Kirke. What is certain is that Spenser approved of EK's presence.) There are two introductory essays, and each poem is followed by a section of glosses. This critical commentary is printed in what was then a modern Italian font, so visually distinguishing it from the neo-Gothic black font of the poetry. It is a layout Elizabethan readers would have associated with scholarly editions of classical works; the modern equivalent would be a poet publishing his first work in the format of an Arden Shakespeare. By contrast, however, the volume's title, and its woodcuts, would have reminded Elizabethan readers of *The Calendar of Shepherds*, a hugely popular sixteenth-century translation of a low-brow French almanac, a kind of self-help manual of its day; and when the reader comes to read the scholarly glosses, they are found to be not only helpful and pedantic by turns (as is the way of glosses), but also sometimes misleading or incorrect . . .¹⁰

The Shepherds' Calendar intrigues, and it delights in doing so. There is an exuberance and daring about the ways in which it declares itself to be erudite, yet popular; of the past, yet present; and serious, yet playful. These qualities are most striking in the archaism of its language, 'the which,' as EK prophesied, 'of many things which in him be strange I know will seem the strangest'. Some have found it too strange. Sir Philip Sidney, though he singled out the *Calendar* as one of the very few – four – works of English poetry that had deserved praise (he was writing in 1580), felt that he 'dare not allow' Spenser's 'framing of his style to an old rustic language'.¹¹ Spenser's archaism is made up in part from his use of Chaucerian words. The novelty of this is sometimes overstated; there was, prior to *The Shepherds' Calendar*, an established if old-fashioned poetic diction which drew on Chaucer. Spenser renewed the currency of this diction. However, he also used many neo-Chaucerianisms, effectively creating new 'old' words, often by applying what he understood to be medieval inflections to Elizabethan words; and he also used many dialect words, refusing to be constrained by any London-based consensus as to what language should be. As Ben Jonson complained, 'Spenser, in affecting the ancients, writ no language.'[12] That, however, was the aim. Spenser's archaism is innovative, not reactionary. *The Shepherds' Calendar* draws on the past to create a new diction, a recognizably Spenserian language. Doing so, Spenser enriched literary English as a whole, opening up the native and dialect resources of the language at a time when most writers were anglicizing Latin and Greek words.

Such innovative archaism has generally led to Spenser's texts being left completely unmodernized.[13] There are valid arguments for such a stance; this edition, however, modernizes. The great general benefit of modernization is that it makes the text more immediately comprehensible and so more pleasant to read. The specific benefit, when applied to Spenser, is that a modernized edition is better able than an unmodernized edition to recreate the sense of strangeness so keenly felt by EK, Sidney and Jonson. Presented with unfamiliar spellings and a system of punctuation based around periods of speech instead of grammatical units, a modern reader loses the ability to differentiate between Elizabethan variation (which might itself be the result of the printer's, as opposed to Spenser's, preferences) and neo-Chaucerian innovation. Take the beginning of 'January' as an example:

> A Shepeheards boye (no better doe him call)
> When Winters wastful spight was almost spent,
> All in a sunneshine day, as did befall,
> Led forth his flock, that had bene long ypent.

Here, unmodernized, all of *The Shepherds' Calendar* appears archaic, and offers difficulties to the eye and ear as well. Modernized, however, the one blatant Chaucerianism – 'ypent' (penned) – stands out, while the lines read and scan without effort:

> A shepherd's boy (no better do him call),
> When winter's wasteful spite was almost spent,
> All in a sunshine day, as did befall,
> Led forth his flock that had been long ypent.

The sense of Spenser's language as 'strange' emerges more clearly as the different times and places of the poet's language make themselves felt. Difficulties of comprehension still remain; but then they were a part of the experience of the original edition, as the need for EK's glosses indicate.

Spenser's archaism serves many different purposes. Allied with the use of dialect, it falls naturally from the mouths of the rural, and sometimes rustic, shepherds who inhabit the eclogues. It creates a unique and flexible soundscape, and contributes to the musicality discussed above. Above all, its strangeness draws attention to the poem as an artifact within a poetic tradition – as do all the other intriguing details, along with their other different purposes. Nothing is simply to be read. The opening of 'January' goes on to introduce a shepherd's boy called Colin Clout. What of that? EK points out that this shepherd's name can also be found in the work of the English poet John Skelton (?1460–1529), and in an eclogue of the French poet Clément Marot (1496–1544). He suggests that Colin is Spenser's poetic persona, and so the equivalent of Tityrus, the famous persona of the Roman poet and writer of eclogues, Virgil (70–29 BC). If EK is here playing his role as the poem's literary memory honestly, then *The Shepherds' Calendar* is a remarkable synthesis of classical, European, and English traditions.[14]

As the poem progresses and it becomes clear that EK was correct, *The Shepherds' Calendar*'s intrigues look increasingly like self-advertisements. The poem is designed to be Spenser's *masterpiece*: that is, 'the piece of work by which a craftsman gained from his guild the recognized rank of "master"' (*OED2*). Spenser had other works written by 1579, some of which he later collected in *Complaints* (1591). Indeed, some ten years earlier, in his final year at school, he had been given the task of translating Clément Marot and another French poet, Joachim Du Bellay (1522–60), for Jan van der Noodt's *A Theatre for Worldings* (1569). None of this poetry, however, was suitable to establish his credentials as a master-poet. *The Shepherds' Calendar* is perfect for this task. It demonstrates a command of technique and tradition allied with an ability to innovate. The poem's dominant mode is pastoral, a mode previously barely attempted in English. In pastoral, shepherds meet and sit down – often in the shade of a tree; they talk briefly about the state of their flocks, before debating an issue, or holding a singing match; they sing in praise of their beloved, or their god; they lament the difficulties of love, or the death of one of their number; then afterwards, as evening draws in, they rise and begin to make their way home. This is Arcadia, where much is spoken and little happens, a landscape passed down and reshaped – and so in its Renaissance and literary sense 'imitated' – by poet after poet since the Greek poet, Theocritus (c. 316 BC – c. 260 BC) had first described it. His remembered countryside became Virgil's landscape of the imagination, an idyllic, literary world and yet, through allusion and allegory, also the world of the Roman Empire and its civil wars. The Italian poets Petrarch (1304–74) and Mantuan (1448–1516), had brought elements of harsh satire to this world, aimed particularly at the Church. As it developed through the centuries, Arcadia became, perhaps above all, the place where the poet goes to meet tradition. Spenser meets it on his own terms. *The Shepherds' Calendar* finds a place for all these different Arcadias in the variety of its eclogues (divided by EK into the three different kinds of 'plaintive', 'recreative', and 'moral'). It blends these with the influences of English poets such as Chaucer, Skelton and William Langland (c. 1367–86). This English Arcadia is a remarkably comprehensive and flexible literary landscape; and Spenser matched its variousness with a previously unseen variety of verse forms, which change from eclogue to eclogue, and sometimes even within eclogues. Doing so, he naturalizes pastoral, whose imagery would go on to dominate the Elizabethan lyric, and transforms the English literary landscape, making *The Shepherds' Calendar* also a poetic manifesto, the equivalent of Wordsworth's and Coleridge's *Lyrical Ballads* (1798).

The Shepherds' Calendar is, then, a self-consciously literary poem. It is, however, also a self-consciously political poem, as deeply engaged with the historical currents of its time as with literary tradition. The shepherds of this English Arcadia are also Elizabethan subjects, who sing odes 'purposely intended', as the April eclogue's introduction states, 'to the honour and praise of our most gracious sovereign, Queen Elizabeth'. Elizabeth becomes 'fair Elisa, queen of shepherds all', daughter of a god and a nymph, about whom, in awe, the sun and moon revolve. This praise may strike the reader as overblown and so lacking in seriousness, but it should not; for it is intimately bound up with the personal nature, and related political culture, of Elizabethan government. This was centred on the Court, where Elizabeth's great courtiers vied for the Queen's attention and favour as part of the continual process of maintaining their influence. The Court was thus in some ways, and at some times, a theatre, and during Elizabeth's reign conventions of behaviour and language developed to unprecedented lengths. Her courtiers behaved as if they were her lovers, devoted in service to their unattainable mistress; they praised her under the names of a variety of goddesses, each of which symbolized aspects of her political role or aspirations. Court politics and Court culture intermingled. 'April', in its praise of Elisa, is related to that culture. It offers a naturalized image of Elizabethan government, imagining the Queen and her rule as a part of the natural order of the cosmos, and as it does so it also makes clear the political power of Spenser's 'maidens with the breasts of cream'. To state that the Queen deserves support accomplishes little; such statements become persuasive and so gain power when they entice the listener to imagine their service to the Queen as an act of beauty – as the equivalent of strewing 'the ground with daffadowndillies;/ and cowslips, and kingcups, and loved lilies'.

Such an 'aestheticization of politics', to use Walter Benjamin's phrase in his description of a key element of German fascism, is likely to make the modern reader edgy.[15] Spenser, however, though clearly a supporter of Elizabeth, is no mouthpiece for Elizabethan propaganda. Rather, he praises in order to shape, and his Arcadia is not simply a refracted, allegorical, image of England as it is or as its rulers would wish it, but also an attempt to fashion a new England. This is clearest when the shepherds become clergymen (pastors of flocks of men) and the poem turns explicitly to religious issues. At first sight, the 'moral' eclogues' warnings against Roman Catholic priests and clergymen with Roman Catholic leanings may seem unexceptional; Elizabeth, after all, was supreme head of a Protestant Church of England. Spenser, however, uses the language of 'hot' or militant Protestantism, in which Roman Catholic priests are foxes and wolves who threaten good Protestant sheep. Militant Protestants, at their most extreme often labelled Puritans, sought both to reform the Church of England further and to pursue a more aggressive foreign policy in Europe in support of the Protestant cause.[16] Religion and politics are always a potent mix, and such militant Protestantism was deeply unwelcome to Elizabeth. Throughout her reign, she attempted to steer a middle way in religious matters, suppressing radicalism of all sorts. The movement towards further reformation from within the Church of England was effectively ended in 1577, when Elizabeth suspended Edmund Grindal, the Archbishop of Canterbury. Yet *The Shepherds' Calendar* not only uses the language and polemic of militant Protestantism, but both laments the silencing of Grindal (as the great shepherd Algrind, at the end of the July eclogue), and celebrates other clerics who share his beliefs. Indeed, it seems likely that the 'November' eclogue warns Elizabeth, now under the name of Dido, not to agree to marry the Catholic Duc d'Alençon. This was dangerous advice: John Stubbs had given Elizabeth similar advice directly in a pamphlet published earlier that year; it had cost him his right hand. *The Shepherds' Calendar* is not so much a reflection or expression of Elizabeth's England, in fact, as an argument with it, carried out on the grounds and terms of the poet's own choosing – Arcadia. This Arcadia is a political, social and religious synthesis every bit as much as it is a synthesis of literary traditions.

The literary historical importance of *The Shepherds' Calendar* passes unchallenged; not so the poem's ability to interest a modern reader. Typically, the acknowledgement that it is 'the first considerable poem of the Elizabethan age' is followed by the qualification that it is 'too engaged a work to have survived as a whole'.[17] The poem's intense awareness of its place in literary and political history contrives, it seems, to leave it stranded on a distant, footnoted Elizabethan shore (or, what is nearly the same, somewhere on a university course). Editions often agree with this opinion by printing only a few eclogues – 'January', 'April', 'October', 'November' and 'December' are the favourites to choose from. This edition, however, disagrees; it is as a whole that *The Shepherds' Calendar* survives to interest us today. For *The Shepherds' Calendar* is more than the sum of its parts and Blake's *Songs of Innocence and of Experience* are again a constructive parallel. Both poems use many-parted structures to set up dialogues between many different voices on many different issues, and so, as whole works, demonstrate a complexity of thought and inclusivity of perspective that goes far beyond that of any single part: as wholes, Spenser's and Blake's poems each seem almost to become – to paraphrase the title of a novel by the late George Perec – a user's manual to life. Yet in the very need to grasp these disparate and various works whole lies their difficulty.

The Shepherds' Calendar is above all a love poem; or, more accurately, a poem concerned with love. Love is explored through the poem's twelve-part structure. Colin Clout's unrequited love for Rosalind supplies the dominant narrative thread. This love is melancholy and oppressive, having taken away Colin's inspiration to sing anything other than the laments with which he begins, turns, and ends the year. The calendrical structure of the poem intertwines this narrative love with the rhythms of the seasons. As the eclogues pass, so the year turns. The barren ground of winter produces the buds that promise spring, which blossom into the flowers of summer and autumn, before withering as winter comes again: the shepherds carry out tasks appropriate to the seasons. Colin reads this progress as an analogue of his life: a carefree spring led to the loves of summer, which turned into autumn's frustrations and finally winter's cares. He finds a kind of sympathetic comfort in the discomforts of winter; while the summer's ease seems to mock his own unhappiness. Colin's love is thus set in a relationship with the natural world, whose changing variety the eclogues celebrate. Spenser's Arcadia, placed within a calendar, gains not only the sense of time's passage, from January to December, but also a sense of the eternal round, as December leads on to January, and the year begins anew. As in *Prothalamion*, the relationship between the finite world of man and the unchanging world of God is shadowed.

There are also other voices, and other loves within *The Shepherds' Calendar*. One of these voices is that of a younger Colin Clout. He is the writer of the ode in praise of Elisa which Hobbinol sings to Thenot in 'April', to show Thenot what the shepherds have lost by Colin's silence. A biography of Colin builds among the poem's different perspectives. 'October' finds Piers and Cuddie discussing the poor present state of poetry. Cuddie complains at the poet's lack of reward. Piers reminds him of the reward of fame, and of the importance of poetry, with its ability to fashion the age. If he wants more practical, immediate rewards, Cuddie should move on from writing in the humble genre of pastoral, and write epic poetry celebrating his Queen and her great nobles. The model for such a progression, and such a happy career, is the Roman poet of empire, Virgil. If Cuddie cannot match him, Colin can. Biography is here developing into autobiography; Colin the shepherd is becoming also Colin the poetic persona of Spenser (a possibility EK had alerted us to in 'January'). Spenser, with *The Shepherds' Calendar*, has begun his career as Virgil was thought to have done, by publishing a collection of eclogues. Spenser writes to reform, and, as Colin, for his Queen; he has an epic in hand. With this calendar, history itself is shown recurring, as Spenser declares his attempt to emulate Virgil, announcing his first step towards becoming the national poet, the poet laureate. (This is another innovation, poetry at this time being considered a rather trifling occupation, to be left behind with one's youth.) Love, meanwhile, is now a political emotion, the love of – in a monarchy – queen and country. Such love tends to be generally

unfashionable and untalked-about at present; it lacks intellectual
credibility. But it is a widespread and manipulable emotion, and
central to the political workings of a nation state, a concept which
the Tudors did much to develop. In *The Shepherds' Calendar* all
these different loves blur into one another, in the complex way that
they do in life. Personal love, in Colin the shepherd's case, seems to
make him forget the service of his Queen, the love of whom provides
a surer inspiration and guide to true poetry. His ode to the queen of
shepherds has already passed from his own hands, and has become a
valued possession of his community, entertaining them and shaping
their habits of thought. Yet love is also the fun, bawdy and cupidic
pleasure of 'March', which blows away the cobwebs of winter for
the shepherds' boys, Willye and Tomalin. Such delight leads on, in
'May', to the question of love's morality, and its relation to estab-
lished religion. Palinode asks Piers why they, as clergymen, should
not join in and enjoy the pleasures and games of love. This argument
shows one of Spenser's finest qualities, and one which unites him
with another fervently Protestant poet and writer of pastoral and
epic – John Milton. Like Milton, Spenser has the imaginative
sympathy and breadth of mind to understand to the full the attrac-
tions of what he believes to be evil. Palinode's arguments in favour
of pleasure are not dismissed, but remain deeply attractive, and are
perhaps more persuasive than Pier's arguments for the virtues of a
more ascetic life. The balance is intriguing, and the debate hangs in
the balance, unresolved. It is quite possible to feel that Spenser is of
the Devil's party without knowing it, as Blake described the Milton
of *Paradise Lost*. Or rather, that Spenser's response when he does
realize his 'error' – to slip from poet to pedagogue and finish the
eclogue off with the crudely 'hot' Protestant fable of the Fox and the
Kid – cannot close down the possibilities he has set in motion.

Love, then, is no one constant or simple thing within *The Shep-
herds' Calendar*. It is many-faceted and unstable, private and public,
changing with time, and place, and person. It offers to fulfil and it
offers dangers. *The Shepherds' Calendar* builds to a complex under-
standing of its breadth and instability by the structural principles of
variation, opposition and repetition. Each eclogue only exists fully in
relation to every other, and together they aspire to comprehensive-
ness. At the end of 'December', the poet steps outside the pastoral
world; 'Lo,' he declares, 'I have made a calendar for every year,/That
steel in strength and time in durance [endurance] shall outwear.'

*

The Shepherds' Calendar was an immediate success, going through five editions during Spenser's lifetime. Such success breeds interest; how, we might wonder, did Spenser feel? Did success change him in any way? For the first Elizabethan readers, there was another, more basic, question: what was this poet's name? Spenser had published *The Shepherds' Calendar* under the Latin pseudonym, 'Immerito'. *Three Proper and Witty Familiar Letters*, a volume of Spenser's and Harvey's correspondence, was designed to exploit and satisfy this interest. Published in 1580, and actually containing five letters, it left the true identity of Immerito unrevealed – though the keen-eyed would spot that the poet's first name was Edmund. The letters date from shortly before and shortly after the publication of *The Shepherds' Calendar*; in piecemeal fashion they tell a story of a nervous pre-debut poet turning into a confident literary figure. In the letter of October 1579, Spenser has only recently been convinced by Harvey to publish, and has only just arrived in the Earl of Leicester's household. Leicester was a powerful noble and the Queen's favourite; with Lord Burghley, he was at the heart of Elizabethan policy-making. He was also the greatest literary patron of his day. Rather breathlessly, Immerito tells Harvey that he hopes to carry out some business of the Earl's on the continent. Furthermore, Immerito has gained access to the literary circle based around the Earl; he is pleased to be able to tell Harvey that he is 'in some use of familiarity' with Sir Philip Sidney and Sir Edward Dyer. By the time of his letter of April 1580, things have changed. Sidney and Dyer are mentioned without comment, and Immerito is quite happy to augment Sidney's own judgement on matters of poetic theory. Spenser has arrived at the centres of Elizabethan literary and political life.

It is hard to know how accurate this picture is: *Three Proper and Witty Familiar Letters* is a carefully designed work of self-publicity, and all that is left of Spenser's life are the receipts of daily living, the various details of where he was, and when, and what he was doing. Spenser exists for us, and probably existed for his Elizabethan readers, mainly as a part and product of his works. That said, however, the excitement and satisfaction of Spenser's letters to Harvey seem justified from what we do know of his life. In arriving at Leicester's household, Spenser had risen greatly, though it could be said that he had not gone far. For he is thought to have been born in London, at some time in the years 1552–4, to a family of very moderate means. His mother was called Elizabeth, and his father was probably a clothier, a trade that allowed Spenser to be sent as a poor scholar to the Merchant Taylors' School, perhaps from the year of its foundation, 1561.[18] From there, he went up in 1569 to Pembroke Hall, Cambridge, as a 'sizar' – a scholar who paid his way by carrying out various servant's duties. (His portrait now hangs in the College's dining hall.) He gained his BA in 1573 and, after further study, his MA in 1576. By virtue of this university education, Spenser would now have been able to call himself a gentleman; for such poor gentlemen there was a relatively limited number of careers. Generally, they might teach, enter the clergy, or become private secretaries. Spenser became a secretary, a career that he would pursue, alongside and perhaps as part of his career as a poet, for the rest of his life.

On entering Leicester's household in 1579, Spenser had moved from the peripheries of Elizabethan society towards its centres. It is hard to imagine a more amenable position for him; Leicester's household not only offered him opportunities both as a secretary and a poet, but was also one of the most influential centres of English militant Protestantism. Leicester himself, as one of the key figures of this movement, was likely both to appreciate and offer protection to Spenser's own political and religious views. Spenser's aim of becoming a new Virgil must have seemed possible, and indeed, to an extent, he went on to achieve it. In 1590 he published the first three books of his romance epic, *The Faerie Queene*. This is a work that follows on in many ways from *The Shepherds' Calendar*, sharing many of the same aims, but realizing them on a far more magnificent scale. The epic, like the eclogues, is 'a continued allegory, or dark conceit', as Spenser described it in his prefatory letter to his friend, Sir Walter Ralegh. Its work is 'to fashion a gentleman or noble person in virtuous and gentle discipline'. England which had become Arcadia now became 'faery land', and Elisa its faery queen, by whom, Spenser says, 'I mean glory in my general intention, but in my particular I conceive the most excellent and glorious person of our sovereign the Queen.' *The Faerie Queene* is the great Elizabethan poem, and the greatest long poem of its century. It won Spenser the public recognition of his Queen's pleasure, and in 1591 Elizabeth awarded him an annual pension of £50, a sum which more or less tripled his annual salary.

Yet, at the same time, Spenser's life resembled more closely that of another Roman poet – Ovid, the poet of exile. For by the end of 1580, Spenser had left London and the Elizabethan Court. Accompanied by his wife (probably the Machabyas Chylde who married 'Edmounde Spenser' at St Margaret's church, Westminster, on 27

October 1579), he had gone to work as the secretary to Lord Grey, the Queen's Lord Deputy in Ireland. Ireland was a country very much on the peripheries of Elizabethan culture; it was a troublesome and dangerous land, refusing to submit either to English rule or English Protestantism, and offering Catholic powers a back door through which to attack England. Spenser's move from London to Ireland has often been taken as a sign that he had fallen into disfavour, perhaps by offending Leicester in some way. Such a fall is unlikely; Grey was the most important representative of the Queen in Ireland, and a man in disfavour would not have been appointed his secretary, a position which would have involved Spenser in many confidential matters of Elizabethan policy. Yet it is hard to picture the Immerito of *The Shepherds' Calendar* and *Three Proper and Witty Familiar Letters* happily imagining his future to lie in Ireland, far from the literary and political centres he knew.

Once in Ireland, Spenser was quickly baptized into the practicalities of Elizabethan colonial policies. In September 1580, a Papal force had landed at Smerwick, on the Kerry coast. Grey besieged them, and forced their surrender on 9 November. All the common soldiers – some six hundred men – were then massacred. Grey defended his action afterwards, arguing that their surrender was unconditional (which at that time allowed the victor to do as he wished with his prisoners). Other witnesses contested Grey's account. Spenser appears to have been untroubled by Grey's actions; perhaps he believed with Milton that if you wish to love some person or some principle truly, you must be willing to hate everything that stands against that person or principle. Some sixteen years later, Spenser formulated his own 'solution' for the Irish problem in *A View of the Present State of Ireland: Discoursed by way of a Dialogue between Eudoxus and Irenius*. (Troubles with the censors meant that it was not published until 1633.) With a care and precision which border at times on admiration, *A View* analyses the ways in which Irish culture was constructed. Yet such a sympathetic ability to understand cultural difference is put to quite ruthless ends; *A View* calls for the brutal suppression, the extermination if necessary, of the Irish by sword and starvation. Grey's solutions, it seems, were the correct ones: Eudoxus describes him as 'a most just, sincere, godly and right noble man'; and Irenius argues that, at Smerwick, Grey had no other rational option but to massacre the Papal force – 'there was no other way but to make that short end of them which was made.'[19]

This was not official policy, though the refusal of such strategies of brutality was a matter of expense as well as principle. Armies and wars are costly, and if Elizabeth's vacillating foreign policies had any unifying principle it was to avoid expense whenever possible. The result of this in Ireland was that the country lurched from one rebellion to another, as Elizabeth spent the bare minimum required to prevent English rule from breaking down entirely. Did Spenser feel betrayed by his Queen? It is tempting to read the greater violence of the second part of *The Faerie Queene*, published in 1595, as a reflection of his growing frustrations with Elizabethan policy in Ireland. Whether such inferences are correct cannot be known; what is certain is that Spenser made Ireland his home, staying there when Grey returned to England in 1582, and gradually acquiring positions and property. When, in June of 1598, the widespread rebellion that had always been threatening finally broke out, Spenser had a considerable amount to lose. On 15 October, Spenser's 3,000-acre estate in Munster was overrun, and his house at Kilcolman burnt. He fled with his family to Cork, from where, as Sheriff of the city, he carried a letter to London, informing the Queen's Privy Council of what had happened. Some three weeks later, still in London, he died, and was buried on the 16th in Westminster Abbey, at the expense of the Earl of Essex. According to the antiquary and historian William Camden, many poets were present, and 'mournful elegies and poems, with the pens that wrote them, [were] thrown into the tomb.'[20]

'HERE LIES (EXPECTING THE SECOND COMING OF OUR SAVIOUR CHRIST JESUS) THE BODY OF EDMUND SPENSER, THE PRINCE OF POETS IN HIS TIME.'

When Spenser's monument was erected in 1620, it managed to give him another forty years of life, by getting wrong both the date of his birth and of his death. Yet its description of Spenser as 'the Prince of Poets' was accurate enough, and perhaps more significant than was intended. To an Elizabethan, 'prince' had the meaning of 'ruler' as well as 'heir to the thone'. The inscription commemorates Spenser as the acknowledged *king* of the poets of his time, as befitted the poet who had sought to give, and succeeded in giving, the English the kingdom of their own language.[21] He was not only a servant of his Queen and country, but also, his epitaph suggests, the legislator of his own world. Our picture of Spenser as a national poet, concerned to give voice and form to the values of his body politic, the

Elizabethan state, is a picture particularly true to the younger pre-1590s Spenser; the Spenser of *The Shepherds' Calendar* and the first three books of *The Faerie Queene*. Alongside this must be added a picture of a later Spenser, a more princely and personal poet who celebrates his own life, creating a distance between the values of his poetic kingdom and those of temporal power; the Spenser in this edition particularly of *Colin Clout's Come Home Again* and *Amoretti and Epithalamion*.

Colin Clout's Come Home Again may be seen as a kind of halfway house between these two different Spensers. Published in 1595, it was completed in substance by the end of 1591.[22] The poem is an extended pastoral, written in a remarkably fluent and easy style. Colin recounts, at the prompting of his audience of curious shepherds, his voyage across the ocean to the kingdom and court of Cynthia. In doing so, Spenser was aligning a traditional pastoral motif – of the shepherd who has returned to the country after visiting the city – with his own life; for most of the details and figures of this narrative are also autobiographical, 'agreeing with the truth', as Spenser puts it in his dedication to Sir Walter Ralegh, 'in circumstances and matter.' Ralegh – in the poem, the Shepherd of the Ocean – had visited Spenser at Kilcolman in 1589, and had persuaded Spenser to accompany him to London. There Spenser had overseen the publication of the first part of *The Faerie Queene* and, through Ralegh's introduction, had read the poem to a delighted Queen Elizabeth.

Yet the attitude of both Colin and the poem to Cynthia's court is ambivalent. This ambivalence can be grasped most clearly in the title: where is the home in *Colin Clout's Come Home Again*? To any reader of *The Shepherds' Calendar*, Colin Clout could only come home to England. Yet, in this poem, Colin Clout comes home by leaving his Queen's Court and country, and returning to a different land, clearly modelled on Ireland. It is not that Spenser is becoming in any meaningful sense an Irish poet; the ruthless hostility to Irish culture displayed in *A View of the Present State of Ireland* makes that implausible. Rather, Spenser is becoming a poet of Ireland, as he values that country's lack (in his eyes) of any established civil culture, and its distance from the Elizabethan Court. Out of Ireland and its natural beauties, Spenser feels able to create another Arcadia, a kind of literary New England. Such a new land allows him to establish a clearer perspective from which to judge the perversions and corruptions of the Old.

Cynthia, his queen, is not dispraised: 'My thought, my heart, my love, my life is she,' declares Colin at the poem's centre, 'And I hers ever only, ever one.' She is surrounded, in life and in the poem, by her poets and ladies, whom, with their qualities, Spenser glorifies, in lyrical flights which threaten to go beyond moderate, pastoral limits. Why then, as Thestylis asks, does he return home? Cynthia's court is also a place of 'enormities', a place in which the language of love, in particular, has come to lack its proper meaning. For the courtiers, like Colin, sing and talk of love; they swim in it, in fact, 'up to the ears'. Yet they use the language of love to achieve their own worldly and sensual ambitions, raising the question of how the true poet of love is to be differentiated from the false. Colin's belief in love is not shaken: he recites a Christian humanist and neo-Platonic philosophy of love, in which love functions as a kind of grand unification theory. Yet it is hard not to see his departure from the Court as a retreat, an acknowledgement that the true practice of love can only continue among the shepherds of the new Arcadia, away from centres of actual power. Along with that retreat, another figure and source of Colin's love and poetry re-emerges; for while *Colin Clout's Come Home Again* centres on Elizabeth, it ends with Rosalind, Colin's own love. The two figures exist independently of each other, in different countries. Public and private love seem to be the point of unravelling: Cynthia no longer sits among her shepherds as did Elisa.

It is quite likely that Spenser's first wife died shortly after *Colin Clout's Come Home Again* was written. In 1594 Spenser married Elizabeth Boyle, some twenty years his junior. *Amoretti and Epithalamion* was published in the following year. It consists of three related parts: a sonnet sequence is followed by a short group of poems known as anacreontics, which is followed by a long ode. The volume celebrates the couple's courtship and marriage, and is offered as a wedding gift to Elizabeth. Spenser the poet is here writing for himself, doing 'great wrong', as sonnet 33 has it, to his 'most sacred Empress [. . . in] not finishing her Queen of Faery'. Though he is indebted to his Queen, it is his new Elizabeth who is his life's 'last ornament', and who is, 'Of all alive most worthy to be praised' (sonnet 74).

In choosing his new queen, Spenser was also throwing off literary authority. The sonnet sequence, as it had been given shape by the Italian poet Petrarch, tells a story of spiritual suffering, based around the lover's devotion to an unattainable mistress. Spenser's sonnets are, by contrast, 'happy leaves' (sonnet 1), telling the story of a love that develops and is brought to fulfilment as the lover is granted his beloved. At the beginning of the sequence, the lover-poet of the *Amoretti* has a tendency to constitute himself and his beloved through the figures of Petrarchan convention: she is the cruel, imperious lady, while he is the submissive yet predatory huntsman of the heart. Escaping from these conventions to a clearer sight of his beloved occupies much of the rest of the sequence; the poet is gradually made to realize his beloved's true virtues and attractions, and so comes to a new understanding of the values of love, and in particular its mutual nature (sonnet 65). The realm of private love, as fashioned by *Amoretti*, is no longer a treacherous place which threatens poetic creativity itself, as it had been in *The Shepherds' Calendar*, where Colin's love for Rosalind was narcissistic, withdrawing the poet into himself and silence. The poet's and his beloved's love for each other is now seen as an echo of God's love for man, shown in his sacrifice of Christ to redeem man's sins. Personal love offers the poet a source of values independent of the temporal world of power, and a way of realizing those values in the physical world. As sonnet 68 concludes:

> So let us love, dear love, like as we ought;
> Love is the lesson which the Lord us taught.

Tensions, however, remain: the poet still tends to think of his success as conquest, and when, at the end of *Amoretti*, he is separated from his beloved, he once more falls into frustration and doubt. This doubt is compounded for the reader by the anacreontics that follow. For these four short poems, with their return to a mythic and comic explanation of love's nature and troubles, recall the beginning of the sonnet sequence. It is only with the marriage ode, *Epithalamion*, that the reader emerges to the morning of the marriage day that will finally bring the lovers together for good.

The poet-groom presides over *Epithalamion* rather as Prospero presides over the island in Shakespeare's *The Tempest*: the world of the poem is intensely his, and under his control. At the heart of *Epithalamion* lies the desire to be able to possess a day, so that it will never fade: 'Let this day, let this one day be mine,' pleads the poet to the father of the muses, 'Let all the rest be thine'. To this end, the poet attempts to create this day through the power of his own poetry; it is as if he hopes, by constructing a perfect simulacrum of the day, to detach it from time. Time is made to pass within the world of the poem, as it passes in the world: a year of days passes with the poem's 365 long lines, and a day of hours passes with its 24 stanzas, the passage of minutes being marked in quarter hour segments by the poem's short lines. At the same time (or times), this day is a particular day: night falls in the poem after 16¼ daylight hours, the number of hours Elizabethan almanacs show 11 June 1594 as having; and that was the day on which Spenser and Elizabeth Boyle were married.[23] *Epithalamion* has claims to be the most overdetermined poem in the English language.[24]

Within this personal and universal day, the poet's dreams are shown being realized. He sends first the Muses to collect his beloved, then all the nymphs of rivers and green forests, then virgins and young boys, minstrels and merchants' daughters. When she arrives in the church, it is almost as if she has emerged from the poet's imagination, Pygmalion-like. Where the sun, moon and shepherds had circled the untouchable Elisa, 'queen of shepherds all', now all of creation circles the poet's bride as she stands before the altar; and this beloved gives the poet her hand, and is eventually brought to his bed. 'Never had man more joyful day than this,' declares the poet; and then the intensity of this joy brings fears, as the groom begins to think of those things that threaten his happiness. These fears do not sour *Epithalamion*'s celebrations; they act, rather, as the sober measures of it. For *Epithalamion*, unlike Prospero in *The Tempest*, needs to make no renunciation of its art to make an accommodation with humanity. Though the poem may recognize its poet's desire to be free of time, it has never agreed to it. Its joy is found as a part of human nature, and its strength is remarkable; it is one of the most purely joyful poems in English. But what did Elizabeth Boyle make of the knowledge that breasts will curdle?

JOHN LEE

References

1. John Keats, 'To Charles Cowden Clarke' (1817).
2. Harold Bloom, *Shelley's Mythmaking* (New Haven: Yale University Press, 1959), p. 153.
3. William Hazlitt provides an important exception. See 'Spenser and his Critics'.
4. Samuel Taylor Coleridge, *Table Talk*, 24 June 1827.

5. See 'Spenser and his Critics'.

6. Heracleitus, *On the Universe*, fragment 41.

7. Edmund Spenser, *Three Proper and Witty Familiar Letters*, 2 April, 1580.

8. The metrical patterns of quantitative verse are based upon the duration of syllables and not, as is usual in English, upon relative degrees of stress.

9. This is discussed in EK's introductory Epistle to *The Shepherds' Calendar*, p. 5.

10. For this reason and because of the demands of space, only 'January' is here printed complete with EK's glosses (and woodcut).

11. Sir Philip Sidney, *An Apology for Poetry* (pubd 1595), ll. 1434–8.

12. Ben Jonson, *Timber: Or, Discoveries* (pubd 1640), ll. 2237–8.

13. A recent exception is Douglas Brooks-Davies, *Edmund Spenser: Selected Shorter Poems* (Harlow: Longman, 1995). The process of modernizing *The Shepherds' Calendar* was begun by the Elizabethan printers of editions subsequent to the first.

14. Lynn Staley Johnson characterizes EK as the poem's 'literary memory' in *The Shepheardes Calender: An Introduction* (University Park: Pennsylvania State University Press, 1990), p. 7.

15. This phrase has, in fact, become associated with Benjamin, as it captures the thrust of his argument regarding fascism and art. See Walter Benjamin, 'The Work of Art in the Age of Mechanical Reproduction', in *Illuminations*, ed. by Hannah Arendt (London: Jonathan Cape, 1970), pp. 219–53.

16. Anthea Hume, *Edmund Spenser: Protestant Poet* (Cambridge: Cambridge University Press, 1984). For details of what reforms were aimed at, see under 'Reformation' in the 'Glossary of Names'.

17. Alastair Fowler, *A History of English Literature* (Oxford: Blackwell, 1987), p. 59.

18. See *Prothalamion* l. 128 (for London), *Amoretti* 74 (for Elizabeth). Also, for the family's (seemingly unprofitable) relation to the rich Spencers of Wormleighton and Althorp in Northamptonshire, see *Colin Clout's Come Home Again* ll. 536–9.

19. *Spenser's Prose Works*, ed. by Rudolf Gottfried (Baltimore: Johns Hopkins Press, 1949), p. 162.

20. Alexander C. Judson, *The Life of Edmund Spenser* (Baltimore: Johns Hopkins Press, 1945), p. 206.

21. For Elizabethan and Jacobean responses, see 'Spenser and his Critics'.

22. There may have been some later revisions; these are detailed in the Notes.
23. A. Kent Hieatt, *Short Time's Endless Monument* (New York: Columbia University Press, 1960). Further details of the numerological structure of *Amoretti and Epithalamion* are given in the Notes and in 'Spenser and his Critics', p. 263.
24. Joseph F. Loewenstein, 'Echo's Ring: Orpheus and Spenser's Career', *English Literary Renaissance* 16 (1986), 287–302, p. 300.

IRELAND

DONEGAL

ULSTER

Dunluce

Dungannon

Blackwater Armagh

Sligo

Newry

Dundalk

CAVAN

LOUTH

Clare I. Clew B.

CONNAUGHT

Drogheda

MEATH

Boyne

Mulingar Trim

Athlone

Galway

Dublin

Naas

Kildare

Kilcullen Glenmalure

LEINSTER

Limerick

Askeaton

Kilkenny

Slaney

Enniscorthy

Cashel

New Ross

Kilmallock

Galtee Mts.

Clonmel

Wexford

MUNSTER

Tralee

Buttevant Kilcolman Cas.

Castletownroche

Waterford

Mallow

Lismore

Dungarvan

Smerwick

Blackwater Fermoy

Youghal

Cork

Kinsale

MILES

0 10 20 30 40 50

NOTE ON THE TEXT

This edition's overriding aim is to provide the most enjoyable text of Spenser's poems. This end has been pursued in a variety of ways:

i. the text has been modernized, except where Spenser is most obviously using an archaism or dialect form.

ii. many single words have been glossed, the glosses being placed at the right hand of the page. The presence of a gloss is indicated – by an asterisk – only when it appears, for reasons of space, opposite the next line. Otherwise glosses are not indicated, as such indications inevitably break the reader's concentration. Instead, whenever necessary, the reader can glance across to find the word explained. The most commonly glossed words are collected in the 'Glossary of Words' at the very back of this book; after their first three appearances, these words are usually only glossed once in a poem, unless a particular usage introduces a nuance of sense.

iii. lengthier annotations and explanations of phrases have been placed in the 'Notes' section at the back of this book, with references being given at the right hand of the page – n. 1, n. 2 etc.

iv. proper names, real and mythical, are explained in the 'Glossary of Names' (after 'Notes'). This section also allows the reader to gain a sense of the various interrelations, political and literary, of which Spenser's poems are a part.

The reader should be willing to knock off prefixes such as 'y' or 'em' to discover the modern sense of a word, and also to read on; obscure words are often paired with more common words of similar meaning – for example, the Epistle to *The Shepherds' Calendar* talks of 'a gallimaufry or hodgepodge of all other speeches'. The reader should also be aware that words such as 'flower' and 'bower' may be monosyllabic; with Spenser it is safe to assume, when in doubt, that the line is meant to be syllabically regular. Relatedly, what may now appear to be half-rhymes are likely to have been full-rhymes; pronunciation has changed significantly since the Elizabethan period.

ABBREVIATIONS

cf.   Compare
c.   About
fl.   Flourished

DBD   Douglas Brooks-Davies, ed., *Edmund Spenser: Selected Shorter Poems* (Harlow: Longmans, 1995)

EK   Author of critical apparatus to 1579 edn of *The Shepherds' Calendar* (see 'Introduction', p. xxi).

EW   Elizabeth Porges Watson, ed., *Spenser: Selected Writings* (London: Routledge, 1992)

Norton   Hugh Maclean and Anne Lake Prescott, eds, *Edmund Spenser's Poetry*, 3rd edn (New York: Norton, 1993)

SE   A. C. Hamilton, ed., *The Spenser Encyclopedia* (Toronto and Buffalo: University of Toronto Press, 1990)

Variorum Edwin Greenlaw *et al.*, eds, *The Works of Edmund Spenser: A Variorum Edition*, 10 vols (Baltimore: Johns Hopkins Press, 1943)

Yale   William A. Oram *et al.*, eds, *Shorter Poems of Edmund Spenser* (New Haven: Yale, 1989)

Am&Ep Spenser, *Amoretti and Epithalamion*
As   Spenser, *Astrophel*, pubd with *Col*
Col   Spenser, *Colin Clout's Come Home Again*
Daph   Spenser, *Daphnaida*
Ecl   *Eclogues* (of various authors)
FH   Spenser, *Four Hymns*
FQ   Spenser, *The Faerie Queene*
Meta   Ovid, *Metamorphoses*
MHT   Spenser, 'Mother Hubbard's Tale', pubd in *Complaints*
Mui   Spenser, 'Muiopotmos', pubd in *Complaints*
PL   Milton, *Paradise Lost*

RT   Spenser, 'The Ruines of Time', pubd in *Complaints*
SC   Spenser, *The Shepherds' Calendar*

All references to Latin and Greek authors are to the Loeb editions.

SHORTER POEMS

containing twelve eclogues proportionable
to the twelve months.

Entitled
to the noble and virtuous
gentleman most worthy of all titles
both of learning and chivalry
Master Philip Sidney. n. 2

At London.
Printed by Hugh Singleton,
dwelling in Creede Lane near unto Ludgate
at the sign of the golden tunny   tuna
and are there to be sold.
1579

To His Book

Go little book: thyself present,   n. 3
As child whose parent is unkent,   unknown
To him that is the president   Sidney
Of noblesse and of chivalry;   nobility
And if that Envy bark at thee,
As sure it will, for succour flee
   Under the shadow of his wing;
And asked who thee forth did bring,
A shepherd's swain say did thee sing,   boy
All as his straying flock he fed;   while
And when his Honour has thee read,
Crave pardon for my hardihead.   boldness
   But if that any ask thy name,   the author's name
Say thou wert base-begot with blame;   lowly born
For-thy thereof thou takest shame.   for this reason
And when thou art past jeopardy,
Come tell me what was said of me:

And I will send more after thee.

Immerito.   'the undeserving one'

            To the most excellent and learned both
            orator and poet, Master Gabriel Harvey, his
        very special and singular good friend E.K. commendeth
                the good liking of this his labour,
                    and the patronage of the   n. 4
                        new poet.

    'Uncouth unkiste,' said the old famous poet   unknown/unkissed
    Chaucer, whom for his excellency and won-   n. 5
    derful skill in making, his scholar Lydgate – a   writing verse
    worthy scholar of so excellent a master –   n. 6
  5 calleth the loadstar of our language; and   guiding star
    whom our Colin Clout in his eclogue calleth
    Tityrus, the god of shepherds, comparing him
    to the worthiness of the Roman Tityrus, Virgil.
    Which proverb, mine own good friend Master
 10 Harvey, as in that good old poet it served well
    Pandarus' purpose for the bolstering of his
    bawdy brokage, so very well taketh place in   match-making
    this our new poet, who for that he is uncouth   it suits for
    (as said Chaucer) is unkissed and, unknown to
 15 most men, is regarded but of few. But I doubt
    not, so soon as his name shall come into the
    knowledge of men and his worthiness be
    sounded in the trump of fame, but that he
    shall be not only kissed but also beloved of all,
 20 embraced of the most, and wondered at of the   admired
    best. No less, I think, deserveth his wittiness in
    devising, his pithiness in uttering, his com-
    plaints of love so lovely, his discourses of
    pleasure so pleasantly, his pastoral rudeness,   homeliness
 25 his moral wiseness, his due observing of
    decorum everywhere – in personages, in sea-   n. 7
    sons, in matter, in speech – and generally in all
    seemly simplicity of handling his matter, and
    framing his words; the which of many things

30 which in him be strange I know will seem the   *unfamiliar*
    strangest, the words themselves being so
    ancient, the knitting of them so short and
    intricate, and the whole period and compass
    of speech so delightsome for the roundness
35 and so grave for the strangeness.

    And first of the words to speak, I grant they
be something hard and of most men unused,
yet both English and also used of most excel-
lent authors and most famous poets. In whom,
40 whenas this our poet hath been much travelled   *since*
and thoroughly read, how could it be (as that
worthy orator said) but that walking in the   *Cicero/n. 8*
sun, although for other cause he walked, yet
needs he mought be sunburnt; and having the   *must*
45 sound of those ancient poets still ringing in his
ears he mought needs, in singing, hit out some   *reproduce*
of their tunes. But whether he useth them by
such casualty and custom, or of set purpose   *chance*
and choice – as thinking them fittest for such
50 rustical rudeness of shepherds (either for that   *homeliness*
their rough sound would make his rhymes
more ragged and rustical, or else because such
old and obsolete words are most used of
country folk) – sure I think, and think I think
55 it not amiss, that they bring great grace and,
as one would say, authority to the verse. For
albe amongst many other faults it specially be   *although*
objected of Valla against Livy, and of other
against Sallust, that with overmuch study they
60 affect antiquity as coveting thereby credence
and honour of elder years, yet I am of opinion,
and eke the best learned are of the like, that   *also*
those ancient solemn words are a great orna-
ment both in the one and in the other: the one
65 labouring to set forth in his work an eternal
image of antiquity; and the other carefully
discoursing matters of gravity and importance.   *discussing*
For if my memory fail not, Tully, in that book
wherein he endeavoureth to set forth the pat-
70 tern of a perfect orator, saith that oft-times an   *n. 9*

ancient word maketh the style seem grave and, as it were, reverend; no otherwise than we honour and reverence grey hairs for a certain religious regard which we have of old age.

75 Yet neither everywhere must old words be stuffed in, nor the common dialect and manner of speaking so corrupted thereby, that – as in old buildings – it seems disorderly and ruinous: but all as in most exquisite pictures they use to *just*
80 blaze and portrait not only the dainty linea- *depict* ments of beauty, but also, round about it, to shadow the rude thickets and craggy cliffs, that by the baseness of such parts more excel- *humbleness* lency may accrue to the principal. For oft-
85 times we find ourselves, I know not how, singularly delighted with the show of such natural rudeness, and take great pleasure in that disorderly order. Even so do those rough and harsh terms enlumine and make more *illuminate*
90 clearly to appear the brightness of brave and glorious words. So, oftentimes, a discord in music maketh a comely concordance; so, great *beautiful harmony* delight took the worthy poet Alcaeus to behold *n. 10* a blemish in the joint of a well-shaped body.

95 But if any will rashly blame such his purpose in choice of old and unwonted words, him *unusual* may I more justly blame and condemn, or of *either* witless headiness in judging, or of heedless *hastiness* hardiness in condemning; for, not marking the *boldness/n. 11*
100 compass of his bent, he will judge of the length of his cast. For in my opinion it is one special praise, of many which are due to this poet, that he hath laboured to restore, as to their rightful heritage, such good and natural Eng-
105 lish words as have been long time out of use and almost clear disherited. Which is the only *disinherited* cause that our mother tongue, which truly of itself is both full enough for prose and stately enough for verse, hath long time been counted
110 most bare and barren of both. Which default whenas some endeavoured to salve and recure, *remedy*

they patched up the holes with pieces and rags
of other languages, borrowing here of the
French, there of the Italian, everywhere of the
115 Latin; not weighing how ill those tongues
accord with themselves, but much worse with   agreed/each other
ours. So now they have made our English
tongue a gallimaufry or hodgepodge of all
other speeches.
120   Other some, no so well seen in the English   skilled
tongue as perhaps in other languages, if they
happen to hear an old word – albeit very
natural and significant – cry out straightway
that we speak no English but gibberish, or
125 rather such as in old time Evander's mother
spoke. Whose first shame is that they are not   n. 12
ashamed in their own mother tongue strangers
to be counted and aliens; the second shame,   foreigners
no less than the first, that what so they under-
130 stand not they straightway deem to be sense-
less and not at all to be understood – much
like to the mole in Aesop's fable that, being
blind herself, would in no wise be persuaded   way
that any beast could see. The last (more shame-
135 ful than both), that of their own country and
natural speech, which together with their
nurse's milk they sucked, they have so base
regard and bastard judgement that they will
not only themselves not labour to garnish and
140 beautify it, but also repine that of other it   are discontent
should be embellished – like to the dog in the
manger that himself can eat no hay and yet
barketh at the hungry bullock, that so fain   gladly
would feed; whose currish kind, though
145 cannot be kept from barking, yet I con them   can
thank that they refrain from biting.   the critics
    Now for the knitting of sentences, which
they call the joints and members thereof, and   limbs
for all the compass of the speech: it is round   proportion/plain
150 without roughness, and learned without hard-
ness – such, indeed, as may be perceived of the
least, understood of the most, but judged only

of the learned. For what in most English
writers useth to be loose, and as it were ungirt,
155 in this author is well grounded, finely framed,
and strongly trussed up together. In regard   n. 13
whereof, I scorn and spew out the rakehelly   immoral
rout of our ragged rhymers (for so themselves
use to hunt the letter) which without learning   n. 14
160 boast, without judgement jangle, without   argue
reason rage and foam, as if some instinct of   impulse
poetical spirit had newly ravished them above
the meanness of common capacity. And being
in the middest of all their bravery, suddenly
165 (either for want of matter, or of rhyme, or
having forgotten their former conceit) they   idea
seem to be so pained and travailed in their   troubled
remembrance, as it were a woman in child-
birth, or as that same Pythia when the trance
170 came upon her:
      Os rabidum fera corda domans, etc.   n. 15
      Netheless, let them a God's name feed on   nevertheless/in
their own folly, so they seek not to darken the
beams of others' glory. As for Colin, under
175 whose person the author self is shadowed,   himself/represented
how far he is from such vaunted titles and
glorious shows, both himself showeth where
he saith:
      Of Muses, Hobbin, I con no skill;   know not
180 and,   n. 16
      Enough is me to paint out my unrest, etc.;   Enough for me
and also appeareth by the baseness of the   humbleness
name, wherein, it seemeth, he chose rather to
unfold great matter of argument covertly than
185 (professing it) not suffice thereto accordingly.
Which moved him rather in eclogues than
otherwise to write, doubting perhaps his abil-
ity (which he little needed); or minding to
furnish our tongue with this kind wherein it   genre
190 faulteth; or following the example of the best   lacks
and most ancient poets which devised this kind
of writing, being both so base for the matter   it being
and so homely for the manner, at the first to

try their abilities – and as young birds, that be
195 newly crept out of the nest, by little first to
prove their tender wings before they make a
greater flight. So flew Theocritus, as you may
perceive he was already fully fledged. So flew
Virgil, as not yet well feeling his wings. So flew
200 Mantuan, as being not full summed. So   feathered
Petrarch. So Boccaccio. So Marot, Sannazar,
and also divers other excellent both Italian and   diverse
French poets, whose footing this author every-   footsteps
where followeth, yet so as few, but they be
205 well scented, can trace him out. So, finally,   have a keen
flieth this our new poet, as a bird whose   sense of smell
principals be scarce grown out, but yet as   main feathers
that in time shall be able to keep wing with
the best.
210   Now, as touching the general drift and
purpose of his eclogues, I mind not to say   intend
much, himself labouring to conceal it. Only
this appeareth; that his unstaid youth had long   unregulated
wandered in the common labyrinth of love, in
215 which time to mitigate and allay the heat of
his passion, or else to warn (as he saith) the
young shepherds – *scilicet* his equals and com-   namely
panions – of his unfortunate folly, he compiled
these twelve eclogues which, for that they be
220 proportioned to the state of the twelve
months, he termeth *The Shepherds' Calendar*,
applying an old name to a new work.   n. 17
    Hereunto have I added a certain gloss or
scholion for the exposition of old words and
225 harder phrases, which manner of glossing and
commenting, well I wote, will seem strange   know
and rare in our tongue. Yet for so much as I
knew many excellent and proper devices both
in words and matter would pass in the speedy
230 course of reading, either as unknown or as not
marked; and that in this kind, as in other, we
might be equal to the learned of other nations:
I thought good to take the pains upon me,
the rather for that, by means of some   especially as

235 familiar acquaintance, I was made privy to his   intimate
counsel and secret meaning in them, as also in
sundry other works of his. Which, albeit I know
he nothing so much hateth as to promulgate, yet   publish his poems
thus much have I adventured upon his friend-
240 ship (himself being for long time far
estranged), hoping that this will the rather   absent
occasion him to put forth divers other excel-   make
lent works of his which sleep in silence, as his
Dreams, his Legends, his Court of Cupid, and
245 sundry others, whose commendations to set   n. 18
out were very vain, the things, though worthy   pointless
of many, yet being known to few.

These my present pains, if to any they be
pleasurable or profitable, be you judge, mine
250 own good Master Harvey, to whom I have –
both in respect of your worthiness generally
and otherwise upon some particular and
special considerations – vowed this my labour
and the maidenhead of this our common
255 friend's poetry, himself having already in the
beginning dedicated it to the noble and worthy
gentleman, the right worshipful Master Philip
Sidney, a special favourer and maintainer of all
kind of learning. Whose cause, I pray you sir,
260 if envy shall stir up any wrongful accusation,
defend with your mighty rhetoric and other
your rare gifts of learning, as you can; and   know how
shield with your good will, as you ought,
against the malice and outrage of so many
265 enemies as I know will be set on fire with the
sparks of his kindled glory.

And thus recommending the author unto
you, as unto his most special good friend, and
myself unto you both, as one making singular
270 account of two so very good and so choice
friends, I bid you both most heartily farewell,
and commit you and your most commendable
studies to the tuition of the greatest.   God

Your own assuredly to
be commanded E. K.

Post scriptum
Now I trust, Master Harvey, that upon sight
of your special friend's and fellow poet's
doings – or else for envy of so many unworthy
quidams, which catch at the garland, which to   somebodies/victor's
you alone is due – you will be persuaded to   garland
pluck out of the hateful darkness those so
many excellent English poems of yours which
lie hid, and bring them forth to eternal light.   n. 19
Trust me, you do both them great wrong, in
depriving them of the desired sun, and also
yourself, in smothering your deserved praises;
and all men generally, in withholding from
them so divine pleasures which they might
conceive of your gallant English verses, as they
have already done of your Latin poems –
which in my opinion, both for invention and
elocution, are very delicate and superexcellent.
And thus again I take my leave of my good
Master Harvey, From my lodging at London
this 10 of April 1579.

The general argument
of the whole book.

Little, I hope, needeth me at large to discourse   discuss
the first original of aeglogues, having already   eclogues/n. 20
touched the same. But, for the word 'aeg-
logues' I know is unknown to most, and also
5 mistaken of some the best learned (as they
think), I will say somewhat thereof, being not
at all impertinent to my present purpose.   unconnected
     They were first of the Greeks, the inventors
of them, called Æglogai as it were αἴγον or
10 αἰγονόμων λόγοι, that is, goatherds' tales.
For although in Virgil and others the speakers
be more shepherds than goatherds, yet Theo-
critus (in whom is more ground of authority
than in Virgil, this specially from that deriving,   n. 21
15 as from the first head and wellspring, the
whole invention of his aeglogues) maketh

goatherds the persons and authors of his tales.
This being, who seeth not the grossness of   being so/stupidity
such as, by colour of learning, would make   semblance
20 us believe that they are more rightly termed
eklogai – as they would say, 'extraordinary
discourses of unnecessary matter'; which defi-
nition, albe in substance and meaning it agree   although
with the nature of the thing, yet no whit   not at all
25 answereth with the ἀνάλυσις and interpre-   analysis
tation of the word. For they be not termed
eclogues, but aeglogues. Which sentence this
author very well observing upon good judge-   opinion
ment, though indeed few goatherds have to do
30 herein, netheless doubteth not to call them by   nevertheless
the used and best-known name. Other curious   subtle
discourses hereof I reserve to greater occasion.

These twelve aeglogues, everywhere answer-
ing to the seasons of the twelve months, may
35 be well divided into three forms or ranks: for
either they be plaintive, as the first, the sixth,
the eleventh and the twelfth; or recreative,
such as all those be which conceive matter of
love, or commendation of special personages;
40 or moral, which for the most part be mixed
with some satirical bitterness – namely the
second of reverence due to old age, the fifth of
coloured deceit, the seventh and ninth of dis-   disguised
solute shepherds and pastors, the tenth of
45 contempt of poetry and pleasant wits. And to
this division may everything herein be reason-
ably applied, a few only except, whose special
purpose and meaning I am not privy too. And   familiar with
thus much generally of these twelve aeglogues.

50   Now will we speak particularly of all, and   of each in turn
first of the first, which he calleth by the first
month's name, January. Wherein to some he
may seem foully to have faulted, in that he
erroneously beginneth with that month which
55 beginneth not the year. For it is well known,
and stoutly maintained with strong reasons of
the learned, that the year beginneth in March;

for then the sun reneweth his finished course,
and the seasonable spring refresheth the earth,
60 and the pleasance thereof, being buried in the   n. 22
sadness of the dead winter now worn away,
reliveth. This opinion maintain the old astrol-
ogers and philosophers, namely the reverend
Andalo, and Macrobius in his *Holidays of*   Holy-days
65 *Saturn* – which account also was generally
observed both of Grecians and Romans.

But, saving the leave of such learned heads,   by the leave
we maintain a custom of counting the seasons
from the month January, upon a more special
70 cause than the heathen philosophers ever could
conceive: that is, for the incarnation of our
mighty Saviour and eternal redeemer, the Lord
Christ, who, as then renewing the state of the
decayed world and returning the compass of
75 expired years to their former date and first
commencement, left to us his heirs a memorial
of his birth in the end of the last year and
beginning of the next. Which reckoning, beside
that eternal monument of our salvation, lean-
80 eth also upon good proof of special judge-
ment. For, albeit that in elder times, whenas
yet the count of the year was not perfected (as
afterwards it was by Julius Caesar), they began
to tell the months from March's beginning,
85 and, according to the same, God (as is said in   agreeing
scripture) commanded the people of the Jews   n. 23
to count the month Abib, that which we call
March, for the first month, in remembrance
that in that month he brought them out of the
90 land of Egypt: yet, according to tradition of
latter times, it hath been otherwise observed,
both in government of the church and rule of
mightiest realms. For from Julius Caesar, who   the time of
first observed the leap year (which he called
95 *bissextilem annum*), and brought into a more
certain course the odd wandering days – which
of the Greeks were called ὑπερβαίνοντες, of
the Romans *intercalares* (for in such matter of   n. 24

learning I am forced to use the terms of the
100 learned) – the months have been numbered
twelve, which in the first ordinance of Romu-
lus were but ten, counting but 304 days in
every year, and beginning with March. But
Numa Pompilius, who was the father of all the
105 Roman ceremonies and religion, seeing that
reckoning to agree neither with the course of
the sun nor of the moon, thereunto added two
months, January and February: wherein it see-
meth that wise king minded upon good reason
110 to begin the year at January, of him therefore
so called *tanquam janua anni* – 'the gate and
entrance of the year' – or of the name of the
god Janus; to which god, for that the old
paynims attributed the birth and beginning of   pagans
115 all creatures new-coming into the world, it
seemeth that he therefore to him assigned the
beginning and first entrance of the year. Which
account, for the most part, hath hitherto con-
tinued, notwithstanding that the Egyptians
120 begin their year in September for that, accord-
ing to the opinion of the best rabbins and very   rabbis
purpose of the scripture itself, God made the
world in that month, that is called to them
Tisri. And therefore he commanded them to
125 keep the feast of Pavilions in the end of the   n. 25
year, in the fifteenth day of the seventh month,
which before that time was the first.
   But our author, respecting neither the sub-
tlety of the one part nor the antiquity of the
130 other, thinketh it fittest, according to the sim-
plicity of common understanding, to begin
with January – weening it, perhaps, no   thinking
decorum that shepherd should be seen in
matter of so deep insight, or canvass a case of   knowledgeable
135 so doubtful judgement. So therefore beginneth
he, and so continueth he throughout.

January

ÆGLOGA PRIMA

ARGUMENT

In this first eclogue, Colin Clout, a shepherd's
boy, complaineth him of his unfortunate love,
being but newly (as seemeth) enamoured of a
country lass called Rosalind. With which
strong affection being very sore travailed, he   troubled
compareth his careful case to the sad season of   woeful
the year, to the frosty ground, to the frozen
trees, and to his own winterbeaten flock. And
lastly, finding himself robbed of all former
pleasance and delights, he breaketh his pipe in   pleasure
pieces, and casteth himself to the ground.

COLIN CLOUT

A shepherd's boy (no better do him call),
When winter's wasteful spite was almost spent,   destructive
All in a sunshine day, as did befall,
Led forth his flock that had been long ypent.   penned
5 So faint they waxed, and feeble in the fold,   pen for animals
That now uneaths their feet could them uphold.   scarcely/EK

All as the sheep, such was the shepherd's look,   just as
For pale and wan he was (alas the while).   sickly
May seem he loved, or else some care he took;   sorrow

10 Well couth he tune his pipe, and frame his style.   knew how to/EK
   Tho to a hill his fainting flock he led,   then
   And thus him plained the while his sheep there fed.   lamented

   'Ye gods of love that pity lovers' pain
   (If any gods the pain of lovers pity),
15 Look from above, where you in joys remain,
   And bow your ears unto my doleful ditty;
   And Pan, thou shepherds' god, that once didst love,
   Pity the pains that thou thyself didst prove.   experience

   'Thou barren ground, whom winter's wrath hath wasted,
20 Art made a mirror to behold my plight:
   Whilom thy fresh spring flowered, and after hasted   formerly
   Thy summer proud with daffadillies dight: dressed/n. 3
   And now is come thy winter's stormy state,
   Thy mantle marred, wherein thou maskedst late.   cloak/concealed

25 'Such rage as winter's reigneth in my heart,
   My life-blood freezing with unkindly cold;   unnatural
   Such stormy stours do breed my baleful smart,   times/painful
   As if my year were waste, and waxen old.   wasted/grown
   And yet, alas, but now my spring begun,
30 And yet, alas, it is already done.

   'You naked trees, whose shady leaves are lost,
   Wherein the birds were wont to build their bower,   used/nest
   And now are clothed with moss and hoary frost,
   Instead of bloss'ms, wherewith your buds did flower –
35 I see your tears that from your boughs do rain,
   Whose drops in dreary icicles remain.

   'All so my lustful leaf is dry and sere,   vigorous/withered/EK
   My timely buds with wailing all are wasted;   seasonable
   The blossom which my branch of youth did bear,
40 With breathed sighs is blown away and blasted,
   And from mine eyes the drizzling tears descend,
   As on your boughs the icicles depend.   hang down

   'Thou feeble flock whose fleece is rough and rent,   torn
   Whose knees are weak through fast and evil fare,   poor food
45 Mayst witness well by thy ill government
   Thy master's mind is overcome with care.

Thou weak, I wan; thou lean, I quite forlorn;   sickly
With mourning pine I, you with pining mourn.

'A thousand sithes I curse that careful hour   times/full of trouble/EK
50 Wherein I longed the neighbour town to see,   EK
And eke ten thousand sithes I bless the stour,   also/moment/EK
Wherein I saw so fair a sight as she:
Yet all for nought; such sight hath bred my bane –   sorrow
Ah, God! that love should breed both joy and pain.

55 'It is not Hobbinol wherefore I plain,   complain
Albe my love he seek with daily suit;   although
His clownish gifts and court'sies I disdain,   rustic/EK
His kids, his cracknels, and his early fruit.   biscuits
Ah, foolish Hobbinol, thy gifts be vain;   EK
60 Colin them gives to Rosalind again.   EK

'I love thilk lass (alas why do I love?)   this same/EK
And am forlorn (alas why am I lorn?)   left alone
She deigns not my good will, but doth reprove,   accepts/reject
And of my rural music holdeth scorn;
65 Shepherd's device she hateth as the snake,   invention
And laughs the songs that Colin Clout doth make.

'Wherefore, my pipe, albe rude Pan thou please,
Yet for thou pleasest not where most I would –
And thou unlucky Muse, that wont'st to ease   were used
70 My musing mind, yet canst not when thou should:
Both pipe and Muse shall sore the while abye.'   pay dearly
So broke his oaten pipe, and down did lie.

By that the welked Phoebus gan avail   faded/began/bring down/EK
His weary waine, and now the frosty Night   wagon
75 Her mantle black through heaven gan overhale.   draw over/EK
Which seen, the pensive boy, half in despite,
Arose, and homeward drove his sunned sheep,
Whose hanging heads did seem his careful case to weep.

                    Colin's emblem   EK
                    Anchôra speme
                  [There is still hope]

[EK's] GLOSS

[l.1] Colin Clout) is a name not greatly used, and yet have I seen a poesy of Master Skelton's under that title. But indeed the word 'Colin' is French, and used of the French poet Marot (if he be worthy of the name of a poet) in a certain eclogue. Under which name this poet secretly shadoweth himself, as sometime did Virgil under the name of Tityrus, thinking it much fitter than such Latin names, for the great unlikelihood of the language.

poem

Spenser

n. 4

[l.6] uneaths) scarcely.

[l.10] couth) cometh of the verb 'con', that is, to know or have skill. As well interpreteth the same the worthy Sir Thomas Smith in his book of government, whereof I have a perfect copy in writing lent me by his kinsman, and my very singular good friend, Master Gabriel Harvey, as also of some other his most grave and excellent writings.

n. 5

[l.49] Sithe) time.

[l.50] Neighbour town) the next town: expressing the Latin *vicina*.

[l.27] stour) a fit [l.37] sere) withered [l.57] his clownish gifts) imitateth Virgil's verse, *Rusticus es, Corydon; nec munera curat Alexis.*

n. 6

[l.55] Hobbinol) is a feigned country name whereby (it being so common and usual) seemeth to be hidden the person of some his very special and most familiar friend, whom he entirely and extraordinarily beloved, as peradventure shall be more largely declared hereafter. In this place seemeth to be some savour of disorderly love, which the learned call *pæderastice*; but it is gathered beside his meaning. For who that hath read Plato his dialogue called *Alcibiades*, Xenophon and Maximus Tyrius of Socrates' opinions, may easily perceive that such love is much to be allowed and liked of, specially so meant as Socrates used it; who saith that indeed he loved Alcibiades

invented/rustic

n. 7
perhaps

n. 8/such savour
n. 9

extremely, yet not Alcibiades' person, but his soul, which is Alcibiades' own self. And so is *pæderastice* much to be preferred before *gynerastice*; that is, the love which inflameth men with lust toward womankind. But yet let no man think that herein I stand with Lucian, or his devilish disciple Unico Aretino, in defence of execrable and horrible sins of forbidden and unlawful fleshliness, whose abominable error is fully confuted of Perionius, and others.

[l.61] I love) a pretty epanorthosis in these two verses, and withal a paronomasia or playing with the word, where he saith, 'I love thilk lass, (alas & c).

repetition
pun

[l.60] Rosalind) is also a feigned name which, being well ordered, will bewray the very name of his love and mistress whom by that name he coloureth: so as Ovid shadoweth his love under the name of Corinna, which of some is supposed to be Julia, the emperor Augustus his daughter, and wife to Agrippa. So doth Aruntius Stella everywhere call his lady 'Asteris' and 'Ianthis', albe it is well known that her right name was Violantilla, as witnesseth Statius in his *Epithalamium*. And so the famous paragon of Italy, Madonna Celia, in her letters envelopeth herself under the name of Zima, and Petrona under the name of Bellochia. And this generally hath been a common custom of counterfeiting the names of secret personages.

reveal

disguises

n. 10
n. 11

[not known]

[l.73] avail) bring down.
[l.75] overhale) draw over.

Emblem

His emblem or poesy is hereunder added in Italian: *Anchôra speme*. The meaning whereof is that, notwithstanding his extreme passion and luckless love, yet leaning on hope, he is somewhat recomforted.

February

This eclogue is rather moral and general than bent to any secret or particular purpose. It specially containeth a discourse of old age in the person of Thenot, an old shepherd, who, for his crookedness and unlustiness, is scorned of Cuddie, an unhappy herdsman's boy. The matter very well accordeth with the season of the month – the year now drooping and, as it were, drawing to his last age. For as in this time of year, so then in our bodies there is a dry and withering cold which congealeth the curdled blood, and freezeth the weather-beaten flesh with storms of fortune and hoar frosts of care. To which purpose the old man telleth a tale of the Oak and the Brier so lively and so feelingly as, if the thing were set forth in some picture before our eyes, more plainly could not appear.

    feebleness

    n. 1

CUDDIE

Ah, for pity! will rank winter's rage   *violent*
These bitter blasts never gin t'assuage?   *begin to*
The keen cold blows through my beaten hide,   *sharp/weather-beaten*
All as I were through the body gride.   *pierced*
5 My ragged runts all shiver and shake,   *small cows*
As doen high towers in an earthquake;   *do*
They wont in the wind wag their wriggle tails,   *used/wriggling*
Perk as peacock, but now it avails.   *lively/n. 2*

THENOT

Lewdly complainest thou, lazy lad,   *foolishly*
10 Of winter's wrack, for making thee sad.   *violence*
Must not the world wend in his common course   *go forward*
From good to bad and from bad to worse,
From worse unto that is worst of all,
And then return to his former fall?   *n. 3*
15 Who will not suffer the stormy time,
Where will he live till the lusty prime?   *cheerful/spring*
Self have I worn out thrice thirty years,
Some in much joy, much in many tears,

Yet never complained of cold nor heat,
20 Of summer's flame nor of winter's threat;
Ne ever was to Fortune foeman,   not/enemy
But gently took that ungently came;
And ever my flock was my chief care,
Winter or summer they mought well fare.   might

CUDDIE
25 No marvel, Thenot, if thou can bear
Cheerfully the winter's wrathful cheer;   mood
For age and winter accord full nigh –   mirror each other
This chill, that cold; this crooked, that wry;   twisted
And as the louring weather looks down,
30 So seemest thou like Good Friday to frown.   n. 4
But my flowering youth is foe to frost,
My ship unwont in storms to be tossed.

THENOT
The sovereign of seas he blames in vain   Neptune
That, once sea-beat, will to sea again.   tossed by the sea
35 So, loit'ring, live you little herdgrooms,   herdsmen/n. 5
Keeping your beasts in the budded brooms,   n. 6
And when the shining sun laugheth once,
You deemen the spring is come at once.   think
Tho gin you, fond flies, the cold to scorn   then/foolish
40 And, crowing in pipes made of green corn,
You thinken to be Lords of the Year.   n. 7
But eft, when ye count you freed from fear,   afterwards
Comes the breme Winter with chamfered brows,   fierce/grooved
Full of wrinkles and frosty furrows,
45 Drearily shooting his stormy dart   cruelly
Which curdles the blood and pricks the heart.
Then is your careless courage accoyed;   vigour/daunted
Your careful herds with cold be annoyed.   troubled
Then pay you the price of your surquedry,   pride
50 With weeping, and wailing, and misery.

CUDDIE
Ah, foolish old man, I scorn thy skill   reasoning
That wouldest me my springing youngth to spill.   youth/waste
I deem thy brain emperished be
Through rusty elde, that hath rotted thee;   age

55 Or sicker thy head very totty is,   certainly/unsteady
    So on thy corbe shoulder it leans, amiss.   bowed
    Now thyself hast lost both lop and top,   small branches
    Als my budding branch thou wouldest crop;   also
    But were thy years green, as now be mine,
60 To other delights they would incline.
    Tho wouldest thou learn to carol of love,   sing
    And hery with hymns thy lass's glove;   praise
    Tho wouldest thou pipe of Phillis' praise –
    But Phillis is mine for many days:
65 I won her with a girdle of gilt,   waist-band
    Embossed with bugle about the belt.   tubular glass beads
    Such an one shepherds would make full fain;   glad
    Such an one would make thee young again.

    THENOT
    Thou art a fon of thy love to boast;   fool
70 All that is lent to love will be lost.

    CUDDIE
    Seest how brag yond bullock bears –   proudly
    So smirk, so smooth – his pricked ears?   neat
    (His horns be as broad as rainbow bent,
    His dewlap as lithe as lass of Kent.)   n. 8/soft
75 See how he venteth into the wind: sniffs
    Weenest of love is not his mind?   Do you think
    Seemeth thy flock thy counsel can,   know
    So lustless be they, so weak, so wan,
    Clothed with cold and hoary with frost.
80 Thy flock's father his courage hath lost;   ram/lustiness
    Thy ewes, that wont to have blowen bags,   swollen udders
    Like wailful widows hangen their crags;   necks
    The rather lambs be starved with cold: earlier born
    All for their master is lustless and old.   All this

    THENOT
85 Cuddie, I wote thou kenst little good   know/understand
    So vainly t'advance thy headless hood.   n. 9
    For youngth is a bubble blown up with breath,
    Whose wit is weakness, whose wage is death,   n. 10
    Whose way is wilderness, whose inn penance,

90 And stoop-gallant age, the host of grievance.*   humbler/n. 11
But shall I tell thee a tale of truth   *suffering
Which I conned of Tityrus in my youth,   EK: Chaucer
Keeping his sheep on the hills of Kent?

CUDDIE
To nought more, Thenot, my mind is bent
95 Than to hear novels of his devise: tales/devising
They be so well thewed and so wise,   EK: morally instructive
Whatever that good old man bespake.

THENOT
Many meet tales of youth did he make,   fitting
And some of love and some of chivalry,
100 But none fitter than this to apply.
Now listen awhile, and hearken the end,   attend to the moral

'There grew an aged tree on the green,   n. 12
A goodly Oak sometime had it been,
With arms full strong and largely displayed,
105 But of their leaves they were disarrayed;   stripped
The body big and mightily pight,   pitched
Throughly rooted and of wonderous height: thoroughly
Whilom had been the king of the field,   formerly
And mochell mast to the husband did yield,   many acorns/farmer
110 And with his nuts larded many swine.   fattened
But now the grey moss marred his rine,   bark
His bared boughs were beaten with storms,
His top was bald and wasted with worms,
His honour decayed, his branches sere.   bare
115 'Hard by his side grew a bragging Brier,   wild rose
Which proudly thrust into th'element,   air
And seemed to threat the firmament.   sky
It was embellished with blossoms fair,
And thereto aye wonned to repair   always/used/go
120 The shepherds' daughters to gather flowers
To paint their garlands with his colours;
And in his small bushes used to shroud
The sweet nightingale singing so loud:
Which made this foolish Brier wax so bold   All of which/grow
125 That on a time he cast him to scold   he decided

And sneb the good Oak for he was old.   snub
'"Why standst there," quoth he, "thou brutish block?
Nor for fruit nor for shadow serves thy stock.   trunk
Seest how fresh my flowers be spread,
130 Dyed in lily white and crimson red,
With leaves engrained in lusty green,
Colours meet to clothe a maiden queen.   fit
Thy waste bigness but cumbers the ground,   wasted/encumbers
And dirks the beauty of my blossoms round.   darkens
135 The mouldy moss which thee accloyeth,   chokes
My cinnamon smell too much annoyeth.
Wherefore soon, I rede thee, hence remove,   advise
Lest thou the price of my displeasure prove."   discover
So spoke this bold Brier with great disdain;
140 Little him answered the Oak again,   in reply
But yielded, with shame and grief adawed   subdued
That of a weed he was overawed.
    'It chanced after, upon a day,
The husbandman self to come that way,   himself
145 Of custom for to surview his ground
And his trees of state in compass round.   round about/n. 13
Him when the spiteful Brier had espied,
Causeless complained and loudly cried
Unto his lord, stirring up stern strife:
150 '"O my liege lord, the god of my life,   n. 14
Pleaseth you ponder your suppliant's plaint,   request
Caused of wrong and cruel constraint,
Which I your poor vassal daily endure:
And but your goodness the same recure,   redress
155 Am like for desperate dool to die   grief
Through felonous force of mine enemy."   cruel
    'Greatly aghast with this piteous plea,
Him rested the goodman on the lea,   meadow
And bade the Brier in his plaint proceed.
160 With painted words tho gan this proud weed   deceitful
(As most usen ambitious folk)
His coloured crime with craft to cloak.   slander
    '"Ah, my sovereign, lord of creatures all,
Thou placer of plants both humble and tall,
165 Was not I planted of thine own hand

To be the primrose of all thy land –
With flowering blossoms to furnish the prime,   spring
And scarlet berries in summer time?
How falls it, then, that this faded Oak –
170 Whose body is sere, whose branches broke,
Whose naked arms stretch unto the fire –   EK: fit for the fire
Unto such tyranny doth aspire,
Hindering with his shade my lovely light,
And robbing me of the sweet sun's sight?
175 So beat his old boughs my tender side
That oft the blood springeth from wounds wide:
Untimely my flowers forced to fall,
That be the honour of your coronal.   garland
And oft he lets his cankerworms light   caterpillars/alight
180 Upon my branches to work me more spite;   harm
And oft his hoary locks down doth cast,
Wherewith my fresh flowerets be defaced.   young blossoms
For this and many more such outrage,
Craving your goodlihead to assuage   goodness
185 The rancorous rigour of his might,   spiteful
Nought ask I but only to hold my right,
Submitting me to your good sufferance,   indulgence
And praying to be guarded from grievance."   injury
   'To this the Oak cast him to reply
190 Well as he couth; but his enemy
Had kindled such coals of displeasure,
That the goodman nould stay his leisure   would not wait
But home him hasted with furious heat,
Increasing his wrath with many a threat.
195 His harmful hatchet he hent in hand,   grasped
(Alas, that it so ready should stand)
And to the field alone he speedeth
(Aye little help to harm there needeth).   always
Anger nould let him speak to the tree,
200 Enaunter his rage mought cooled be;   lest/might
But to the root bent his sturdy stroke,
And made many wounds in the waste Oak.
The axe's edge did oft turn again,   become blunt
As half-unwilling to cut the grain;
205 Seemed the senseless iron did fear,

Or to wrong holy eld did forbear.   age
For it had been an ancient tree,
Sacred with many a mystery,
And often crossed with the priest's crewe,   holy-water pot
210 And often hallowed with holy-water dew.
But sike fancies weren foolery   such
And broughten this Oak to this misery;
For nought mought they quitten him from decay, deliver from ruin
For fiercely the goodman at him did lay.
215 The block oft groaned under the blow,   trunk
And sighed to see his near overthrow.
In fine, the steel had pierced his pith,   at last
Tho down to the earth he fell forthwith;
His wondrous weight made the ground to quake,
220 Th'earth shrank under him, and seemed to shake.
There lieth the Oak, pitied of none.
'Now stands the Brier like a lord, alone,
Puffed up with pride and vain pleasance;   delight
But all this glee had no continuance.
225 For eftsones winter gan to approach;   soon afterwards
The blust'ring Boreas did encroach
And beat upon the solitary Brier –
For now no succour was seen him near.
Now gan he repent his pride too late;
230 For, naked left and disconsolate,
The biting frost nipped his stalk dead,
The wat'ry wet weighed down his head,
And heaped snow burdened him so sore
That now upright he can stand no more
235 And, being down, is trod in the dirt
Of cattle, and bruised, and sorely hurt.
Such was th'end of this ambitious Brier,
For scorning eld – '

CUDDIE
Now I pray thee, shepherd, tell it not forth;   no more
240 Here is a long tale, and little worth.
So long have I listened to thy speech
That graffed to the ground is my breech;   grafted/rump
My heart's-blood is well nigh frorne I feel,   frozen
And my galage grown fast to my heel;   clog

245 But little ease of thy lewd tale I tasted.   foolish
    Hie thee home, shepherd, the day is nigh wasted.   nearly

Thenot's emblem
Iddio perche è vecchio,
Fa suoi al suo essempio.
[God, being old, makes his own in his image]

Cuddie's emblem
Niuno vecchio,
Spaventa Iddio
[No old man fears God]

March

In this eclogue two shepherds' boys, taking
occasion of the season, begin to make purpose   *to talk of*
of love and other pleasance which to spring-
time is most agreeable. The special meaning
hereof is to give certain marks and tokens to
know Cupid, the poets' god of love. But more
particularly, I think, in the person of Thomalin
is meant some secret friend who scorned Love
and his knights so long till at length himself
was entangled and unawares wounded with   *unexpectedly*
the dart of some beautiful regard, which is   *sight*
Cupid's arrow.

WILLYE

Thomalin, why sitten we so,
As weren overwent with woe,   *overcome*
   Upon so fair a morrow?
The joyous time now nigheth fast   *nears*
5 That shall allege this bitter blast   *assuage*
   And slake the winter's sorrow.   *abate*

THOMALIN

Sicker, Willye, thou warnest well,   *certainly/admonish*
For winter's wrath begins to quell,   *abate*
   And pleasant spring appeareth.
10 The grass now gins to be refreshed,
The swallow peeps out of her nest,
   And cloudy welkin cleareth.   *sky*

WILLYE

Seest not thilk same hawthorn stud,   *trunk*
How bragly it begins to bud   *showily*
15   And utter his tender head?   *put forth*
Flora now calleth forth each flower
And bids make ready Maia's bower,
   That new is uprist from bed.   *risen*
Tho shall we sporten in delight   *then*
20 And learn with Lettice to wax light,   *grow/wanton*
   That scornfully looks askance.   *with disdain at us*
Tho will we little Love awake,

That now sleepeth in Lethe lake,
   And pray him leaden our dance.

THOMALIN

25 Willye, I ween thou be assot,   think/bewildered
For lusty Love still sleepeth not,   lively
   But is abroad at his game.

WILLYE

How kenst thou that he is awoke?   know
Or hast thyself his slumber broke?   n. 1
30   Or made privy to the same?   Or been made/intimate

THOMALIN

No, but happily I him spied   fortunately
Where in a bush he did him hide,
   With wings of purple and blue.
And were not that my sheep would stray,
35 The privy marks I would bewray,   peculiar/reveal
   Whereby by chance I him knew.

WILLYE

Thomalin, have no care for-thy;   about that
Myself will have a double eye,
   Ylike to my flock and thine.
40 For als at home I have a sire   father/n. 2
(A stepdame eke, as hot as fire)   stepmother/also
   That duly adays counts mine.   everyday

THOMALIN

Nay, but thy seeing will not serve;   watching
My sheep for that may chance to swerve   wander
45   And fall into some mischief.
For sithence is but the third morrow   from that time
That I chanced to fall asleep with sorrow
   And waked again with grief;
The while thilk same unhappy ewe,   During which time/that
50 Whose clouted leg her hurt doth show,   wrapped in cloth
   Fell headlong into a dell
And there unjointed both her bones;   dislocated
Mought her neck been jointed attones,   might/at the same time
   She should have need no more spell.   healing charms
55 Th'elf was so wanton and so wood   ewe/wild

(But now, I trow, can better good)   trust/knows
    She mought ne gang on the green.   (be content to) wander

WILLYE
Let be as may be, that is past;
That is to come, let be forecast.   n. 3
60 Now tell us what thou hast seen.

THOMALIN
It was upon a holiday,
When shepherds' grooms han leave to play,   servants/are allowed
    I cast to go a-shooting.   decided
Long wand'ring up and down the land
65 With bow and bolts in either hand   arrows
    For birds in bushes tooting,   looking
At length, within an ivy tod   bush
(There shrouded was the little god)
    I heard a busy bustling.
70 I bent my bolt against the bush,   aimed
Listening if anything did rush,
    But then heard no more rustling.
Tho, peeping close into the thick,   closely/thicket
Might see the moving of some quick   something alive
75   Whose shape appeared not.   was not distinguishable
But were it faery, fiend, or snake,
My courage earned it to awake,   yearned
    And manfully thereat shot.   and so
With that sprang forth a naked swain,   boy
80 With spotted wings like peacock's train;   tail-feathers
    And, laughing, lope to a tree,   leapt
His gilden quiver at his back,   golden
And silver bow, which was but slack –   not drawn
    Which lightly he bent at me.   swiftly
85 That seeing, I levelled again,   aimed
And shot at him with might and main,   vigorously
    As thick as it had hailed.
So long I shot that all was spent;
Tho pumice stones I hast'ly hent,   grabbed/n. 4
90   And threw, but nought availed;   helped
He was so wimble and so wight,   nimble/quick
From bough to bough he leaped light,
    And oft the pumies latched.   pumices/caught

Therewith afraid I ran away,
95 But he, that erst seemed but to play,   at first
   A shaft in earnest snatched,
   And hit me, running, in the heel.   n. 5
   For then I little smart did feel,
   But soon it sore increased,
100 And now it rankleth more and more,
   And inwardly it fest'reth sore,
   Ne wote I how to cease it.   know

WILLYE
Thomalin, I pity thy plight.
Perdie with Love thou diddest fight –   truly
105 I know him by a token;
   For once I heard my father say
   How he him caught upon a day   one day
   (Whereof he will be wroken)   Love/avenged
   Entangled in a fowling net
110 Which he for carrion crows had set   father
   That in our pear-tree haunted.
   Tho said, he was a winged lad,
   But bow and shafts as then none had
   Else had he sore been daunted.
115 But see the welkin thicks apace,   sky/darkens quickly
   And stooping Phoebus steeps his face: bathes (in the ocean)
   It's time to haste us homeward.

Willye's emblem
To be wise and eke to love,
Is granted scarce to God above.   barely

Thomalin's emblem
Of honey and of gall in love there is store;
The honey is much, but the gall is more.

April

This eclogue is purposely intended to the
honour and praise of our most gracious sover-
eign, Queen Elizabeth. The speakers herein
be Hobbinol and Thenot, two shepherds;
the which Hobbinol being before mentioned
greatly to have loved Colin, is here set forth
more largely, complaining him of that boy's   *lamenting*
great misadventure in love, whereby his mind
was alienate and withdrawn not only from
him who most loved him, but also from all
former delights and studies, as well in pleasant
piping as cunning rhyming and singing, and
other his laudable exercises. Whereby he taketh
occasion – for proof of his more excellency
and skill in poetry – to record a song which   *sing*
the said Colin sometime made in honour of
her Majesty, whom abruptly he termeth Elisa.   *concisely*

THENOT
Tell me, good Hobbinol, what gars thee greet?   *makes/weep*
What, hath some wolf thy tender lambs ytorn?
Or is thy bagpipe broke, that sounds so sweet?
Or art thou of thy loved lass forlorn?   *forsaken*

5   Or be thine eyes attempered to the year,   *attuned*
Quenching the gasping furrows' thirst with rain?
Like April shower, so streams the trickling tears
Adown thy cheek to quench thy thirsty pain.

HOBBINOL
Nor this, nor that, so much doth make me mourn,
10 But for the lad whom long I loved so dear   *because/Colin*
Now loves a lass that all his love doth scorn: *Rosalind*
He, plunged in pain, his tressed locks doth tear.   *curled*

Shepherds' delights he doth them all forswear;   *renounce*
His pleasant pipe, which made us merriment,
15 He wilfully hath broke, and doth forbear   *abstain from*
His wonted songs, wherein he all outwent.   *usual/surpassed*

THENOT
What is he for a lad you so lament?   what kind of lad is he
Is love such pinching pain to them that prove?   try it
And hath he skill to make so excellent,   versify
20 Yet hath so little skill to bridle love?   control

HOBBINOL
Colin thou kenst, the southern shepherd's boy:
Him Love hath wounded with a deadly dart.
Whilom on him was all my care and joy,   once
Forcing with gifts to win his wanton heart.   attempting/ungoverned

25 But now from me his madding mind is start,   foolish/started
And woos the widow's daughter of the glen.
So now fair Rosalind hath bred his smart;
So now his friend is changed for a fren.   stranger

THENOT
But if his ditties be so trimly dight,   composed
30 I pray thee, Hobbinol, record some one,   sing
The whiles our flocks do graze about in sight,
And we close shrouded in this shade alone.   well sheltered

HOBBINOL
Contented, I. Then will I sing his lay   song/n. 1
Of fair Elisa, queen of shepherds all,
35 Which once he made as by a spring he lay,
And tuned it unto the waters' fall.

'Ye dainty nymphs, that in this blessed brook
    Do bathe your breast,
Forsake your wat'ry bowers, and hither look,
40   At my request.
And eke you Virgins that on Parnass dwell,   Muses
Whence floweth Helicon the learned well,
    Help me to blaze
    Her worthy praise,
45 Which in her sex doth all excel.

'Of fair Elisa be your silver song,
    That blessed wight,   person
The flower of virgins; may she flourish long
    In princely plight.   condition
50 For she is Syrinx' daughter, without spot,   immaculate/n. 2

Which Pan, the shepherds' god, of her begot.
   So sprung her grace
   Of heavenly race;
No mortal blemish may her blot.

55 'See where she sits upon the grassy green,
   (O seemly sight!)
Yclad in scarlet, like a maiden queen,
   And ermines white.
Upon her head a crimson coronet,
60 With damask roses and daffadillies set;
   Bay leaves between,
   And primroses green,
Embellish the sweet violet.

'Tell me, have ye seen her angelic face,
65   Like Pheobe fair?
Her heavenly haviour, her princely grace,   bearing
   Can you well compare?
The red rose meddled with the white yfere,   mingled/together
In either cheek depeincten lively cheer.   depicts
70   Her modest eye,
   Her majesty,
Where have you seen the like but there?

'I saw Phoebus thrust out his golden head
   Upon her to gaze;
75 But when he saw how broad her beams did spread,
   It did him amaze.
He blushed to see another sun below,
Ne durst again his fiery face outshow.   dared/exhibit
   Let him, if he dare,
80   His brightness compare
With hers, to have the overthrow.   to be defeated

'Show thyself, Cynthia, with thy silver rays,   Diana
   And be not abashed:
When she the beams of her beauty displays,
85   Oh how art thou dashed!
But I will not match her with Latona's seed,
Such folly great sorrow to Niobe did breed.
   Now she is a stone,

And makes daily moan,
90 Warning all other to take heed.

    'Pan may be proud that ever he begot
        Such a bellibone;   fair lass
    And Syrinx rejoice that ever was her lot
        To bear such an one.
95 Soon as my younglings cryen for the dam,
    To her will I offer a milk-white lamb:
        She is my goddess plain,
        And I her shepherd swain,
    Albe forswonk and forswat I am.   overworked/sweating

100 'I see Calliope speed her to the place
        Where my goddess shines;
    And after her the other Muses trace,
        With their violins.
    Be they not bay branches which they do bear,   n. 3
105 All for Elisa in her hand to wear?
        So sweetly they play,
        And sing all the way,
    That it a heaven is to hear.

    'Lo, how finely the Graces can it foot   dance
110   To the instrument;   pipe
    They dancen deftly and singen soot   sweetly
        In their merriment.
    Wants not a fourth Grace, to make the dance even?
    Let that room to my Lady be yeven: given
115   She shall be a Grace
        To fill the fourth place,
    And reign with the rest in heaven.

    'And whither rennes this bevy of ladies bright,   runs/group
        Ranged in a row?
120 They be all Ladies of the Lake behight,   called/n. 4
        That unto her go.
    Chloris, that is the chiefest nymph of all,
    Of olive branches bears a coronal;
        Olives be for peace
125   When wars do surcease;   cease
    Such for a princess be principal.   n. 5

'Ye shepherds' daughters that dwell on the green,
 Hie you there apace;   *hurry/quickly*
Let none come there but that virgins bene,   *are*
130 To adorn her grace.
 And when you come whereas she is in place,
 See that your rudeness do not you disgrace: *rustic nature*
  Bind your fillets fast,   *hair ribbons*
  And gird in your waist   *tie*
135 (For more finesse) with a tawdry lace. *refinement/silk band*

'Bring hither the pink and purple columbine,   *n. 6*
 With gillyflowers;
Bring coronations, and sops-in-wine, *carnations/clove-pink*
 Worn of paramours;
140 Strew me the ground with daffadowndillies,   *daffodils*
 And cowslips, and kingcups, and loved lilies;   *buttercup*
  The pretty paunce   *pansy*
  And the chevisance   *[not known]*
 Shall match with the fair flower-de-lys.   *an iris/n. 7*

145 'Now rise up, Elisa, decked as thou art
  In royal array;
 And now ye dainty damsels may depart,
  Each one her way.
 I fear I have troubled your troops too long;
150 Let dame Elisa thank you for her song;
  And if you come hither
  When damsons I gather,
 I will part them all you among.'   *divide*

THENOT
And was thilk same song of Colin's own making? *this*
155 Ah, foolish boy, that is with love yblent.   *blinded*
Great pity is, he be in such taking,   *condition*
For nought caren that be so lewdly bent. *bent on such foolishness*

HOBBINOL
Sicker I hold him for a greater fon   *fool*
That loves the thing he cannot purchase.
160 But let us homeward; for night draweth on,
 And twinkling stars the daylight hence chase.

Thenot's emblem
O quam te memorem virgo?   n. 8
[What should I call you, maiden?]

Hobbinol's emblem
O dea certe
[Goddess surely!]

May

In this fifth eclogue, under the persons of two   n. 1
shepherds, Piers and Palinode, be represented
two forms of pastors or ministers – or the
Protestant and the Catholic – whose chief talk
standeth in reasoning whether the life of the
one must be like the other. With whom having
showed that it is dangerous to maintain any
fellowship, or give too much credit to their
colourable and feigned goodwill, he telleth him   Piers
a tale of the fox that, by such a counterpoint   deception
of craftiness, deceived and devoured the cred-
ulous kid.

PALINODE
Is not thilk the merry month of May,
When love-lads masken in fresh array?   lovers/dress
How falls it, then, we no merrier bene,   are
Ylike as others, girt in gaudy-green?   clothed
5 Our bluncket liveries be all too sad   grey coats
For thilk same season, when all is yclad
With pleasance: the ground with grass, the woods
With green leaves, the bushes with bloss'ming buds.
Youth's folk now flocken in everywhere,
10 To gather May-buskets and smelling-brier;   hawthorn/sweet-brier
And home they hasten the posts to dight,   adorn
And all the kirk pillars ere daylight,   church-pillars/before
With hawthorn buds and sweet eglantine,   sweet-brier
And garlands of roses and sops-in-wine.   a flower (the clove-pink)
15 Such merry-make holy saints doth queme,   please
But we here sitten as drowned in a dream.

PIERS
For younkers, Palinode, such follies fit,   young men
But we tway be men of elder wit.   two

PALINODE
Sicker this morrow, ne lenger ago,   not longer
20 I saw a shoal of shepherds outgo   clergy
With singing, and shouting, and jolly cheer.
Before them yode a lusty tab'rer,   went/drummer

That to the many a hornpipe played,   company/n. 2
Whereto they dancen, each one with his maid:
25 To see those folks make such jouisance   merriment
Made my heart after the pipe to dance.
Tho to the grene wood they speeden hem all,
To fetchen home May with their musical;   n. 3/music
And home they bringen in a royal throne,
30 Crowned as king; and his queen attone   agreed
Was Lady Flora, on whom did attend
A fair flock of faeries and a fresh band
Of lovely nymphs. (O that I were there,
To helpen the ladies their May-bush bear!)
35 Ah, Piers, be not thy teeth on edge, to think
How great sport they gainen with little swink?   work

PIERS
Perdie, so far am I from envy   truly
That their fondness inly I pity.   foolishness/heartily
Those faitours little regarden their charge   vagabonds
40 While they, letting their sheep run at large,
Passen their time, that should be sparely spent,   carefully
In lustihead and wanton merriment.   pleasure
Thilk same be shepherds for the devil's stead,   place
That playen while their flocks be unfed.
45 Well is it seen their sheep be not their own,
That letten them run at random alone;
But they be hired for little pay   n. 4
Of other, that caren as little as they   by another
What fallen the flock, so they han the fleece,   befalls
50 And get all the gain, paying but a piece.
I muse what account both these will make,
The one for the hire which he doth take,
And th'other for leaving his Lord's task,
When great Pan account of shepherds shall ask.   EK: Christ

PALINODE
55 Sicker, now I see thou speakest of spite,   from spite
All for thou lackest somedeal their delight.   in some measure
I (as I am) had rather be envied,
All were it of my foe, then fonly pitied: although/foolishly
And yet if need were, pitied would be,
60 Rather than other should scorn at me;

For pitied is mishap that n'as remedy,   has no
But scorned be deeds of fond foolery.
What shoulden shepherds other things tend
Than, sith their God his good does them send,   since
65 Reapen the fruit thereof (that is pleasure),
The while they here liven at ease and leisure?
For when they be dead, their good is ygo,   gone
They sleepen in rest, well as other moe.   just as/more
Tho with them wends what they spent in cost,   goes
70 But what they left behind them is lost.   n. 5
Good is no good but if it be spend;   unless
God giveth good for none other end.

PIERS
Ah, Palinodie, thou art a world's child:
Who touches pitch mought needs be defiled.   bitumen/must
75 But shepherds (as Algrind used to say)
Mought not live ylike as men of the lay: like laymen
With them it sits to care for their heir,   for laymen it's proper
Enaunter their heritage do impair;   lest/inheritance
They must provide for means of maintenance,
80 And to continue their wont countenance.   usual/standing
But shepherd must walk another way;
Sike worldly sovenance he must forsay.   remembrance/renounce
The son of his loins why should he regard   take care
To leave enriched with that he hath spared?   put aside
85 Should not thilk God that gave him that good
Eke cherish his child, if in his ways he stood?   also/Godly paths
For if he mislive in lewdness and lust,   the son
Little boots all the wealth and the trust   helps/estate
That his father left by inheritance:
90 All will be soon wasted with misgovernance.
But through this and other their miscreance,   false belief
They maken many a wrong chevisance,   EK: enterprise
Heaping up waves of wealth and woe,
The floods whereof shall them overflow.
95 Sike men's folly I cannot compare
Better than to the ape's foolish care,
That is so enamoured of her young one,
(And yet, God wote, such cause hath she none)   knows
That with her hard hold and straight embracing   tight

100 She stoppeth the breath of her youngling.
    So, oftentimes, whenas good is meant,   when
    Evil ensueth of wrong entent.   because of/judgement
       The time was once and may again retorn   return
    (For ought may happen that hath been beforn)   anything
105 When shepherds had none inheritance,
    Ne of land, nor fee in sufferance,   neither/n. 6
    But what might arise of the bare sheep,   from
    (Were it more, or less) which they did keep.
    Well, ywis, was it with shepherds tho: truly
110 Nought having, nought feared they to forgo;   do without
    For Pan himself was their inheritance,   EK: God
    And little them served for their maintenance.   they needed little
    The shepherds' God so well them guided
    That of nought they were unprovided:
115 Butter enough, honey, milk, and whey,   they had
    And their flocks' fleeces them to array.   to clothe themselves
    But tract of time, and long prosperity –   the passing
    That, nurse of vice, this of insolency –
    Lulled the shepherds in such security
120 That, not content with loyal obeisance,   obedience
    Some gan to gape for greedy governance   desire/n. 7
    And match themself with mighty potentates,
    Lovers of lordship, and troublers of states.   nations
    Tho gan shepherds' swains to look aloft   servants/at their masters
125 And leave to live hard, and learn to ligge soft.   cease/lie
    Tho, under colour of shepherds, somewhile   disguise/at some time
    There crept in wolves, full of fraud and guile,   'false' clergy
    That often devoured their own sheep
    And often the shepherds that did hem keep.   them
130 This was the first source of shepherds' sorrow,
    That now nill be quit with bail nor borrow.   will not/surety or pledge

PALINODE
    Three things to bear be very burdenous,
    But the fourth to forbear is outrageous.   endure/[proverbial]
    Women that of love's longing once lust,   desire
135 Hardly forbearen, but have it they must: with difficulty abstain
    So when choler is inflamed with rage,   anger
    Wanting revenge, is hard to assuage.   desiring
    And who can counsel a thirsty soul

With patience to forbear the offer'd bowl?
140 But of all burdens that a man can bear,
    Most is, a fool's talk to bear and to hear: worst
    I ween the giant has not such a weight,   think/Atlas
    That bears on his shoulders the heaven's height.
    Thou findest fault where n'is to be found,
145 And buildest strong wark upon a weak ground;   work
    Thou railest on right without reason,
    And blamest hem much for small encheason.   occasion
    How shoulden shepherds live, if not so?
    What? should they pinen in pain and woe?
150 Nay, said I thereto, by my dear borrow,   pledge
    If I may rest, I nill live in sorrow.   will not
       Sorrow ne need be hastened on,   does not
    For he will come without calling anon.   soon
    While times enduren of tranquillity,
155 Usen we freely our felicity;
    For when approachen the stormy stours,   times of turmoil
    We mought with our shoulders bear off the sharp   ward off
       showers.
    And, sooth to say, nought seemeth sike strife,   truth/unseemly
    That shepherds so witen each other's life,   blame
160 And layen her faults the world beforn,   their
    The while their foes done each of hem scorn.   do
    Let none mislike of that may not be mended:
    So conteck soon by concord mought be ended.   contention/might

    PIERS
    Shepherd, I list none accordance make   choose/agreement
165 With shepherd that does the right way forsake;
    And of the twain, if choice were to me,
    Had liefer my foe than my friend he be.   rather
    For what concord han light and dark sam?   have/together
    Or what peace has the lion with the lamb?
170 Such faitours, when their false hearts be hid,   imposters
    Will do as did the Fox by the Kid.   n. 8

    PALINODE
    Now, Piers, of fellowship, tell us that saying;   out of
    For the lad can keep both our flocks from straying.

PIERS
    Thilk same Kid (as I can well devise)   imagine
175 Was too very foolish and unwise.   extremely
    For on a time, in summer season,
    The Gate, her dam, that had good reason,   Goat/her = his
    Yode forth abroad unto the green wood,   went
    To browse, or play, or what she thought good.
180 But, for she had a motherly care
    Of her young son, and wit to beware,
    She set her youngling before her knee,
    That was both fresh and lovely to see,   he that
    And full of favour as kid mought be: as attractive as
185 His velvet head began to shoot out,
    And his wreathed horns gan newly sprout;
    The blossoms of lust to bud did begin   n. 9
    And spring forth rankly under his chin.
      'My son,' quoth she (and with that gan weep,
190 For careful thoughts in her heart did creep),   full of care
    'God bless thee, poor orphan, as he mought me,   may
    And send thee joy of thy jollity.
    Thy father – ' (that word she spake with pain;
    For a sigh had nigh rent her heart in twain)
195 'Thy father, had he lived this day
    To see the branch of his body display,   offspring
    How would he have joyed at this sweet sight!
    But ah, false Fortune such joy did him spite,   deny
    And cut off his days with untimely woe,
200 Betraying him into the traines of his foe.   snares
    Now I, a wailful widow behight,   ordained
    Of my old age have this one delight:
    To see thee succeed in thy father's stead,   place
    And flourish in flowers of lustihead;   n. 10
205 For even so thy father his head upheld,
    And so his haughty horns did he weld.'   imposing/wield
      Tho, marking him with melting eyes,
    A thrilling throb from her heart did arise,   EK: a piercing sob
    And interrupted all her other speech
210 With some old sorrow that made a new breach: appearance
    Seemed she saw in the youngling's face
    The old lineaments of his father's grace.   features
    At last her sullen silence she broke,   sad

And gan his new-budded beard to stroke.
215   'Kiddie,' quoth she, 'thou kenst the great care
      I have of thy health and thy welfare,   moral well-being
      Which many wild beasts liggen in wait   for which/lie
      For to entrap in thy tender state;
      But most the Fox, master of collusion,   trickery
220   For he has vowed thy last confusion.   final destruction
      For-thy, my Kiddie, be ruled by me,
      And never give trust to his treachery.
      And if he chance come, when I am abroad,   away
      Spar the yate fast, for fear of fraud;   shut/gate
225   Ne for all his worst, nor for his best,
      Open the door at his request.'
         So schooled the Gate her wanton son,   Goat
      That answered his mother, all should be done.
      Tho went the pensive dam out of door,
230   And chanced to stumble at the threshold floor:
      Her stumbling step somewhat her amazed
      (For such, as signs of ill luck, be dispraised),   censured
      Yet forth she yode, thereat half-aghast,   went
      And Kiddie the door sparred after her fast.   shut
235   It was not long after she was gone
      But the false Fox came to the door anon: straightaway
      Not as a Fox, for then he had been kend,   known
      But all as a poor pedlar he did wend,   go
      Bearing a truss of trifles at his back,   bundle
240   As bells, and babes, and glasses in his pack.   dolls/mirrors/n. 11
      A biggen he had got about his brain,   cap
      For in his headpiece he felt a sore pain;
      His hinder heel was wrapped in a clout,   rag
      For with great cold he had got the gout.
245   There at the door he cast me down his pack,   n. 12
      And laid him down, and groaned, 'Alack, alack!
      Ah, dear Lord, and sweet Saint Charity,
      That some good body would once pity me!'
         Well heard Kiddie all this sore constraint,   distress
250   And lenged to know the cause of his complaint.   longed
      Tho, creeping close behind the wicket's clink,   door's keyhole/n. 13
      Privily he peeped out through a chink: stealthily
      Yet not so privily but the Fox him spied –
      For deceitful meaning is double-eyed.

255 'Ah, good young master,' then gan he cry,
    'Jesus bless that sweet face I espy,
    And keep your corpse from the careful stounds   pains
    That in my carrion carcase abounds.'   rotten
      The Kid, pitying his heaviness,   dejection
260 Asked the cause of his great distress,
    And also who, and whence, that he were.   from where
    Tho he, that had well yconned his lear,   learnt/lesson
    Thus meddled his talk with many a tear: mingled
    'Sick, sick, alas, and little lack of dead,   almost
265 But I be relieved by your beastlihead.   unless/humanity
    I am a poor sheep, albe my colour dun,
    For with long travail I am brent in the sun.   n. 14/burnt
    And if that my grandsire me said be true,   the Pope
    Sicker I am very sib to you: closely related
270 So, be your goodlihead, do not disdain   goodness
    The base kindred of so simple swain.   kinship
    Of mercy and favour, then, I you pray
    With your aid to forestall my near decay.'   prevent
      Tho out of his pack a glass he took,   mirror
275 Wherein while Kiddie unwares did look,   unintentionally
    He was so enamoured with the newel,   novelty
    That nought he deemed dear for the jewel.   judged
    Tho opened he the door, and in came
    The false Fox, as he were stark lame   quite
280 (His tail he clapped betwixt his legs twain,
    Lest he should be descried by his train).   revealed/tail
      Being within, the Kid made him good glee,   n. 15
    All for the love of the glass he did see.
    After his cheer, the pedlar can chat   n. 16
285 And tell many leasings of this and that,   lies
    And how he could show many a fine knack.   trick
    Tho showed his ware, and opened his pack – goods/spread out
    All save a bell which he left behind   except
    In the basket for the Kid to find:
290 Which when the Kid stooped down to catch,
    He popped him in, and his basket did latch.   close
    Ne stayed he once the door to make fast,   even
    But ran away with him in all haste.
      Home when the doubtful dam had her hied, worried/hurried
295 She mought see the door stand open wide.

All aghast, loudly she gan to call
Her Kid, but he nould answer at all.   would not
Tho on the floor she saw the merchandise
Of which her son had set too dear a price.
300 What help? Her Kid she knew well was gone:
She wept, and wailed, and made great moan.
Such end had the Kid for he nould warned be
Of craft coloured with simplicity;   disguised
And such end, perdie, does all hem remain   truly/await
305 That of such falsers' friendship be fain.   deceivers'/glad

PALINODE
Truly, Piers, thou art beside thy wit,   have misunderstood
Furthest fro the mark, weening it to hit.   from/thinking
Now I pray thee, let me thy tale borrow
For our Sir John to say tomorrow   n. 17
310 At the kirk, when it is holiday;   church
For well he means but little can say.
But and if foxes be so crafty as so,   But if
Much needeth all shepherds hem to know.

PIERS
Of their falsehood more could I recount,
315 But now the bright sun ginneth to dismount,
And for the dewy night now doth nigh,   draw near
I hold it best for us home to hie.

Palinode's emblem
Πᾶς μὲν ἄπιστος ἀπιστεῖ.   n. 18
[The faithless do not trust.]

Pier's his emblem
Τίς δ' ἄρα πίστις ἀπίστῳ;
[What trust, then, in the faithless?]

June

This eclogue is wholly vowed to the complain-
ing of Colin's ill success in his love. For being
(as is aforesaid) enamoured of a country lass,   *in love with*
Rosalind, and having (as seemeth) found place
in her heart, he lamenteth to his dear friend
Hobbinol that he is now forsaken unfaithfully,
and in his stead Menalcas, another shepherd,   *place*
received disloyally. And this is the whole argu-
ment of this eclogue.

HOBBINOL
Lo, Colin, here the place whose pleasant site
From other shades hath weaned my wand'ring mind.
Tell me, what wants me here to work delight?   *do I lack/that gives*
The simple air, the gentle warbling wind
5 So calm, so cool, as nowhere else I find –
The grassy ground with dainty daisies dight,   *adorned*
The bramble bush, where birds of every kind
To the waters' fall their tunes attemper right.   *attune*

COLIN
O happy Hobbinol, I bless thy state,   *condition*
10 That paradise hast found which Adam lost.   *n. 1*
Here wander may thy flock early or late,
Withouten dread of wolves to be ytossed: *harried*
Thy lovely lays here mayst thou freely boast.   *short poems/recite*
But I, unhappy man, whom cruel fate
15 And angry gods pursue from coast to coast,   *n. 2*
Can nowhere find to shroud my luckless pate.   *shelter/head*

HOBBINOL
Then if by me thou list advised be,   *wish to*
Forsake the soil that so doth thee bewitch: *place*
Leave me those hills where harbour n'is to see, *[omit 'me']/habitation*
20 Nor holly-bush, nor brier, nor winding witch;   *witch elm*
And to the dales resort, where shepherds rich
And fruitful flocks be everywhere to see.
Here no night-ravens lodge, more black than pitch,   *n. 3/bitumen*
Nor elvish ghosts, nor ghastly owls do flee;
25 But friendly faeries, met with many Graces   *instead*

And lightfoot nymphs, can chase the ling'ring night
With hay-de-guys, and trimly-trodden traces,*   country dances
Whilst sisters nine,* which dwell on Parnass height,   *dance-steps
Do make them music for their more delight;   *the Muses/greater
30 And Pan himself, to kiss their crystal faces,
Will pipe and dance when Phoebe shineth bright:
Such peerless pleasures have we in these places.   unequalled

COLIN
And I, whilst youth and course of careless years the passage/carefree
Did let me walk withouten links of love,   chains
35 In such delights did joy amongst my peers: enjoy myself
But riper age such pleasures doth reprove;
My fancy eke from former follies move   also/moves
To stayed steps; for time, in passing, wears,   restrained
(As garments doen, which waxen old above)   do/show surface wear
40 And draweth new delights with hoary hairs.   white

Tho couth I sing of love and tune my pipe   could
Unto my plaintive pleas in verses made;
Tho would I seek for queen-apples unripe   n. 4
To give my Rosalind; and in summer shade
45 Dight gaudy garlands was my common trade,   fashioning/ornate
To crown her golden locks: but years more ripe,
And loss of her, whose love as life I weighed,
Those weary wanton toys away did wipe.

HOBBINOL
Colin, to hear thy rhymes and roundelays   short songs
50 Which thou were wont on wasteful hills to sing,   desolate
I more delight than lark in summer days;   than to hear a
Whose echo made the neighbour groves to ring,   you whose
And taught the birds (which in the lower spring   young trees
Did shroud in shady leaves from sunny rays)   hide
55 Frame to thy song their cheerful chirruping,   to tune
Or hold their peace for shame of thy sweet lays.   being abashed by

I saw Calliope, with Muses moe,   more
Soon as thy oaten pipe began to sound,
Their ivory lutes and tamburins forgo,   small drums/left
60 And from the fountain, where they sat around,
Renne after hastily thy silver sound.   run
But when they came where thou thy skill didst show,

They drew aback, as half with shame confound   as if/confounded
Shepherd to see them in their art outgo.   outdo

COLIN

65 Of Muses, Hobbinol, I con no skill,   know nothing
   For they be daughters of the highest Jove,
   And holden scorn of homely shepherd's quill.   simple/pipe
   For sith I heard that Pan with Phoebus strove,   since
   Which him to much rebuke and danger drove,   Pan
70 I never list presume to Parnass hill;   n. 5
   But, piping low in shade of lowly grove,   humbly
   I play to please myself, all be it ill.   even if it be poorly

   Nought weigh I who my song doth praise or blame, care
   Ne strive to win renown or pass the rest: surpass
75 With shepherd sits not follow flying fame,   it suits not
   But feed his flock in fields where falls hem best.   it's best for them
   I wot my rhymes be rough, and rudely dressed;   unpolished
   The fitter they, my careful case to frame: troubled/condition/express
   Enough is me to paint out my unrest,   for me/to depict
80 And pour my piteous plaints out in the same.   laments

   The god of shepherds, Tityrus, is dead,   EK: Chaucer
   Who taught me, homely as I can, to make,   roughly/versify
   He, whilst he lived, was the sovereign head
   Of shepherds all that be with love ytake:
85 Well couth he wail his woes, and lightly slake   could/quickly ease
   The flames which love within his heart had bred,
   And tell us merry tales to keep us wake,   awake
   The while our sheep about us safely fed.

   Now dead he is, and lieth wrapped in lead –
90 O why should death on him such outrage show? –
   And all his passing skill with him is fled,   surpassing
   The fame whereof doth daily greater grow.
   But if on me some little drops would flow
   Of that the spring was in his learned head,
95 I soon would learn these woods to wail my woe,   teach
   And teach the trees their trickling tears to shed.

   Then should my plaints, caused of discourtesy, Rosalind's discourtesy
   As messengers of all my painful plight,
   Fly to my love, wherever that she be,

100 And pierce her heart with point of worthy wite,   just blame
    As she deserves, that wrought so deadly spite.   harm
    And thou, Menalcas, that by treachery
    Didst underfong my lass to wax so light,   seduce/so wanton
    Shouldest well be known for such thy villainy.

105 But since I am not as I wish I were,
    Ye gentle shepherds (which your flocks do feed,
    Whether on hills, or dales, or otherwhere),
    Bear witness all of this so wicked deed,   all of you
    And tell the lass, whose flower is waxed a weed,   beauty
110 And faultless faith is turned to faithless fere,   companion
    That she the truest shepherd's heart made bleed
    That lives on earth, and loved her most dear.

    HOBBINOL
    O careful Colin, I lament thy case:
    Thy tears would make the hardest flint to flow.
115 And faithless Rosalind, and void of grace,
    That art the root of all this ruthful woe.   piteous
    But now is time, I guess, homeward to go:
    Then rise, ye blessed flocks, and home apace,   quickly
    Lest night with stealing steps do you forslow,   impede
120 And wet your tender lambs that by you trace.   go

                    Colin's emblem
                    Gia speme spenta
                    [Already hope is lost]   n. 6

July

This eclogue is made in the honour and com-   n. 1
mendation of good shepherds, and to the
shame and dispraise of proud and ambitious
pastors – such as Morell is here imagined to be.

THOMALIN
Is not thilk same a goatherd proud,   this
    that sits on yonder bank,   hill
Whose straying herd themself doth shroud   hide
    among the bushes rank?   thick

MORRELL
5 What ho, thou jolly shepherd's swain,   servant
    come up the hill to me;
Better is than the lowly plain
    als for thy flock and thee.   also

THOMALIN
Ah, God shield, man, that I should climb,   forbid
10   and learn to look aloft:
This rede is rife, that oftentime   saying/commonplace
    great climbers fall unsoft.
In humble dales is footing fast,   safe
    the trod is not so trickle;   path/precarious
15 And though one fall through heedless haste,   careless
    yet is his miss not mickle.   much
And now the sun hath reared up   n. 2
    his fiery-footed team,
Making his way between the Cup
20   and golden Diadem;
The rampant Lion hunts he fast,   Leo
    with Dog of noisome breath,   EK: Dog star/noxious
Whose baleful barking brings in haste
    pine, plagues, and dreary death.   suffering
25 Against his cruel scorching heat
    where hast thou coverture?   cover
The wasteful hills unto his threat   desolate
    is a plain overture.   open place
But, if thee lust to holden chat
30   with seely shepherd's swain,   simple

Come down and learn the little what
    that Thomalin can sayn.   say

MORRELL
Sicker thou's but a lazy lord,   certainly/lout
    and recks much of thy swink,   reckons/work
35 That with fond terms and witless words   foolish
    to blear mine eyes dost think.   dim/do
In evil hour thou hentest in hond   take/hand
    Thus holy hills to blame,
For sacred unto saints they stond,
40   and of them han their name.
St Michael's Mount who dost now know,   n. 3
    that wards the western coast?   guards
And of St Bridget's Bower, I trow,   [unlocated]/believe
    all Kent can rightly boast;
45 And they that con of Muses' skill,   know
    say mostwhat that they dwell   most say
(As goatherds wont) upon a hill,   used to
    beside a learned well.   EK: Parnassus
And wonned not the great god Pan,   dwelt/Christ
50   upon Mount Olivet,   Mt of Olives
Feeding the blessed flock of Dan,   Israelites
    which did himself beget?

THOMALIN
O blessed sheep! O shepherd great!
    that bought his flock so dear,
55 And them did save with bloody sweat   n. 4
    from wolves that would them tear.

MORRELL
Beside, as holy fathers say,   besides
    there is a hilly place
Where Titan riseth from the main   Hyperion/ocean
60   to renne his daily race,
Upon whose top the stars be stayed,   supported
    and all the sky doth lean:
There is the cave where Phoebe laid
    the shepherd long to dream.   Endymion
65 Whilom there used shepherds all   formerly
    to feed their flocks at will,

Till by his folly one did fall   n. 5
    that all the rest did spill;   ruin
And sithence shepherds be foresaid   ever since/banished
70   from places of delight:
For-thy I ween thou be afraid,   think
    to climb this hill's height.
Of Sinai can I tell thee more,
    and of Our Lady's Bower;   n. 6
75 But little needs to strew my store —   display my knowledge
    suffice this hill of our.
Here han the holy fauns recourse,   a gathering place/n. 7
    and sylvans hauten rathe;   early
Here has the salt Medway his source,
80   wherein the nymphs do bathe —
The salt Medway that trickling streams
    adown the dales of Kent,
Till with his elder brother, Thames,
    his brackish waves be meynt.   salty tasting/mingled
85 Here grows melampod everywhere,   black hellebore
    and terebinth, good for goats: the turpentine tree
The one my madding kids to smear,
    the next to heal their throats.
Hereto, the hills be nigher heaven,   nearer
90   and thence the passage eath,   easy
As well can prove the piercing levin   lightning
    that seldom falls beneath.   n. 8

THOMALIN
Sicker thou speaks like a lewd lorel,   ignorant fellow
    of heaven to deemen so: judge
95 How be I am but rude and borrel,   although/unlearned
    yet nearer ways I know.   better
'To kirk the nar, from God more far,'   church/nearer
    has been an old-said saw;   proverb
And he that strives to touch the stars
100   oft stumbles at a straw.
Alsoon may shepherd climb to sky   as soon may a
    that leads in lowly dales,   leads his flock
As goatherd proud that, sitting high,
    upon the mountain sails.
105 My seely sheep like well below,   innocent

they need not melampod;
For they be hale enough, I trow,   healthy/believe
  and liken their abode.
But if they with thy goats should yede,   go
110   they soon might be corrupted,
Or like not of the frowy feed,   musty
  or with the weeds be glutted.
The hills, where dwelled holy saints,
  I reverence and adore –
115 Not for themself, but for the saints,
  which han been dead of yore.   long ago
And now they be to heaven forewent,   gone before
  their good is with them go;   gone
Their sample only to us lent,   example
120   that als we mought do so.   might
Shepherds they weren of the best,
  and lived in lowly leas;   meadows
And sith their souls be now at rest,
  why done we them disease?   do/disturb
125 Such one he was (as I have heard
  old Algrind often sayn)   say
That whilom was the first shepherd,   once/Abel
  and lived with little gain: material wealth
As meek he was as meek mought be,
130   simple, as simple sheep;
Humble, and like in each degree   in every way
  the flock which he did keep.
Often he used of his keep   charge
  a sacrifice to bring –
135 Now with a kid, now with a sheep,
  the altars hallowing.
So louted he unto his Lord,   made reverence
  such favour couth he find,   could
That sithence never was abhorred   ever since
140   the simple shepherds' kind.
And such, I ween, the brethren were   believe
  that came from Canaan:
The brethren twelve, that kept yfere   n. 9/together
  the flocks of mighty Pan.
145 But nothing such thilk shepherd was   Paris
  whom Ida hill did bear,

That left his flock to fetch a lass   Helen
    whose love he bought too dear.
For he was proud, that ill was paid,
150   (no such mought shepherds be)   not/must
And with lewd lust was overlaid: mastered
    tway things doen ill agree,   the two/do
But shepherd mought be meek and mild,
    well-eyed (as Argus was),   sharp-eyed
155 With fleshy follies undefiled,
    and stout as steed of brass.   horse/n. 10
Sike one (said Algrind) Moses was,   such
    that saw his Maker's face –   n. 11
His face, more clear than crystal glass –
160   and spake to him in place.   straightaway
This had a brother (his name I knew),   Aaron
    the first of all his cote,   house
A shepherd true, yet not so true   n. 12
    as he that erst I hote.   formerly/named
165 Whilom all these were low, and lief,   humble/willing
    and loved their flocks to feed:
They never stroven to be chief,
    and simple was their weed.   dress
But now (thanked be God therefore)
170   the world is well amend:
Their weeds be not so nighly wore –   niggardly
    such simplesse might then shend.   disgrace
They be yclad in purple and pall,   rich cloth
    so hath their god them blist;   blessed
175 They reign and rulen over all,
    and lord it, as they list.   please
Ygirt with belts of glitterand gold,
    mought they good shepherds bene?   be
Their Pan their sheep to them has sold –   EK: the Pope
180   I say as some have seen.
For Palinode, if thou him ken,   know
    yode late on pilgrimage   went/lately
To Rome (if such be Rome) and then   n. 13
    he saw thilk misusage.   abuse
185 For shepherds, said he, there doen lead   live
    as lords done otherwhere: do
Their sheep han crusts, and they the bread,

the chips, and they the cheer;   crumbs
They han the fleece, and eke the flesh,   also
190   (O seely sheep the while!)   helpless
The corn is theirs – let other thresh,
     their hands they may not file.   defile
They han great stores and thrifty stocks,   flourishing flocks
     great friends and feeble foes:
195 What need hem caren for their flocks? –   them
     their boys can look to those.
These wizards welter in wealth's waves,   wise men/wallow
     pampered in pleasures deep;
They han fat kerns and leany knaves,   farmers/lean servants
200   their fasting flocks to keep.
Sike mister men be all misgone,   kind of/gone astray
     they heapen hills of wrath;   store up
Such surly shepherds han we none,   vainglorious
     they keepen all the path.

MORRELL
205 Here is a great deal of good matter
          lost for lack of telling: being poorly told
Now sicker I see thou dost but clatter;   chatter
     harm may come of melling.   meddling
Thou meddlest more than shall have thank,
210   to witen shepherds' wealth;   censure
When folk be fat, and riches rank,
     it is a sign of health.
But say me, what is Algrind he,   who
     that is so oft benempt?   named

THOMALIN
215 He is a shepherd great in gree,   degree
     but hath been long ypent.   confined
One day he sat upon a hill,
     as now thou wouldest me –
But I am taught by Algrind's ill,
220   to love the low degree.
For, sitting so with bared scalp,
     an eagle soared high   n. 14
That, weening his white head was chalk,
     a shell-fish down let fly:
225 She weened the shell-fish to have broke,

but therewith bruised his brain;
So now, astonied with the stroke,   stunned
        he lies in ling'ring pain.

MORRELL
Ah, good Algrind, his hap was ill,   fortune
230   but shall be bet in time.   better
Now farewell, shepherd, sith this hill
        thou hast such doubt to climb.   fear

Thomalin's emblem
In medio virtus
[Virtue dwells in the middle]

Morrell's emblem
In summo felicitas
[Happiness is in the highest]   n. 15

August

In this eclogue is set forth a delectable contro-   singing match
versy made in imitation of that in Theocritus,
whereto also Virgil fashioned his third and   after which
seventh eclogue. They choose for umpire of   n. 1
their strife Cuddie, a neatherd's boy, who –   cowherd's/n. 2
having ended their cause – reciteth also himself
a proper song, whereof Colin (he saith) was   admirable
author.

WILLYE
Tell me, Perigot, what shall be the game?
Wherefore with mine thou dare thy music match?   why/singing
Or be thy bagpipes renne far out of frame?   tune
Or hath the cramp thy joints benumbed with ache?

PERIGOT
5 Ah, Willye, when the heart is ill-assayed,   afflicted
How can bagpipe or joints be well apaid?   in good condition

WILLYE
What the foul evil hath thee so bestad?   beset
Whilom thou was peregal to the best,   formerly/equal
And wont to make the jolly shepherds glad   used
10 With piping, and dancing didst pass the rest.   at dancing/surpass

PERIGOT
Ah, Willye, now I have learned a new dance –
My old music marred by a new mischance.   misfortune

WILLYE
Mischief mought to that new mischance befall,   might
That so hath reft us of our merriment.
15 But rede me, what pain doth thee so appall?   advise
Or lovest thou, or be thy younglings miswent? young sheep/strayed

PERIGOT
Love hath misled both my younglings and me;
I pine for pain, and they my pain to see.

WILLYE
Perdie and wellaway, ill may they thrive: truly/alas/n. 3
20 Never knew I lover's sheep in good plight.   condition

But and if in rhymes with me thou dare strive,   *But if*
Such fond fant'sies shall soon be put to flight.   *foolish*

PERIGOT
That shall I do, though mochell worse I fared: *much*
Never shall be said that Perigot was dared.

WILLYE
25 Then lo, Perigot, the pledge which I plight: *put up*
A mazer ywrought of the maple ware,   *drinking bowl*
Wherein is enchased many a fair sight   *engraved/n. 4*
Of bears and tigers that maken fierce war;
And over them spread a goodly wild vine
30 Entrailed with a wanton ivy twine.   *entwined/wandering*

Thereby is a lamb in the wolf's jaws: *near that/wolf's*
But see how fast renneth the shepherd swain   *boy*
To save the innocent from the beast's paws;
And here with his sheep-hook hath him slain.
35 Tell me, such a cup hast thou ever seen?
Well mought it beseem any harvest queen.   *might/suit*

PERIGOT
Thereto will I pawn yonder spotted lamb: *pledge*
Of all my flock there n'is sike another,   *is not/such*
For I brought him up without the dam;
40 But Colin Clout reft me of his brother,
That he purchased of me in the plain field: *won from me*
Sore against my will was I forced to yield.

WILLYE
Sicker, make like account of his brother.   *Truly, expect the same for*
But who shall judge the wager won or lost?

PERIGOT
45 That shall yonder herd-groom and none other,   *shepherd's lad*
Which over the pulse hitherward doth post.   *pea-field/come*

WILLYE
But for the sunbeam so sore doth us beat,
Were not better to shun the scorching heat?

PERIGOT
Well agreed, Willye. Then sit thee down, swain: *good point/Cuddie*
50 Sike a song never heardest thou but Colin sing.

CUDDIE
Gin, when ye list, ye jolly shepherds twain: wish
Sike a judge, as Cuddie, were for a king.   fit for

PERIGOT It fell upon a holy eve,   happened/n. 5
WILLYE   Hey, ho, holiday,
55 PERIGOT When holy fathers wont to shrieve,   hear confession
WILLYE   – Now ginneth this roundelay.   n. 6
PERIGOT Sitting upon a hill so high,
WILLYE   Hey, ho, the high hill,
PERIGOT The while my flock did feed thereby   near by
60 WILLYE   (The while the shepherd self did spill),   himself/idle
PERIGOT I saw the bouncing bellibone,   bonny lass
WILLYE   Hey, ho, bonibell,
PERIGOT Tripping over the dale alone,
WILLYE   – She can trip it very well.   n. 7
65 PERIGOT Well decked in a frock of grey   dressed
WILLYE   (Hey, ho, grey is greet),   EK: signifies mourning
PERIGOT And in a kirtle of green say   skirt/fine cloth
WILLYE   (The green is for maidens meet),   n. 8/fitting
PERIGOT A chapelet on her head she wore,   garland
70 WILLYE   Hey, ho, chapelet,
PERIGOT Of sweet violets therein was store,
WILLYE   – She sweeter than the violet.
PERIGOT My sheep did leave their wonted food,
WILLYE   Hey, ho, seely sheep,   poor
75 PERIGOT And gazed on her as they were wood,   mad
WILLYE   Wood as he that did them keep.
PERIGOT As the bonny lass passed by,
WILLYE   Hey, ho, bonny lass,
PERIGOT She roved at me with glancing eye,   looked
80 WILLYE   As clear as the crystal glass.
PERIGOT All as the sunny beam so bright,   just as
WILLYE   Hey, ho, the sun beam,
PERIGOT Glanceth from Phoebus' face forthright,
WILLYE   So love into thy heart did stream;
85 PERIGOT Or as the thunder cleaves the clouds,
WILLYE   Hey, ho, the thunder,
PERIGOT Wherein the lightsome levin shrouds, bright lightning/hides
WILLYE   So cleaves thy soul asunder;
PERIGOT Or as Dame Cynthia's silver ray,   Diana's

90 WILLYE	Hey, ho, the moonlight,	
PERIGOT	Upon the glittering wave doth play,	
WILLYE	– Such play is a piteous plight.	*moving sight*
PERIGOT	The glance into my heart did glide,	
WILLYE	Hey, ho, the glider,	
95 PERIGOT	Therewith my soul was sharply gride,	*pierced*
WILLYE	– Such wounds soon waxen wider.	
PERIGOT	Hasting to ranch the arrow out,	*pull*
WILLYE	Hey, ho, Perigot,	
PERIGOT	I left the head in my heart-root,	
100 WILLYE	– It was a desperate shot.	*dangerous*
PERIGOT	There it rankleth aye more and more,	*always*
WILLYE	Hey, ho, the arrow,	
PERIGOT	Ne can I find salve for my sore,	*nor*
WILLYE	– Love is a careless sorrow.	*n. 9*
105 PERIGOT	And though my bail with death I bought,	*even if/release*
WILLYE	Hey, ho, heavy cheer,	
PERIGOT	Yet should thilk lass not from my thought,	*this*
WILLYE	– So you may buy gold too dear.	
PERIGOT	But whether in painful love I pine,	
110 WILLYE	Hey, ho, pinching pain,	
PERIGOT	Or thrive in wealth, she shall be mine,	
WILLYE	– But if thou can her obtain.	*only if*
PERIGOT	And if for graceless grief I die,	*grief at lacking favour*
WILLYE	Hey, ho, graceless grief,	
115 PERIGOT	Witness she slew me with her eye,	
WILLYE	– Let thy folly be the prief.	*proof*
PERIGOT	And you that saw it, simple sheep,	
WILLYE	Hey, ho, the fair flock,	
PERIGOT	For prief thereof, my death shall weep,	
120 WILLYE	And moan with many a mock.	*grimace*
PERIGOT	So learned I love on a holy eve,	
WILLYE	Hey, ho, holiday,	
PERIGOT	That ever since my heart did grieve,	
WILLYE	– Now endeth our roundelay.	

CUDDIE

125 Sicker, sike a roundel never heard I none: *roundelay*
Little lacketh Perigot of the best,
And Willye is not greatly overgone, *surpassed*
So weren his undersongs well addressed. *responses/arranged*

WILLYE
Herd-groom, I fear me thou have a squint eye; *are biased*
130 Arede uprightly, who has the victory? *declare plainly*

CUDDIE
Faith of my soul, I deem each have gained. *judge/won/no. 10*
For-thy let the lamb be Willye his own, *therefore*
And for Perigot (so well hath him pained), *exerted himself*
To him be the wroughten mazer alone. *drinking bowl*

PERIGOT
135 Perigot is well pleased with the doom; *judgement*
Ne can Willye wite the witeless herd-groom. *blame*

WILLYE
Never dempt more right of beauty, I ween, *judged/believe*
The shepherd of Ida that judged beauty's queen. *Paris/Venus*

CUDDIE
But tell me, shepherds, should it not yshend *disparage*
140 Your roundels fresh to hear a doleful verse *new/sorrowful*
Of Rosalind – who knows not Rosalind? –
That Colin made, ilk can I you rehearse. *the same*

PERIGOT
Now say it, Cuddie, as thou art a lad;
With merry thing it's good to meddle sad. *mix*

WILLYE
145 Faith of my soul, thou shalt ycrowned be
In Colin's stead, if thou this song arede; *place/recite*
For never thing on earth so pleaseth me
As him to hear, or matter of his deed. *work/composing*

CUDDIE
Then listneth each unto my heavy lay, *sad/poem, song*
150 And tune your pipes as ruthful as ye may. *piteously*

'Ye wasteful woods, bear witness of my woe, *unfrequented*
Wherein my plaints did oftentimes resound; *laments*
Ye careless birds are privy to my cries, *carefree/intimate with*
Which in your songs were wont to make a part;
155 Thou, pleasant Spring, hast lulled me oft asleep,
Whose streams my trickling tears did oft augment.

'Resort of people doth my griefs augment;   company
The walled towns do work my greater woe;
The forest wide is fitter to resound
160 The hollow echo of my careful cries;   troubled
I hate the house, since thence my love did part,
Whose wailful want debars mine eyes from sleep. absence

'Let streams of tears supply the place of sleep;
Let all that sweet is, void; and all that may augment depart
165 My dole, draw near. More meet to wail my woe sorrow/fitting
Be the wild woods my sorrows to resound
Than bed or bower, both which I fill with cries cottage
When I them see so waste, and I find no part empty

'Of pleasure past. Here will I dwell apart
170 In ghastful grove therefore, till my last sleep dreadful
Do close mine eyes; so shall I not augment
With sight of such a change my restless woe. constant
Help me, ye baneful birds whose shrieking sound injurious
Is sign of dreary death, my deadly cries mortal

175 'Most ruthfully to tune. And as my cries – piteously
Which of my woe cannot bewray least part – reveal
You hear all night – when nature craveth sleep –
Increase, so let your irksome yells augment. distressing/calls
Thus all the night in plaints, the day in woe,
180 I vowed have to waste, till safe and sound

'She home return, whose voice's silver sound
To cheerful songs can change my cheerless cries.
Hence with the nightingale will I take part;
That blessed bird that spends her time of sleep
185 In songs and plaintive pleas the more t'augment
The memory of his misdeed that bred her woe. Philomela

'And you that feel no woe, whenas the sound when
Of these my nightly cries ye hear apart, at a distance
Let break your sounder sleep, and pity augment.'

PERIGOT
190 O Colin, Colin, the shepherds' joy,
 How I admire each turning of thy verse;
And Cuddie, fresh Cuddie, the liefest boy, dearest
 How dolefully his dole thou didst rehearse.

CUDDIE
Then blow your pipes, shepherds, till you be at home:
195 The night nigheth fast, it's time to be gone.   comes

Perigot his emblem
Vincenti gloria victi
[To the conqueror belongs the glory of the conquered]

Willye's emblem
Vinto non vitto
[Conquered, not overcome]

Cuddie's emblem
Felice chi puo
[He is happy who can]   n. 11

September

Herein Diggon Davie is devised to be a shep-   imagined
herd that, in hope of more gain, drove his
sheep into a far country. The abuses whereof,
and loose living of Popish prelates, by occasion
of Hobbinol's demand, he discourseth at large.

HOBBINOL
Diggon Davie, I bid her good day;   him/n. 1
Or Diggon her is, or I missay.   him/mistake

DIGGON
Her was her, while it was daylight,
But now her is a most wretched wight.   man
5 For day, that was, is wightly past,   quickly
And now at erst the dark night doth haste.   at once

HOBBINOL
Diggon, arede, who has thee so dight?   explain/dealt with
Never I wist thee in so poor a plight.   knew
Where is the fair flock thou was wont to lead?   used
10 Or be they chaffered? Or at mischief dead?   sold/through misfortune

DIGGON
Ah, for love of that is to thee most lief,   which is/dear
Hobbinol, I pray thee gall not my old grief;   chafe
Sike question rippeth up cause of new woe,   such/opens up
For one opened mote unfold many moe.   might/more

HOBBINOL
15 Nay, but sorrow close shrouded in heart
(I know) to keep is a burdenous smart.
Each thing imparted is more eath to bear: easy
When the rain is fall'n, the clouds waxen clear.
And now, sithence I saw thy head last,   since
20 Thrice three moons be fully spent and past,
Since when thou hast measured much ground,   travelled
And wandered, I ween, about the world round,   think/n. 2
So as thou can many things relate:
But tell me first of thy flock's estate.   condition

DIGGON

25 My sheep be wasted (wae is me therefore):   lost/woe
The jolly shepherd that was of yore,   used to be
Is now nor jolly, nor shepherd more.
In foreign coasts, men said, was plenty;
And so there is, but all of misery.

30 I deemed there much to have eked my store, thought/increased
But such eking hath made my heart sore.
In tho countries whereas I have been,   those
No being for those that truly mean; livelihood/act properly
But for such as of guile maken gain,   from guile

35 No such country as there to remain.   no better place
They setten to sale their shops of shame,   set out for sale
And maken a mart of their good name.   n. 3
The shepherds there robben one another,
And layen baits to beguile her brother: their

40 Or they will buy his sheep out of the cote, shelter for sheep
Or they will carven the shepherd's throat.   cut/n. 4
The shepherd's swain you cannot well ken   boy/know
(But it be by his pride) from other men;
They looken as big as bulls that be bate,   fed/n. 5

45 And bearen the crag so stiff and so state,   neck/proudly
As cock on his dunghill crowing crank.   boldly

HOBBINOL

Diggon, I am so stiff and so stank   weary
That uneath may I stand any more;   scarcely
And now the western wind bloweth sore,   bitingly

50 That now is in his chief sovereignty,
Beating the withered leaf from the tree.
Sit we down here under the hill;
Tho may we talk, and tellen our fill,   then
And make a mock at the blust'ring blast: n. 6

55 Now say on, Diggon, whatever thou hast.

DIGGON

Hobbin, ah Hobbin, I curse the stound   hour
That ever I cast to have lorn this ground.   purposed/left
Wellaway the while I was so fond   alas/time/foolish
To leave the good that I had in hand

60 In hope of better that was uncouth: unknown
So lost the dog the flesh in his mouth.   n. 7

My seely sheep (ah, seely sheep)   *innocent*
That here by there I whilom used to keep, *here & there/formerly*
All were they lusty, as thou didst see,   *healthy*
65 Be all starved with pine and penury.   *suffering/poverty*
Hardly myself escaped thilk pain,   *the same*
Driven for need to come home again.   *out of*

HOBBINOL

Ah, fon, now by thy loss art taught   *fool*
That seldom change the better brought:
70 Content who lives with tried state,   *He is*
Need fear no change of frowning Fate;
But who will seek for unknown gain
Oft lives by loss and leaves with pain.

DIGGON

I wote ne, Hobbin, how I was bewitched   *know not*
75 With vain desire and hope to be enriched:
But sicker, so it is – as the bright star   *certainly/n. 8*
Seemeth ay greater when it is far,
I thought the soil would have made me rich.
But now I wote it is nothing sich,   *such*
80 For either the shepherds be idle and still,
And led of their sheep what way they will,   *by*
Or they be false and full of covetise,   *covetousness*
And casten to compass many wrong emprise. *try/achieve/enterprise*
But the more be freight with fraud and spite, *most/loaded with*
85 Ne in good nor goodness taken delight,
But kindle coals of conteck and ire   *discord*
Wherewith they set all the world on fire;
Which when they thinken again to quench,
With holy water they doen hem all drench. *them/drown*
90 They say they con to heaven the highway,   *know*
But by my soul I dare undersay   *say in contradiction*
They never set foot in that same troad,   *path*
But balk the right way and strayen abroad.
They boast they han the devil at command –
95 But ask hem therefore what they han pawned:
Marry, that great Pan bought with dear borrow *security*
To quit it from the black bower of sorrow. *deliver/hell*
But they han sold thilk same long ago;   *n. 9*
For-thy woulden draw with hem many moe.

100 But let hem gang alone, a God's name: go/in
    As they han brewed, so let hem bear blame.   brought about evil

HOBBINOL
Diggon, I pray thee speak not so dirk;   dark
Such mister saying me seemeth to mirk.   kind of/obscure

DIGGON
Then, plainly to speak of shepherds' most what,   relevant affairs
105 Bad is the best (this English is flat).   plain/n. 10
    Their ill haviour gars men missay,*   behaviour/makes
    Both of their doctrine, and of their fay.   *speak against them/faith
    They say the world is much war than it wont,   men/worse
    All for her shepherds be beastly and blunt;   because/their
110 Other say (but how truly I note)   do not know
    All for they holden shame of their cote;   Church
    Some stick not to say (hot coal on her tongue!) hesitate/their
    That sike mischief grazeth them among   they feed on
    All for they casten too much of world's care, attend too much to
115 To deck her dame and enrich her heir.   their/mistress
    For such encheason, if you go nigh,   reason
    Few chimneys reeking you shall espy: smoking
    The fat ox that wont ligge in the stall   lie
    Is now fast stalled in her crumenal.   purse/n. 11
120 Thus chatten the people in their steads,   villages, farms
    Ylike as a monster of many heads.   Hydra
    But they that shooten nearest the prick   mark
    Say other the fat from their beards doen lick;   n. 12
    For big bulls of Bashan brace them about,   surround
125 That with their horns butten the more stout,
    But the lean souls treaden underfoot.
    And to seek redress mought little boot,   might/help little
    For liker be they to pluck away more   as likely
    Than ought of the gotten good to restore;
130 For they be like foul quagmires overgrassed,
    That, if thy galage once sticketh fast,   shoe
    The more to wind it out thou does swink,   work
    Thou mought aye deeper and deeper sink: must
    Yet better leave off with a little loss,
135 Than by much wrestling to leese the gross.   lose/whole

HOBBINOL
Now, Diggon, I see thou speakest too plain:
Better it were a little to feign,
And cleanly cover that cannot be cured –   draw a veil over
Such ill as is forced mought needs be endured.   unavoidable
140 But of sike pastors how done the flocks creep?   with/do/manage

DIGGON
Sike as the shepherds, sike be her sheep:
For they nill listen to the shepherd's voice,   will not
But, if he call hem, at their good choice   as it suits them
They wander at will, and stray at pleasure,
145 And to their folds yield at their own leisure;   pens/n. 13
But they had be better come at their call,   been better to
For many han into mischief fall
And been of ravenous wolves yrent,
All for they nould be buxom and bent.   would not/meek/obedient

HOBBINOL
150 Fie on thee, Diggon, and all thy foul leasing: lying
Well is known that, sith the Saxon king,   n. 14
Never was wolf seen – many or some –
Nor in all Kent, nor in Christendom;   n. 15
But the fewer wolves (the sooth to sayn),   truth/say
155 The more be the foxes that here remain.

DIGGON
Yes, but they gang in more secret wise,   go/manner
And with sheep's clothing doen hem disguise.
They walk not widely as they were wont,
For fear of rangers and the great hunt,   n. 16
160 But privily prowling, to and fro,   stealthily
Enaunter they mought be inly know.   lest/inwardly

HOBBINOL
Or privy or pert if any bene,   concealed/open/be
We han great bandogs will tear their skin.   mastiffs

DIGGON
Indeed thy Ball is a bold big cur,
165 And could make a jolly hole in their fur.
But not good dogs hem needeth to chase,
But heedy shepherds to discern their face;   attentive

For all their craft is in their countenance,
They be so grave and full of maintenance.   upright behaviour
170 But shall I tell thee what myself know
Chanced to Roffynn not long ygo?   Young/n. 17

HOBBINOL
Say it out, Diggon, whatever it hight,   purports
For not but well mought him betight.   nothing/betide
He is so meek, wise, and merciable,   merciful
175 And with his word his work is convenable.   consistent
Colin Clout, I ween, be his self boy   own/n. 18
(Ah, for Colin! he whilom my joy).
Shepherds sich, God mought us many send,
That doen so carefully their flocks tend.

DIGGON
180 Thilk same shepherd mought I well mark.   draw attention to
He has a dog to bite or to bark;
Never had shepherd so keen a cur,
That waketh and if but a leaf stir.   [omit 'and']
Whilom there wonned a wicked wolf   lived
185 That with many a lamb had glutted his gulf,   appetite
And ever at night wont to repair
Unto the flock, when the welkin shone fair,   sky
Yclad in clothing of seely sheep,
When the good old man used to sleep.
190 Tho at midnight he would bark and bawl
(For he had eft learned a cur's call)
As if a wolf were among the sheep.
With that the shepherd would break his sleep,
And send out Lowder (for so his dog hote)   was called
195 To range the fields with wide open throat.
Tho, whenas Lowder was far away,
This wolvish sheep would catchen his prey –
A lamb, or a kid, or a weanel waste;   EK: weaned youngling
With that to the wood would he speed him fast.
200 Long time he used this slippery prank
Ere Roffy could for his labour him thank.   before
At end, the shepherd his practice spied
(For Roffy is wise and as Argus eyed),
And when at even he came to the flock,   evening
205 Fast in their folds he did them lock,   pens

And took out the wolf in his counterfeit coat,
And let out the sheep's blood at his throat.

HOBBINOL
Marry, Diggon, what should him affray   _frighten_
To take his own where ever it lay?
210 For had his weasand been a little wider,   _throat_
He would have devoured both hidder and   _EK: male and_
  shidder.   _female sheep_

DIGGON
Mischief light on him, and God's great curse –   _alight_
Too good for him had been a great deal worse.
For it was a perilous beast above all,   _dangerous_
215 And eke had he conned the shepherd's call, _also/learned_
And oft in the night came to the sheep-cote
And called 'Lowder!' with a hollow throat,
As if it the old man self had been.   _himself_
The dog his master's voice did it ween,
220 Yet half in doubt he opened the door
And ran out as he was wont of yore.   _formerly_
No sooner was out, but, swifter than thought,
Fast by the hide the wolf Lowder caught,
And had not Roffy renne to the steven,   _noise_
225 Lowder had been slain thilk same even.   _evening_

HOBBINOL
God shield, man, he should so ill have thrive,   _forbid_
All for he did his devoir belive.   _duty/promptly_
If sike be wolves, as thou hast told,
How mought we, Diggon, hem behold?

DIGGON
230 How but with heed and watchfulness,
Forstallen hem of their wiliness?   _to prevent_
For-thy with shepherd sits not play,   _suits_
Or sleep, as some doen, all the long day;
But ever liggen in watch and ward,   _to lie/in guard_
235 From sudden force their flocks for to guard.

HOBBINOL
Ah, Diggon, thilk same rule were too strait –   _strict_
All the cold season to watch and wait.

We be of flesh, men as other be,
Why should we be bound to such misery?
240 Whatever thing lacketh changeable rest,   as a change/n. 19
Mought needs decay, when it is at best.

DIGGON
Ah, but Hobbinol, all this long tale
Nought easeth the care that doth me forhale,   distress
What shall I do? What way shall I wend,   go
245 My piteous plight and loss to amend?
Ah, good Hobbinol, mought I thee pray
Of aid or counsel in my decay?

HOBBINOL
Now by my soul, Diggon, I lament
The hapless mischief that has thee hent.   unlucky/seized
250 Netheless, thou seest my lowly sail,   nevertheless/condition
That froward Fortune doth ever avail.   contrary/lower
But were Hobbinol as God mought please,
Diggon should soon find favour and ease.
But if to my cottage thou wilt resort,
255 So as I can I will thee comfort;
There mayst thou lig in a vetchy bed,   lie/pea-straw
Till fairer Fortune show forth her head.

DIGGON
Ah, Hobbinol, God mought it thee requite: may/repay
Diggon on few such friends did ever light.   alight

Diggon's emblem
Inopem me copia fecit
[Plenty has made me poor]   n. 20

October

In Cuddie is set out the perfect pattern of
a poet which, finding no maintenance of his
state and studies, complaineth of the contempt
of poetry (and the causes thereof): specially
having been in all ages, and even amongst the
most barbarous, always of singular account
and honour; and being indeed so worthy and
commendable an art; or rather no art, but a
divine gift and heavenly instinct not to be
gotten by labour and learning, but adorned
with both, and poured into the wit by a certain
ἐνθουσιασμός and celestial inspiration – as   enthusiasm
the author hereof elsewhere at large discour-
seth in his book called *The English Poet*, which   n. 1
book being lately come to my hands, I mind
also, by God's grace, upon further advisement   consideration
to publish.

PIERS

Cuddie, for shame, hold up thy heavy head,   n. 2
And let us cast with what delight to chase   consider
And weary this long ling'ring Phoebus' race.   the day
Whilom thou wont the shepherds' lads to lead   formerly/used
5 In rhymes, in riddles, and in bidding base: n. 3
Now they in thee, and thou in sleep, art dead.

CUDDIE

Piers, I have piped erst so long with pain   before
That all mine oaten reeds be rent and wore,   worn
And my poor Muse hath spent her spared store,   hoarded
10 Yet little good hath got, and much less gain.
Such pleasance makes the grasshopper so poor,   n. 4
And lig so laid when winter doth her strain.   lie/faint/oppress

The dapper ditties that I wont devise   pretty songs
To feed youth's fancy and the flocking fry,   young people
15 Delighten much: what I the bet for-thy?   better/therefore
They han the pleasure, I a slender prize;
I beat the bush, the birds to them do fly;
What good thereof to Cuddie can arise?

PIERS

    Cuddie, the praise is better than the prize,
20 The glory eke much greater than the gain: also
    O what an honour is it to restrain
    The lust of lawless youth with good advice,   desires
    Or prick them forth, with pleasance of thy vein, spur/through poetry
    Whereto thou list their trained wills entice.   wish/captivated/n. 5

25 Soon as thou ginn'st to set thy notes in frame,   begin/tune
    O how the rural routs to thee do cleave!   crowds
    Seemeth thou dost their soul of sense bereave,
    All as the shepherd that did fetch his dame   just/Orpheus
    From Pluto's baleful bower withouten leave: underworld/n. 6
30 His music's might the hellish hound did tame.   Cerberus

CUDDIE

    So praisen babes the peacock's spotted train,
    And wondren at bright Argus' blazing eye:
    But who rewards him ere the more for-thy?   ever
    Or feeds him once the fuller by a grain?
35 Sike praise is smoke that sheddeth in the sky;   such/disperses
    Sike words be wind, and wasten soon in vain.

PIERS

    Abandon then the base and viler clown.   n. 7
    Lift up thyself out of the lowly dust
    And sing of bloody Mars, of wars, of jousts.
40 Turn thee to those that wield the awful crown,   awe-inspiring
    To doubted knights, whose woundless* armour rusts dreaded
    And helms unbruised waxen daily brown.   *unscratched/helmets

    There may thy Muse display her flutt'ring wing,   n. 8
    And stretch herself at large from east to west –
45 Whether thou list in fair Elisa rest,   wish/keep as a subject
    Or, if thee please in bigger notes to sing,   grander
    Advance the worthy whom she loveth best,   praise/Leicester
    That first the white bear to the stake did bring.

    And when the stubborn stroke of stronger sounds   blows
50 Has somewhat slacked the tenor of thy string,   pitch
    Of love and lustihead tho mayst thou sing   pleasure/then

And carol loud, and lead the Miller's round,   a dance
All were Elisa one of thilk same ring: although/that
So mought our Cuddie's name to heaven sound.

CUDDIE

55 Indeed the Romish Tityrus, I hear,
Through his Maecenas, left his oaten reed –
Whereon he erst had taught his flocks to feed,   on which/previously
And laboured lands to yield the timely ear –   n. 9
And eft did sing of wars and deadly dread   afterwards/danger
60 So as the heavens did quake his verse to hear.

But ah! Maecenas is yclad in clay,
And great Augustus long ygo is dead,
And all the worthies liggen wrapped in lead   lie
That matter made for poets on to play: made material/to sing of
65 For ever, who in derring-do were dread,   always/feared
The lofty verse of hem was loved aye.

But after virtue gan for age to stoop,   courage/began
And mighty manhood brought abed of ease,
The vaunting poets found nought worth a   ambitious/no subject
pease   pea
70 To put in press among the learned troop.   n. 10
Tho gan the streams of flowing wits to cease,
And sunbright honour penned in shameful coop.   cage

And if that any buds of poesy,
Yet of the old stock, gan to shoot again,
75 Or it men's follies mote be forced to feign,   must/conceal
And roll with rest in rhymes of ribaldry,   obscenity
Or, as it sprung, it wither must again: as soon as
Tom Piper makes us better melody.   a rustic piper

PIERS

O peerless Poesy, where is then thy place?
80 If nor in prince's palace thou do sit
(And yet is prince's palace the most fit),
Ne breast of baser birth doth thee embrace,   nor
Then make thee wings of thine aspiring wit
And, whence thou cam'st, fly back to heaven apace.   quickly

CUDDIE

85 Ah, Percy, it is all too weak and wan   my Muse/entirely/faint
So high to soar and make so large a flight;
Her pierced pinions be not so in plight.   patched wings/inadequate
For Colin fits such famous flight to scan;   befits/attempt
He, were he not with love so ill bedight,   affected
90 Would mount as high and sing as soot as swan.   sweet/n. 11

PIERS

Ah fon, for Love does teach him climb so high,   fool/it is love
And lifts him up out of the loathsome mire: the world
Such immortal mirror as he doth admire   n. 12
Would raise one's mind above the starry sky,
95 And cause a caitiff courage to aspire;   wretched
For lofty love doth loathe a lowly eye.

CUDDIE

All otherwise the state of Poet stands,
For lordly Love is such a tyrant fell   ruthless
That, where he rules, all power he doth expel.   of other action
100 The vaunted verse a vacant head demands,   celebrated/untroubled
Ne wont with crabbed care the Muses dwell: harsh
Unwisely weaves, that takes two webs in hand.   half-finished cloths

Who ever casts to compass weighty prize,   tries/achieve
And thinks to throw out thund'ring words of threat,   denunciation
105 Let pour in lavish cups and thrifty bits of meat;   nourishing/n. 13
For Bacchus' fruit is friend to Phoebus wise,   wine
And when with wine the brain begins to sweat,
The numbers flow as fast as spring doth rise.   verses

Thou kenst not, Percie, how the rhyme should rage.   knows
110 O, if my temples were distained with wine   stained
And girt in garlands of wild ivy twine,   encircled with
How I could rear the Muse on stately stage,
And teach her tread aloft in buskin fine,   n. 14
With quaint Bellona in her equipage!   strange/retinue

115 But ah, my courage cools ere it be warm: before
For-thy content us in this humble shade,
Where no such troublous tides han us assayed;   times of war
Here we our slender pipes may safely charm.   play

PIERS
And when my gates shall han their bellies laid,   goats/given birth
120 Cuddie shall have a kid to store his farm.   stock

Cuddie's emblem
Agitante calescimus illo etc.   n. 15
[When he stirs we glow]

November

In this eleventh eclogue he bewaileth the death
of some maiden of great blood, whom he
calleth Dido. The personage is secret, and to   n. 1
me altogether unknown, albe of himself I often   although
required the same. This eclogue is made in   asked
imitation of Marot his song, which he made   n. 2
upon the death of Louise, the French Queen;
but far passing his reach, and in mine opinion
all other eclogues of this book.

THENOT
Colin, my dear, when shall it please thee sing,
As thou were wont, songs of some jouisance?   used to/mirth
Thy Muse too long slumb'reth in sorrowing,
Lulled asleep through Love's misgovernance.   bad government
5 Now somewhat sing, whose endless sovenance   something/memory
Among the shepherds' swains may aye remain,   boys/always
Whether thee list thy loved lass advance,   wish/praise
Or honour Pan with hymns of higher vein.

COLIN
Thenot, now n'is the time of merrymake,   is not
10 Nor Pan to hery, nor with Love to play: honour
Sike mirth in May is meetest for to make,   such/fittest
Or summer shade under the cocked hay.   stacked
But now sad winter welked hath the day,   shortened
And Phoebus, weary of his yearly task,
15 Ystabled hath his steeds in lowly lay,   meadow
And taken up his inn in fishes' hask.   abode/basket/n. 3
Thilk sullen season sadder plight doth ask,   this/mood
And loatheth such delights as thou dost praise:
The mournful Muse in mirth now list ne mask,   wishes not to mask
20 As she was wont in youngth and summer days.   her youth
But if thou algate lust light virelays   in any case/desire/songs
And looser songs of love to underfong,   undertake
Who but thyself deserves sike poet's praise?
Relieve thy oaten pipes that sleepen long.   take up

THENOT
25 The nightingale is sovereign of song –
Before him sits the titmouse silent be;   suits/tit

And I, unfit to thrust in skilful throng,
Should Colin make judge of my foolery?
Nay, better learn of hem that learned be,
30 And han been watered at the Muses' well: Hippocrene
The kindly dew drops from the higher tree,
And wets the little plants that lowly dwell.
But if sad winter's wrath, and season chill,
Accord not with thy Muse's merriment,
35 To sadder times thou mayst attune thy quill,   pipe
And sing of sorrow and death's dreariment.   dreariness
For dead is Dido, dead alas, and drent,   drowned
Dido, the great shepherd his daughter sheen;   beautiful/n. 4
The fairest may she was that ever went –   maid
40 Her like she has not left behind, I ween.   believe
And if thou wilt bewail my woeful teen,   grief
I shall thee give yond cosset for thy pain;   hand-reared lamb
And if thy rhymes as round and rueful been   perfect
As those that did thy Rosalind complain,
45 Much greater gifts for guerdon thou shalt gain   reward
Than kid or cosset, which I thee benempt: promised
Then up, I say, thou jolly shepherd swain;
Let not my small demand be so contempt.   despised

COLIN
Thenot, to that I choose thou dost me tempt;
50 But ah, too well I wot my humble vein,   know
And how my rhymes be rugged and unkempt;   harsh
Yet as I con, my conning I will strain.   can/ability

'Up, then, Melpomene! thou mournful'st Muse of nine,
Such cause of mourning never hadst afore;   before
55 Up, grisly ghosts! and up, my rueful rhyme!   Furies
Matter of mirth now shalt thou have no more;
For dead she is that mirth thee made of yore.   previously
Dido, my dear, alas, is dead,
Dead and lieth wrapped in lead.
60   O heavy hearse;   funeral rites
Let streaming tears be poured out in store;   plenty
O careful verse.   sorrowful

'Shepherds that by your flocks on Kentish downs abide,
Wail ye this woeful waste of nature's wark;   work

65 Wail we the wight whose presence was our pride;   person
   Wail we the wight whose absence is our cark.   grief
   The sun of all the world is dim and dark;
      The earth now lacks her wonted light,
      And all we dwell in deadly night.
70   O heavy hearse;
   Break we our pipes that shrilled as loud as lark;
      O careful verse.

   'Why do we longer live (ah, why live we so long)
   Whose better days death hath shut up in woe?
75 The fairest flower our garland all among   among all our
   Is faded quite and into dust ygo.   gone
   Sing now, ye shepherds' daughters, sing no moe   more
      The songs that Colin made in her praise,
      But into weeping turn your wanton lays.   happy songs
80   O heavy hearse;
   Now is time to die. Nay, time was long ygo;
      O careful verse.

   'Whence is it that the floweret of the field doth fade,   why
   And lieth buried long in winter's bale,   miseries
85 Yet soon as spring his mantle doth display   cloak
   It flowereth fresh, as it should never fail,
   But thing on earth that is of most avail –   value
      As virtue's branch and beauty's bud –
      Reliven not for any good?   revive
90   O heavy hearse;
   The branch once dead, the bud eke needs must quail;   also/wither
      O careful verse.

   'She, while she was (that *was* a woeful word to sayn),
   For beauty's praise and pleasance had no peer: ability to delight
95 So well she couth the shepherds entertain   knew how to
   With cakes and cracknels and such country cheer.   biscuits/food
   Ne would she scorn the simple shepherd's swain,
      For she would call hem often heme,   home
      And give hem curds and clotted cream.   them
100   O heavy hearse;
   Als Colin Clout she would not once disdain;   also
      O careful verse.

'But now sike happy cheer is turned to heavy chance,   fortune
Such pleasance now displaced by dolour's dint;   delight/grief's blow
105 All music sleeps where Death doth lead the dance,
And shepherds' wonted solace is extinct.
The blue in black, the green in grey, is tinct;   coloured
   The gaudy garlands deck her grave,   gay
   The faded flowers her corse embrave.   adorn
110   O heavy hearse;
Mourn now, my Muse, now mourn with tears besprint; besprinkled
     O careful verse.

'O thou great shepherd, Lobbin, how great is thy grief!
Where be the nosegays that she dight for thee?   made/n. 5
115 The coloured chaplets wrought with a chief,   coronets/flower-head
The knotted rush-rings and gilt rosemary?   n. 6/painted
For she deemed nothing too dear for thee.   thought
   Ah, they be all yclad in clay;
   One bitter blast blew all away.
120   O heavy hearse;
Thereof nought remains but the memory;
     O careful verse.

'Ay me, that dreary Death should strike so mortal stroke
That can undo Dame Nature's kindly course:
125 The faded locks fall from the lofty oak,
The floods do gasp – for dried is their source –   rivers
And floods of tears flow in their stead perforce.   place
   The mantled meadows mourn,   n. 7
   Their sundry colours turn.
130   O heavy hearse;
The heavens do melt in tears without remorse;   unceasing
     O careful verse.

'The feeble flocks in field refuse their former food,
And hang their heads as they would learn to weep;
135 The beasts in forest wail as they were wood   mad
(Except the wolves that chase the wand'ring sheep)
Now she is gone that safely did hem keep;
   The turtle on the bared branch   turtle-dove/n. 8
   Laments the wound that death did launch.   give
140   O heavy hearse;

And Philomele her song with tears doth steep;   bathe
    O careful verse.

'The water nymphs, that wont with her to sing and dance,
    And for her garland olive branches bear,   n. 9
145 Now baleful boughs of cypress doen advance;
    The Muses, that were wont green bays to wear,   laurel
    Now bringen bitter elder branches sere;   dry
        The Fatal Sisters eke repent   regret
        Her vital thread so soon was spent.
150   O heavy hearse;
    Mourn now, my Muse, now mourn with heavy cheer;
        O careful verse.

'O trustless state of earthly things, and slipper hope slippery
    Of mortal men, that swink and sweat for nought,   work
155 And, shooting wide, do miss the marked scope: target
    Now have I learned (a lesson dearly bought)
    That n'is on earth assurance to be sought;
        For what might be in earthly mould,   substance/n. 10
        That did her buried body hold:
160   O heavy hearse;
    Yet saw I on the bier when it was brought;   looked
        O careful verse.

'But maugre Death, and Dreaded Sisters'* deadly spite, despite
    And gates of hell, and fiery Furies' force,   *Fates
165 She hath the bonds broke of eternal night,   EK: darkness of hell
    Her soul unbodied of the burdenous corpse.
    Why then weeps Lobbin so without remorse?   unceasingly
        O Lobb, thy loss no longer lament,
        Dido n'is dead, but into heaven hent.   taken
170   O happy hearse;
    Cease now, my Muse, now cease thy sorrow's source;
        O joyful verse.

'Why wail we then? Why weary we the gods with plaints laments
    As if some evil were to her betight?   befallen
175 She reigns a goddess now among the saints,
    That whilom was the saint of shepherds' light,   formerly/simple
    And is installed now in heaven's height:
        I see thee, blessed soul, I see,
        Walk in Elysian fields so free.

180   O happy hearse;
      Might I once come to thee (O that I might!)
            O joyful verse.

      'Unwise and wretched men to weet what's good or ill: judge
      We deem of death as doom of ill desert;   judgement for
185   But knew we fools what it us brings until,   unto
      Die would we daily, once it to expert.   experience
      No danger there the shepherd can astert: befall
            Fair fields and pleasant leas there bene,   meadows/are
            The fields aye fresh, the grass aye green.
190   O happy hearse;
      Make haste ye shepherds, thither to revert;   return
            O joyful verse.

      'Dido is gone afore (whose turn shall be the next?)   ahead
      There lives she with the blessed gods in bliss,
195   There drinks she nectar with ambrosia mixt,   n. 11
      And joys enjoys that mortal men do miss.   lack
      The honour now of highest gods she is,
            That whilom was poor shepherds' pride,
            While here on earth she did abide.
200   O happy hearse;
      Cease now, my song, my woe now wasted is;   spent
            O joyful verse.'

THENOT
      Ay, frank shepherd, how be thy verses meynt   honest/mingled
      With doleful pleasance, so as I ne wot
205   Whether rejoice or weep for great constraint?   distress
      Thine be the cosset; well hast thou it got.   lamb
      Up, Colin, up! enough thou mourned hast:
      Now gins to mizzle, hie we homeward fast.   drizzle/hasten

                    Colin's emblem
                    La mort ny mord
                  [EK: Death biteth not]

December

This eclogue – even as the first began – is   n. 1
ended with a complaint of Colin to god Pan
wherein, as weary of his former ways, he
proportioneth his life to the four seasons of
the year: comparing his youth to the spring
time, when he was fresh, and free from love's
folly; his manhood to the summer, which he
saith was consumed with great heat and exces-
sive drouth caused through a comet or blazing   drought
star (by which he meaneth love, which passion
is commonly compared to such flames and
immoderate heat). His riper years he resem-   compares
bleth to an unseasonable harvest wherein the
fruits fall ere they be ripe; his latter age to   before
winter's chill and frosty season, now drawing
near to his last end.

The gentle shepherd sat beside a spring,   n. 2
All in the shadow of a bushy brier,
That Colin hight, which well could pipe and sing,   was called/who
For he of Tityrus his songs did lere.   learn
5   There as he sat in secret shade alone,
       Thus gan he make of love his piteous moan.   began

'O sovereign Pan, thou god of shepherds all,
Which of our tender lambkins takest keep;   care
And when our flocks into mischance mought fall,
10 Dost save from mischief the unwary sheep;
       Als of their masters hast no less regard   who also/n. 3
       Than of the flocks which thou dost watch and ward:

'I thee beseech (so be thou deign to hear   if it be
Rude ditties tuned to shepherd's oaten reed,   rustic
15 Or if I ever sonnet sung so clear,   short poem
As it with pleasance mought thy fancy feed)
       Hearken awhile from thy green cabinet   bower
       The rural song of careful Colinet.   troubled

'Whilom in youth, when flowered my joyful spring,   formerly
20 Like swallow swift I wandered here and there;
For heat of heedless lust me so did sting   desire

That I of doubted danger had no fear: dreaded
   I went the wasteful woods and forest wide,   uninhabited
   Withouten dread of wolves to be espied.

25 'I wont to range amid the mazy thicket,   used
   And gather nuts to make me Christmas game,   pleasure
   And joyed oft to chase the trembling pricket,   young buck
   Or hunt the heartless hare till she were tame.   timid/n. 4
     What recked I of wintry Age's waste?   reckoned/wasteland
30   Tho deemed I my spring would ever last.   then thought

'How often have I scaled the craggy oak,
   All to dislodge the raven off her nest?
   How have I wearied with many a stroke
   The stately walnut tree, the while the rest
35   Under the tree fell all for nuts at strife?
     For ylike to me was liberty and life.

'And for I was in thilk same looser years   those
   (Whether the Muse so wrought me from my birth,
   Or I too much believed my shepherd peers)
40 Somedeal ybent to song and music's mirth,   somewhat inclined
   A good old shepherd, Wrenock was his name,
   Made me by art more cunning in the same.

'Fro thence I durst in derring-do compare   poetic contests
   With shepherd's swain whatever fed in field;
45 And if that Hobbinol right judgement bear,
   To Pan his own self pipe I need not yield: himself/cf. Marsyas
     For, if the flocking nymphs did follow Pan,
     The wiser Muses after Colin ran.

'But ah, such pride at length was ill repaid;
50 The shepherd's god (perdie, god was he none)   in truth
   My hurtless pleasance did me ill upbraid –   harmless/reprove
   My freedom lorn, my life he left to moan.   lost/lamentation
     "Love" they him called that gave me checkmate,
     But better mought they have behote him "Hate".   called

55 'Tho gan my lovely spring bid me farewell,
   And summer season sped him to display
   (For Love then in the Lion's house did dwell)   Leo
   The raging fire that kindled at his ray:

A comet stirred up that unkindly heat,
60   That reigned (as men said) in Venus' seat.   astrological house

'Forth was I led, not as I wont afore   before
When choice I had to choose my wand'ring way,
But whither luck and Love's unbridled lore   creed
Would lead me forth on Fancy's bit to play: n. 5
65   The bush my bed, the bramble was my bower,
The woods can witness many a woeful stour.   affliction

'Where I was wont to seek the honey bee
Working her formal rooms in waxen frame,   symmetrical
The grisly toadstool grown there mought I see,
70 And loathed paddocks lording on the same;   toads
And where the chanting birds lulled me asleep,
The ghastly owl her grievous inn doth keep.   dreary/abode

'Then as the spring gives place to elder time
And bringeth forth the fruit of summer's pride,
75 Also my age, now passed youngthly prime,   even so/youthful
To things of riper reason self applied,   itself
And learned of lighter timber cotes to frame,   shelters/make
Such as might save my sheep and me fro shame.   disaster

'To make fine cages for the nightingale
80 And baskets of bulrushes was my wont:
Who to entrap the fish in winding sale   net
Was better seen, or hurtful beasts to hont?   hunt
I learned als the signs of heaven to ken –   know
How Phoebe fails, where Venus sits and when.   eclipses

85 'And tried time yet taught me greater things: experience
The sudden rising of the raging seas,
The sooth of birds by beating of their wings,   soothsaying
The power of herbs, both which can hurt and ease –
And which be wont t'enrage the restless sheep,   arouse
90   And which be wont to work eternal sleep.

'But ah, unwise and witless Colin Clout,
That kydst the hidden kinds of many a weed,   knew/natures
Yet kydst not ene to cure thy sore heart-root,   even
Whose rankling wound as yet does rifely bleed: copiously
95   Why livest thou still, and yet hast thy death's wound?
Why diest thou still, and yet alive art found?

'Thus is my summer worn away and wasted,
Thus is my harvest hastened all too rathe;   soon
The ear that budded fair is burnt and blasted,   ear of corn/withered
100 And all my hoped gain is turned to scathe: loss
        Of all the seed that in my youth was sown,
        Was nought but brakes and brambles to be mown?   bracken

'My boughs with bloss'ms that crowned were at first,
And promised of timely fruit such store,   in its season
105 Are left both bare and barren now at erst;   at once
The flatt'ring fruit is fallen to ground before,   promising/already
And rotted ere they were half mellow-ripe: sweet
        My harvest waste, my hope away did wipe.   perished

'The fragrant flowers that in my garden grew   n. 6
110 Be withered, as they had been gathered long: as if
Their roots be dried up for lack of dew,
Yet dewed with tears they han been ever among.
        Ah, who has wrought my Rosalind this spite,   to this
        To spill the flowers that should her garland   destroy
        dight?   adorn

115 'And I, that whilom wont to frame my pipe
Unto the shifting of the shepherd's foot,
Sike follies now have gathered as too ripe,   such
And cast them out as rotten and unsoot.   unsweet
        The looser lass I cast to please no more: fickle/resolve
120   One if I please, enough is me therefore.   God

'And thus of all my harvest-hope I have
Nought reaped but a weedy crop of care;
Which when I thought have threshed in swelling sheave,   bundle
Cockle for corn, and chaff for barley, bare: n. 7/bore
125   Soon as the chaff should in the fan be fined,   sifted
        All was blown away of the wavering wind.   by

'So now my year draws to his latter term: limit
My spring is spent, my summer burnt up quite,
My harvest hastes to stir up winter stern,
130 And bids him claim with rigourous rage his right:
        So now he storms with many a sturdy stour,   assault
        So now his blust'ring blast each coast doth scour.

'The careful cold hath nipped my rugged rind,
And in my face deep furrows eld hath pight;   old age/put
135 My head besprent with hoary frost I find,   besprinkled
And by mine eye the crow his claw doth write;
    Delight is laid abed, and pleasure past;
    No sun now shines, clouds han all overcast.

'Now leave, ye shepherds' boys, your merry glee;
140 My Muse is hoarse and weary of this stound.   struggle
Here will I hang my pipe upon this tree –
Was never pipe of reed did better sound.
    Winter is come that blows the bitter blast,
    And after winter dreary death does haste.

145 'Gather ye together, my little flock,
My little flock that was to me so lief;   dear
Let me, ah, let me in your folds ye lock,   pens
Ere the breme winter breed you greater grief.   sharp
    Winter is come that blows the baleful breath,
150   And after winter cometh timely death.

'Adieu delights, that lulled me asleep,
Adieu my dear, whose love I bought so dear;
Adieu my little lambs and loved sheep,
Adieu ye woods that oft my witness were:
155   Adieu good Hobbinol, that was so true,
    Tell Rosalind, her Colin bids her adieu.'

                    Colin's emblem   n. 8

[Epilogue]   n. 9

    Lo, I have made a calendar for every year,
That steel in strength and time in durance* shall outwear: n. 10
And if I marked well the stars' revolution,   *endurance
    It shall continue till the world's dissolution   the calendar
5 To teach the ruder shepherd how to feed his sheep,
And from the falser's fraud his folded* flock to keep.   deceiver's
    Go, little calendar, thou hast a free passport,   *penned
Go but a lowly gate amongst the meaner sort: But go/way
Dare not to match thy pipe with Tityrus his style,
10   Nor with the pilgrim that the ploughman played awhile,   n. 11

But follow them far off, and their high steps adore.
The better please, the worse despise: I ask no more.

Merce non mercede
[Grace not wages]   n. 12

MUIOPOTMOS: OR,
THE FATE OF THE BUTTERFLY

By Ed. Sp.

Dedicated to the most fair and
virtuous lady, the Lady
Carey.

London. Imprinted for William Ponsonby, dwelling
in Paul's Churchyard at the sign of the Bishop's
head.

To the right worthy and virtuous Lady, the
Lady Carey.

Most brave and bountiful Lady, for so excel-
lent favours as I have received at your sweet
hands, to offer these few leaves as in recom-   pages
pense should be as to offer flowers to the gods
for their divine benefits. Therefore I have
determined to give myself wholly to you, as
quite abandoned from myself and absolutely
vowed to your services – which in all right is   justice
ever held for full recompense of debt or
damage, to have the person yielded.
  My person I wot well how little worth it is.   know
But the faithful mind and humble zeal which I
bear unto your Ladyship may perhaps be more
of price, as may please you to account and use
the poor service thereof: which taketh glory to   accounts it
advance your excellent parts and noble virtues,   qualities
and to spend itself in honouring you, not so
much for your great bounty to myself (which
yet may not be unminded), nor for name or   forgotten
kindred's sake by you vouchsafed (being also   acknowledged
regardable), as for that honourable name
which ye have by your brave deserts purchased   excellent qualities
to yourself, and spread in the mouths of all
men; with which I have also presumed to grace

my verses, and under your name to commend
to the world this small poem.

The which beseeching your Ladyship to take   accept kindly
in worth, and of all things therein according to
your wonted graciousness to make a mild con-   usual
struction, I humbly pray for your happiness.   n. 2

Your Ladyship, ever humbly,
E. S.

I sing of deadly dolorous debate,   strife/n. 3
Stirred up through wrathful Nemesis' despite   malice
Betwixt two mighty ones of great estate,
Drawn into arms and proof of mortal fight   the trial
5 Through proud ambition and heart-swelling hate,
Whilst neither could the other's greater might
And sdeignful scorn endure: that from small jar   disdainful/discord
Their wraths at length broke into open war.

The root whereof and tragical effect   outcome
10 Vouchsafe, O thou the mournful'st Muse of nine grant/Melpomene
(That wont'st the tragic stage for to direct   are used
In funeral complaints and wailful tine),   affliction
Reveal to me, and all the means detect,
Through which sad Clarion did at last decline
15 To lowest wretchedness – and is there then
Such rancour in the hearts of mighty men?

Of all the race of silver-winged flies   insects/n. 4
Which do possess the empire of the air
Betwixt the centred earth and azure skies,
20 Was none more favourable nor more fair   fortunate
(Whilst heaven did favour his felicities)
Than Clarion, the eldest son and heir
Of Muscaroll – and in his father's sight   n. 5
Of all alive did seem the fairest wight.   creature

25 With fruitful hope his aged breast he fed
Of future good, which his young toward years –   Clarion's/obliging
Full of brave courage and bold hardihead   spirit/audacity
Above th'ensample of his equal peers –
Did largely promise; and to him fore-read   foretold

30 (Whilst oft his heart did melt in tender tears)   Muscaroll's
   That he in time would sure prove such an one
   As should be worthy of his father's throne.

   The fresh young fly, in whom the kindly fire   natural
   Of lustful youngth began to kindle fast,   vigorous youth
35 Did much disdain to subject his desire
   To loathsome sloth, or hours in ease to waste,
   But joyed to range abroad in fresh attire,
   Through the wide compass of the airy coast,   region
   And with unwearied wings each part t'inquire   explore
40 Of the wide rule of his renowned sire.

   For he so swift and nimble was of flight
   That from this lower tract he dared to stie   region/climb
   Up to the clouds and thence with pinions light   wings
   To mount aloft unto the crystal sky,   Ptolemaic
45 To view the workmanship of heaven's height:
   Whence down descending he along would fly
   Upon the streaming rivers, sport to find,
   And oft would dare to tempt the troublous wind.

   So on a summer's day, when season mild
50 With gentle calm the world had quieted,
   And high in heaven Hyperion's fiery child   Helios
   Ascending did his beams abroad dispread,   spread out
   Whiles all the heavens on lower creatures smiled –
   Young Clarion, with vauntful lustihead,   boastful vigour
55 After his guise did cast abroad to fare,   custom/decide/go
   And thereto gan his furnitures prepare.   began/equipment

   His breast-plate first, that was of substance pure,
   Before his noble heart he firmly bound,
   That mought his life from iron death assure,   might/protect
60 And ward his gentle corpse from cruel wound;   guard/body
   For it by art was framed to endure
   The bite of baleful steel and bitter stound,   attack
   No less than that which Vulcan made to shield
   Achilles' life from fate of Trojan field.   doom

65 And then about his shoulders broad he threw
   A hairy hide of some wild beast, whom he
   In savage forest by adventure slew,   wild/chance

And reft the spoil his ornament to be;   took
Which, sprading all his back with dreadful view,   covering/sight
70 Made all, that him so horrible did see,
Think him Alcides with the lion's skin,   Heracles
When the Nemean conquest he did win.

Upon his head his glistering burgonet,   glittering/helmet
The which was wrought by wonderous device
75 And curiously engraven, he did set.   finely
The metal was of rare and passing price: surpassing
Not Bilbo steel, nor brass from Corinth fet,   n. 6/fetched
Nor costly orichalc from strange Phoenice,   foreign/Phoenicia
But such as could both Phoebus' arrows ward
80 And th'hailing darts of heaven beating hard.   rain

Therein two deadly weapons fixed he bore,
Strongly outlanced towards either side,   out-thrust
Like two sharp spears, his enemies to gore:
Like as a war-like brigantine, applied   small galley/prepared
85 To fight, lays forth her threatful pikes afore –
The engines which in them sad death do hide –   weapons
So did this fly outstretch his fearful horns,
Yet so as him their terror more adorns.

Lastly his shiny wings as silver bright,
90 Painted with thousand colours passing far
All painters' skill, he did about him dight: draw
Not half so many sundry colours are   different
In Iris' bow; ne heaven doth shine so bright,   nor
Distinguished with many a twinkling star;
95 Nor Juno's bird in her eye-spotted train
So many goodly colours doth contain;

Ne (may it be withouten peril spoken)
The archer god, the son of Cytheree –   Venus
That joys on wretched lovers to be wroken   avenged
100 And heaped spoils of bleeding hearts to see –
Bears in his wings so many a changeful token.   n. 7
Ah my liege lord, forgive it unto me,
If ought against thine honour I have told:
Yet sure those wings were fairer manifold.   many times

105 Full many a lady fair, in court full oft
    Beholding them, him secretly envied,
    And wished that two such fans, so silken soft
    And golden fair, her love would her provide;
    Or that, when them the gorgeous fly had doffed,   taken off
110 Some one that would with grace be gratified,   rewarded/n. 8
    From him would steal them privily away,   secretly
    And bring to her so precious a prey.

    Report is that dame Venus, on a day
    In spring when flowers do clothe the fruitful ground,
115 Walking abroad with all her nymphs to play,
    Bade her fair damsels flocking her around
    To gather flowers, her forehead to array.
    Amongst the rest a gentle nymph was found,
    Hight Astery, excelling all the crew   called/n. 9
120 In courteous usage and unstained hue,   behaviour/appearance

    Who being nimbler jointed than the rest,
    And more industrious, gathered more store
    Of the field's honour than the others' best.   flowers
    Which they in secret hearts envying sore,
125 Told Venus, when her as the worthiest   Astery
    She praised, that Cupid (as they heard before)
    Did lend her secret aid in gathering
    Into her lap the children of the spring.

    Whereof the goddess gathering jealous fear   from which
130 (Not yet unmindful how not long ago   forgetful
    Her son to Psyche secret love did bear,
    And long it close concealed, till mickle woe   much
    Thereof arose and many a rueful tear),
    Reason with sudden rage did overgo   she overwhelmed
135 And, giving hasty credit to th'accuser,
    Was led away of them that did abuse her.   by/deceive

    Eftsoons that damsel, by her heavenly might,   presently
    She turned into a winged butterfly,   Venus
    In the wide air to make her wand'ring flight;
140 And all those flowers, with which so plenteously
    Her lap she filled had, that bred her spite,
    She placed in her wings for memory

Of her pretended crime, though crime none were:
Since which that fly them in her wings doth bear.

145 Thus the fresh Clarion being ready dight,   attired
    Unto his journey did himself address,
    And with good speed began to take his flight:
    Over the fields – in his frank lustiness –   unchecked vigour
    And all the champian he soared light,   plain
150 And all the country wide he did possess,
    Feeding upon their pleasures bounteously;
    That none gainsaid, nor did him envy.   spoke against

    The woods, the rivers, and the meadows green,
    With his air-cutting wings he measured wide;
155 Ne did he leave the mountains bare unseen,
    Nor the rank grassy fens' delights untried.   (over-)luxuriant
    But none of these, however sweet they been,   be
    Mote please his fancy nor him cause t'abide: might/stay
    His choiceful sense with every change doth flit;   fickle
160 No common things may please a wavering wit.

    To the gay gardens his unstaid desire   unsettled
    Him wholly carried, to refresh his sprites: spirits
    There lavish Nature, in her best attire,
    Pours forth sweet odours and alluring sights;
165 And Art, with her contending, doth aspire
    T'excel the natural with made delights;
    And all that fair or pleasant may be found,
    In riotous excess doth there abound.

    There he arriving, round about doth fly
170 From bed to bed, from one to other border,
    And takes survey with curious busy eye   attentive
    Of every flower and herb there set in order:
    Now this, now that, he tasteth tenderly,
    Yet none of them he rudely doth disorder,
175 Ne with his feet their silken leaves deface,
    But pastures on the pleasures of each place.

    And evermore with most variety   constantly
    And change of sweetness (for all change is sweet),
    He casts his glutton sense to satisfy –   seeks
180 Now sucking of the sap of herb most meet,   suitable

Or of the dew which yet on them does lie,
Now in the same bathing his tender feet:
And then he percheth on some branch thereby   near by
To weather him, and his moist wings to dry.   to air himself

185 And then again he turneth to his play,
     To spoil the pleasures of that paradise: plunder
     The wholesome sage, and lavender still grey,
     Rank-smelling rue, and cumin good for eyes,   strong
     The roses reigning in the pride of May,
190 Sharp hyssop, good for green wounds' remedies,   unhealing
     Fair marigolds, and bees-alluring thyme,
     Sweet marjoram, and daisies decking prime;   spring

     Cool violets, and orpine growing still,   n. 10
     Embathed balm, and cheerful galingale,
195 Fresh costmary, and breathful camomile,
     Dull poppy, and drink-quick'ning setvale,   valerian
     Vein-healing vervain, and head-purging dill,
     Sound savory, and basil hearty-hale,
     Fat coleworts, and comforting perseline,   cabbages
200 Cold lettuce, and refreshing rosemarine;   rosemary

     And whatso else of virtue good or ill
     Grew in this garden, fetched from far away,
     Of every one he takes and tastes at will
     And on their pleasures greedily doth prey.
205 Then when he hath both played and fed his fill,
     In the warm sun he doth himself embay,   bathe
     And there him rests in riotous suffisance   abundance
     Of all his gladfulness and kingly joyance.

     What more felicity can fall to creature
210 Than to enjoy delight with liberty,
     And to be lord of all the works of nature? –
     To reign in th'air from earth to highest sky,
     To feed on flowers and weeds of glorious feature,
     To take whatever thing doth please the eye.
215 Who rests not pleased with such happiness,
     Well worthy he to taste of wretchedness.

     But what on earth can long abide in state?   one state
     Or who can him assure of happy day,

Sith morning fair may bring foul evening late,   *since*
220 And least mishap the most bliss alter may?
    For thousand perils lie in close await   *secret ambush*
    About us daily, to work our decay;
    That none, except a god (or god him guide)
    May them avoid or remedy provide.

225 And whatso heavens in their secret doom   *judgement*
    Ordained have, how can frail fleshly wight   *man*
    Forecast, but it must needs to issue come?
    The sea, the air, the fire, the day, the night,
    And th'armies of their creatures all and some   *one and all*
230 Do serve to them, and with importune might   *severe*
    War against us the vassals of their will.
    Who then can save what they dispose to spill?   *destroy*

    Not thou, O Clarion, though fairest thou
    Of all thy kind; unhappy happy fly,
235 Whose cruel fate is woven even now
    Of Jove's own hand, to work thy misery.
    Ne may thee help the many-hearty vow   *heart-felt*
    Which thy old sire with sacred piety
    Hath poured forth for thee, and th'altars sprent –   *sprinkled*
240 Nought may thee save from heaven's avengement.

    It fortuned (as heavens had behight)   *ordained*
    That in this garden where young Clarion
    Was wont to solace him, a wicked wight –   *enjoy himself/creature*
    The foe of fair things, th'author of confusion,
245 The shame of nature, the bondslave of spite –
    Had lately built his hateful mansion   *malignant*
    And, lurking closely, in await now lay,
    How he might any in his trap betray.

    But when he spied the joyous butterfly
250 In this fair plot dispacing to and fro,   *moving*
    Fearless of foes and hidden jeopardy,
    Lord how he gan for to bestir him tho,   *then*
    And to his wicked work each part apply!
    His heart did earn against his hated foe,   *rage*
255 And bowels so with rankling poison swelled   *corrosive*
    That scarce the skin the strong contagion held.   *poison*

The cause why he this fly so maliced   hated
Was (as in stories it is written found)
For that his mother, which him bore and bred,
260 The most fine-fingered workwoman on ground,   earth
Arachne, by his means was vanquished   Clarion's
Of Pallas, and in her own skill confound   By/defeated
When she with her for excellence contended:
That wrought her shame, and sorrow never ended.

265 For the Tritonian goddess having heard
Her blazed fame, which all the world had filled,   proclaimed
Came down to prove the truth, and due reward
For her praiseworthy workmanship to yield:
But the presumptuous damsel rashly dared
270 The goddess self to challenge to the field,
And to compare with her in curious skill   intricate
Of works with loom, with needle, and with quill.   spool

Minerva did the challenge not refuse,
But deigned with her the paragon to make: contest
275 So to their work they sit, and each doth choose
What story she will for her tapet take.   tapestry
Arachne figured how Jove did abuse   deceive
Europa like a bull, and on his back
Her through the sea did bear; so lively seen,
280 That it true sea and true bull ye would ween.   think

She seemed still back unto the land to look
And her play-fellows' aid to call, and fear
The dashing of the waves, that up she took   so that
Her dainty feet and garments gathered near:
285 But Lord! how she in every member shook
Whenas the land she saw no more appear   when
But a wild wilderness of waters deep –
Then gan she greatly to lament and weep.

Before the bull she pictured winged Love,   Arachne/Cupid
290 With his young brother, Sport, light fluttering
Upon the waves, as each had been a dove;   as if
The one his bow and shafts, the other spring   youth
A burning tede about his head did move,   wood-torch
As in their sire's new love both triumphing:

295 And many nymphs about them flocking round,
And many tritons which their horns did sound.   mermen

And, round about, her work she did empale   enclose
With a fair border wrought of sundry flowers,
Enwoven with an ivy winding trail –
300 A goodly work, full fit for kingly bowers,
Such as dame Pallas, such as Envy pale
(That all good things with venomous tooth devours)
Could not accuse. Then gan the goddess bright   find fault with
Herself likewise, unto her work to dight.   to address

305 She made the story of the old debate
Which she with Neptune did for Athens try: engage in
Twelve gods do sit around in royal state,
And Jove in midst with awful majesty,
To judge the strife between them stirred late;
310 Each of the gods by his like visnomy   face
Eath to be known; but Jove above them all,   easy
By his great looks and power imperial.

Before them stands the god of seas in place,
Claiming the sea-coast city as his right,
315 And strikes the rocks with his three-forked mace;   trident
Whenceforth issues a warlike steed in sight,
The sign by which he challengeth the place,   claims
That all the gods, which saw his wondrous might,   so that
Did surely deem the victory his due: judge
320 But seldom seen, forejudgement proveth true.

Then to herself she gives her Aegide shield   [see Athene]
And steel-head spear, and morion on her head –   helmet
Such as she oft is seen in war-like field.
Then sets she forth how with her weapon dread   fearsome
325 She smote the ground, the which straightforth did yield
A fruitful olive tree, with berries spread,
That all the gods admired; then all the story
She compassed with a wreath of olives hoary.   framed

Amongst those leaves she made a butterfly,
330 With excellent device and wondrous sleight,   skill
Flutt'ring among the olives wantonly,
That seemed to live, so like it was in sight: appearance

The velvet nap which on his wings doth lie,
The silken down with which his back is dight,   adorned
335 His broad outstretched horns, his hairy thighs,
His glorious colours, and his glistering eyes.

Which when Arachne saw, as overlaid   overcome
And mastered with workmanship so rare,
She stood astonied long, ne ought gainsaid,   astonished/said
340 And with fast-fixed eyes on her did stare,
And by her silence, sign of one dismayed,
The victory did yield her as her share.
Yet did she inly fret, and felly burn,   inwardly/fiercely
And all her blood to poisonous rancour turn,

345 That shortly from the shape of womanhead –   womanhood
Such as she was when Pallas she attempted –   challenged
She grew to hideous shape of drearihead,   wretchedness
Pined with grief of folly late repented:
Eftsoons her white straight legs were altered
350 To crooked crawling shanks, of marrow emptied,   shins
And her fair face to foul and loathsome hue,
And her fine corpse to a bag of venom grew.

This cursed creature, mindful of that old
Enfestered grudge (the which his mother felt),
355 So soon as Clarion he did behold,
His heart with vengeful malice inly swelt;   boiled
And weaving straight a net with many a fold   immediately
About the cave, in which he lurking dwelt,
With fine small cords about it stretched wide –
360 So finely spun that scarce they could be spied.

Not any damsel, which her vaunteth most
In skilful knitting of soft silken twine,
Nor any weaver, which his work doth boast
In diaper, in damask, or in line,   linen/n. 11
365 Nor any skilled in workmanship embossed,   embroidery
Nor any skilled in loops of fing'ring fine,   lacework
Might in their diverse cunning ever dare   skill
With this so curious network to compare.   intricate

Ne do I think that that same subtle gin,   net
370 The which the Lemnian god framed craftily,   Vulcan/made

Mars sleeping with his wife to compass in,   entrap
That all the gods with common mockery
Might laugh at them, and scorn their shameful sin,
Was like to this. This same he did apply
375 For to entrap the careless Clarion,
That ranged each-where without suspicion.   everywhere

Suspicion of friend, nor fear of foe,   no suspicion
That hazarded his health, had he at all,
But walked at will and wandered to and fro,
380 In the pride of his freedom principal.   princely
Little wist he his fatal future woe,   knew
But was secure; the liker he to fall: content/more likely
He likest is to fall into mischance,
That is regardless of his governance.   conduct

385 Yet still Aragnoll (so his foe was hight)   called/n. 12
Lay lurking covertly him to surprise;
And all his gins that him entangle might,   traps
Dressed in good order as he could devise.   prepared
At length, the foolish fly without foresight,
390 As he that did all danger quite despise,
Toward those parts came flying carelessly,
Where hidden was his hateful enemy.

Who seeing him, with secret joy therefore
Did tickle inwardly in every vein;   thrill
395 And his false heart, fraught with all treasons' store,
Was filled with hope his purpose to obtain:
Himself he close upgathered more and more
Into his den, that his deceitful train   trap
By his there being might not be bewrayed,   betrayed
400 Ne any noise, ne any motion made.

Like as a wily fox that, having spied
Where on a sunny bank the lambs do play,
Full closely creeping by the hinder side,   further
Lies in ambushment of his hoped prey,
405 Ne stirreth limb, till seeing ready tide   opportunity
He rusheth forth, and snatcheth quite away
One of the little younglings unawares:

So to his work Aragnoll him prepares.

Who now shall give unto my heavy eyes
410 A well of tears that all may overflow?
Or where shall I find lamentable cries
And mournful tunes enough my grief to show?
Help, O thou tragic Muse, me to devise
Notes sad enough t'express this bitter throw: *turn of events*
415 For lo, the dreary stound is now arrived,   *moment*
That of all happiness hath us deprived.

The luckless Clarion – whether cruel Fate,
Or wicked Fortune faultless him misled,
Or some ungracious blast out of the gate
420 Of Aeole's reign perforce him drove on head –   *kingdom/headlong*
Was (O sad hap and hour unfortunate!)   *chance*
With violent swift flight forth carried
Into the cursed cobweb which his foe
Had framed for his final overthrow.

425 There the fond fly, entangled, struggled long   *foolish*
Himself to free thereout; but all in vain.
For striving more, the more in laces strong
Himself he tied, and wrapped his wings twain
In limey snares the subtle loops among,   *sticky*
430 That in the end he breathless did remain,
And, all his youthly forces idly spent,   *fruitlessly*
Him to the mercy of th'avenger lent.   *himself/gave*

Which when the grisly tyrant did espy,
Like a grim lion rushing with fierce might
435 Out of his den, he seized greedily
On the resistless prey, and with fell spite,   *ruthless*
Under the left wing struck his weapon sly
Into his heart, that his deep-groaning sprite   *spirit*
In bloody streams forth fled into the air,
440 His body left the spectacle of care.   *image of grief/n. 13*

FINIS

COLIN CLOUT'S
COME HOME AGAIN

By Ed. Spenser

London. Printed for William Ponsonby. 1595

To the right worthy and noble Knight, Sir
Walter Ralegh, Captain of Her Majesty's
Guard, Lord Warden of the Stanneries, and   n. 1
Lieutenant of the county of Cornwall.

Sir, that you may see that I am not always idle
as ye think (though not greatly well occupied),
nor altogether undutiful (though not precisely   zealously
officious), I make you present of this simple
pastoral, unworthy of your higher conceit for   imagination
the meanness of the style, but agreeing with
the truth in circumstance and matter. The   n. 2
which I humbly beseech you to accept in part
of payment of the infinite debt in which I
acknowledge myself bounden unto you, for
your singular favours and sundry good turns
showed to me at my late being in England; and
with your good countenance protect against
the malice of evil mouths, which are always
wide open to carp at and misconstrue my
simple meaning. I pray continually for your
happiness. From my house of Kilcolman, the
27th of December, 1591.

Yours ever humbly,
Ed. Sp.

The shepherd's boy (best knowen by that name)
That after Tityrus first sung his lay –   song
Lays of sweet love, without rebuke or blame –
Sat (as his custom was) upon a day
5 Charming his oaten pipe unto his peers,   playing
The shepherd swains that did about him play: boys

Who all the while, with greedy listful ears,   attentive
Did stand astonished at his curious skill,   exquisite
Like heartless deer dismayed with thunder's sound.   timid
10 At last, whenas he piped had his fill,   when
He rested him; and, sitting then around,
One of those grooms (a jolly groom was he
As ever piped on an oaten reed,
And loved this shepherd dearest in degree,
15 Hight Hobbinol) gan thus to him arede.   called/began/speak
      'Colin, my lief, my life, how great a loss   dear
Had all the shepherds' nation by thy lack!   absence
And, I, poor swain, of many, greatest cross!   affliction
That sith thy Muse – first since thy turning back –   since/return
20 Was heard to sound as she was wont on high,   used
Hast made us all so blessed and so blithe.   You/happy
Whilst thou was hence all dead in dole did lie: sorrow
The woods were heard to wail full many a sithe,   time
And all their birds with silence to complain;   lament
25 The fields with faded flowers did seem to mourn,
And all their flocks from feeding to refrain;
The running waters wept for thy return,
And all their fish with languor did lament.
But now both woods and fields, and floods revive,
30 Sith thou art come, their cause of merriment,
That us, late dead, hast made again alive.
But were it not too painful to repeat
The passed fortunes which to thee befell
In thy late voyage, we thee would entreat,
35 Now at thy leisure them to us to tell.'
      To whom the shepherd gently answered thus:
'Hobbin, thou temptest me to that I covet;
For of good passed newly to discuss,   recount
By double usury doth twice renew it.   n. 3
40 And since I saw that angel's blessed eye,   Elizabeth's
Her world's bright sun, her heaven's fairest light,
My mind – full of my thought's satiety –   gratification
Doth feed on sweet contentment of that sight.
Since that same day in nought I take delight,
45 Ne feeling have in any earthly pleasure,   nor
But in remembrance of that glorious bright,   radiance
My life's sole bliss, my heart's eternal treasure.

Wake then, my pipe; my sleepy Muse, awake,
Till I have told her praises lasting long:
50 Hobbin desires, thou mayst it not forsake –   refuse
Hark then, ye jolly shepherds, to my song.'
      With that they all gan throng about him near,
With hungry ears to hear his harmony;
The whiles their flocks, devoid of danger's fear,
55 Did round about them feed at liberty.
      'One day,' quoth he, 'I sat (as was my trade)   habit
Under the foot of Mole, that mountain hoar,   ancient
Keeping my sheep amongst the cooly shade
Of the green alders by the Mulla's shore.
60 There a strange shepherd chanced to find me out –
Whether allured with my pipe's delight,
Whose pleasing sound yshrilled far about,
Or thither led by chance, I know not right:
Whom when I asked from what place he came,
65 And how he hight, himself he did ycleep   call
The Shepherd of the Ocean by name,   Ralegh
And said he came far, from the main-sea deep.
He, sitting me beside in that same shade,
Provoked me to play some pleasant fit,   urged/song
70 And when he heard the music which I made,
He found himself full greatly pleased at it.
Yet, æmuling my pipe, he took in hand   emulating
My pipe, before that æmuled of many,
And played thereon (for well that skill he cond),   knew
75 Himself as skilful in that art as any.
He piped, I sung, and when he sung, I piped,
By change of turns each making other merry:
Neither envying other, nor envied,
So piped we, until we both were weary.'
80   There interrupting him, a bonny swain,
That Cuddy hight, him thus atween bespake: broke in
'And should it not thy ready course restrain,   if/n. 4
I would request thee, Colin, for my sake,
To tell what thou didst sing when he did play.
85 For well I ween it worth recounting was,   imagine
Whether it were some hymn, or moral lay,
Or carol made to praise thy loved lass.'
      'Nor of my love, nor of my loss,' quoth he,

'I then did sing, as then occasion fell;   it happened
90 For love had me forlorn, forlorn of me,   since/n. 5
    That made me in that desert choose to dwell.   deserted place
    But of my river Bregog's love I sung,
    Which to the shiny Mulla he did bear,
    And yet doth bear, and ever will, so long
95 As water doth within his banks appear.'
        'Of fellowship,' said then that bonny boy,
    'Record to us that lovely lay again: sing
    The stay whereof shall nought these ears annoy,   duration
    Who all that Colin makes do covet fain.'   which/earnestly
100   'Hear then,' quoth he, 'the tenor of my tale,   import
    In sort as I it to that shepherd told: just as
    No leasing new, nor grandam's fable stale,   falsehood
    But ancient truth confirmed with credence old.
        'Old father Mole (Mole hight that mountain grey
105 That walls the northside of Armulla dale),
    He had a daughter fresh as flower of May,
    Which gave that name unto that pleasant vale: who
    Mulla, the daughter of Mole, so hight
    The nymph which of that water course has charge,
110 That springing out of Mole doth run down right
    To Buttevant, where spreading forth at large
    It giveth name unto that ancient city
    Which Kilnemullah cleped is of old,   named
    Whose ragged ruins breed great ruth and pity
115 To travellers which it from far behold.
    Full fain she loved, as was beloved full fain
    Of her own brother river, Bregog hight –
    So hight because of this deceitful train,   scheme
    Which he with Mulla wrought to win delight.
120 But her old sire more careful of her good,
    And meaning her much better to prefer,   advance
    Did think to match her with the neighbour flood
    Which Allo hight, Broad-water called far;
    And wrought so well with his continual pain
125 That he that river for his daughter won –
    The dower agreed, the day assigned plain,   dowry
    The place appointed where it should be done.
        'Nathless the nymph her former liking held;
    For love will not be drawn, but must be led,

130 And Bregog did so well her fancy weld   *sway*
    That her good will he got her first to wed.   *with her consent*
    But for her father, sitting still on high,   *always*
    Did warily still watch which way she went,
    And eke from far observed, with jealous eye,   *also*
135 Which way his course the wanton Bregog bent,
    Him to deceive, for all his watchful ward,   *guard*
    The wily lover did devise this sleight: *trick*
    First into many parts his stream he shared,   *divided*
    That, whilst the one was watched, the other might
140 Pass unespied to meet her by the way;
    And then, besides, those little streams so broken   *further*
    He underground so closely did convey   *secretly*
    That of their passage doth appear no token,
    Till they into the Mulla's water slide.
145 So, secretly, did he his love enjoy:
    Yet not so secret but it was descried   *discovered*
    And told her father by a shepherd's boy.
    Who, wondrous wroth for that so foul despite,   *angry/injury*
    In great avenge did roll down from his hill
150 Huge mighty stones, the which encumber might
    His passage and his watercourses spill.   *Bregog's/spoil*
    So of a river, which he was of old,
    He none was made; but scatter'd all to nought,
    And lost among those rocks into him rolled,
155 Did lose his name – so dear his love he bought.'
        Which having said, him Thestylis bespake:
    'Now by my life this was a merry lay,   *song*
    Worthy of Colin self, that did it make.   *himself*
    But read now eke, of friendship I thee pray,   *tell*
160 What ditty did that other shepherd sing?   *Ralegh*
    For I do covet most the same to hear,
    As men use most to covet foreign thing.'
        'That shall I eke,' said he, 'to you declare.
    His song was all a lamentable lay,   *n. 6*
165 Of great unkindness, and of usage hard,
    Of Cynthia, the Lady of the Sea,
    Which from her presence faultless him debarred.
    And ever and anon, with singults rife,   *frequent sobs*
    He cried out, to make his undersong: *refrain*
170 "Ah, my love's queen, and goddess of my life,

Who shall me pity, when thou dost me wrong?"'
  Then gan a gentle bonny lass to speak,
That Marin hight: 'Right well he sure did plain,   lament
That could great Cynthia's sore displeasure break,
175 And move to take him to her grace again.
But tell on further, Colin, as befell   what
Twixt him and thee, that thee did hence dissuade.'   persuade
  'When thus our pipes we both had wearied well,'
Quoth he, 'and each an end of singing made,
180 He gan to cast great liking to my lore,   express/skill
And great disliking to my luckless lot
That banished had myself, like wight forlorn,   man
Into that waste where I was quite forgot.   desolate place
The which to leave, thenceforth he counselled me –
185 Unmeet for man in whom was ought regardful –   n. 7
And wend with him, his Cynthia to see,   go
Whose grace was great, and bounty most rewardful,
Besides her peerless skill in making well   versifying
And all the ornaments of wondrous wit,
190 Such as all womankind did far excel,
Such as the world admired and praised it.
    'So, what with hope of good, and hate of ill,
He me persuaded forth with him to fare:
Nought took I with me but mine oaten quill –
195 Small needments else need shepherd to prepare.
So to the sea we came. The sea? That is
A world of waters heaped up on high,
Rolling like mountains in wide wilderness,
Horrible, hideous, roaring with hoarse cry.'
200   'And is the sea,' quoth Coridon, 'so fearful?'
    'Fearful much more,' quoth he, 'than heart can fear:
Thousand wild beasts, with deep mouths gaping direful,
Therein still await poor passengers to tear.   always
Who life doth loathe, and longs death to behold
205 Before he die, already dead with fear,
And yet would live with heart half stony-cold,
Let him to sea, and he shall see it there.
And yet as ghastly dreadful as it seems,   appallingly
Bold men presuming life for gain to sell   willing
210 Dare tempt that gulf, and in those wand'ring streams
Seek ways unknown, ways leading down to hell.

For as we stood there waiting on the strand,
Behold a huge great vessel to us came
Dancing upon the waters' back to land,
215 As if it scorned the danger of the same.
Yet was it but a wooden frame and frail,
Glued together with some subtle matter;
Yet had it arms and wings, and head and tail,
And life to move itself upon the water.
220 Strange thing, how bold and swift the monster was,
That neither cared for wind, nor hail, nor rain,
Nor swelling waves, but thorough them did pass
So proudly, that she made them roar again.
The same aboard us gently did receive,
225 And without harm us far away did bear,
So far that land, our mother, us did leave,
And nought but sea and heaven to us appear.
Then heartless quite and full of inward fear,   disheartened
That shepherd I besought to me to tell
230 Under what sky, or in what world we were,
In which I saw no living people dwell.
Who me recomforting all that he might,
Told me that that same was the regiment   kingdom
Of a great shepherdess, that Cynthia hight,
235 His liege, his lady, and his life's regent.
   '"If then," quoth I, "a shepherdess she be,
Where be the flocks and herds which she doth keep?
And where may I the hills and pastures see,
On which she useth for to feed her sheep?"   is accustomed
240   '"These be the hills," quoth he, "the surges high,
On which fair Cynthia her herds doth feed:
Her herds be thousand fishes with their fry,
Which in the bosom of the billows breed.
Of them the shepherd which hath charge in chief
245 Is Triton, blowing loud his wreathed horn: a conch/n. 8
At sound whereof, they all for their relief
Wend to and fro at evening and at morn.
And Proteus eke with him does drive his herd   n. 9
Of stinking seals and porcpisces together,   porpoises/n. 10
250 With hoary head and dewy dropping beard,
Compelling them which way he list, and whither.   pleases
And I, among the rest, of many least,

Have in the ocean charge to me assigned,
Where I will live or die at her behest,   *command*
255 And serve and honour her with faithfull mind.
    Besides, a hundred nymphs all heavenly born,   *also*
    And of immortal race, do still attend   *always*
    To wash fair Cynthia's sheep when they be shorn,
    And fold them up when they have made an end.
260 Those be the shepherds which my Cynthia serve
    At sea, beside a thousand moe at land: *more*
    For land and sea my Cynthia doth deserve
    To have in her commandement at hand."   *ready command*
      'Thereat I wondered much, till wond'ring more
265 And more, at length we land far off descried,
    Which sight gladed me; for much afore   *previously*
    I feared, lest land we never should have eyed.
    Thereto our ship her course directly bent,
    As if the way she perfectly had known.
270 We Lundy pass; by that same name is meant
    An island, which the first to west was shown.
    From thence another world of land we kend,   *saw*
    Floating amid the sea in jeopardy,
    And round about with mighty white rocks hemmed,
275 Against the sea's encroaching cruelty.
    Those same, the shepherd told me, were the fields
    In which dame Cynthia her landherds fed;
    Fair goodly fields, than which Armulla yields
    None fairer, nor more fruitful to be redd.   *cultivated*
280 The first, to which we nigh approached, was
    A high headland thrust far into the sea,
    Like to a horn, whereof the name it has,   *Cornwall/n. 11*
    Yet seemed to be a goodly pleasant lea.   *place*
    There did a lofty mount at first us greet,   *n. 12*
285 Which did a stately heap of stones uprear,
    That seemed amid the surges for to fleet,   *float*
    Much greater than the frame which us did bear.
    There did our ship her fruitful womb unlade,
    And put us all ashore on Cynthia's land.'
290   'What land is that thou meanst,' then Cuddy said,
    'And is there other than whereon we stand?'
      'Ah, Cuddy,' then quoth Colin, 'thou's a fon   *fool*
    That has not seen least part of nature's work:

Much more there is unkend than thou dost con,   unknown/know
295 And much more that does from men's knowledge lurk.
For that same land much larger is than this,
And other men and beasts and birds doth feed:
There fruitful corn, fair trees, fresh herbage is,
And all things else that living creatures need.
300 Besides, most goodly rivers there appear,
No whit inferior to thy Funcheon's praise,   not at all
Or unto Allo, or to Mulla clear –
Nought hast thou, foolish boy, seen in thy days.'
'But if that land be there,' quoth he, 'as here,
305 And is their heaven likewise there all one?   the same
And, if like heaven, be heavenly graces there,
Like as in this same world where we do wone?'   dwell
'Both heaven and heavenly graces do much more,'
Quoth he, 'abound in that same land than this.
310 For there all happy peace and plenteous store
Conspire in one to make contented bliss:
No wailing there nor wretchedness is heard,
No bloody issues nor no leprosies,   n. 13
No grisly famine, nor no raging sword,
315 No nightly bodrags, nor no hue and cries.   raids/n. 14
The shepherds there abroad may safely lie   pass the night
On hills and down, withouten dread or danger;
No ravenous wolves the good man's hope destroy,
Nor outlaws fell affray the forest ranger.   fierce/attack
320 There learned arts do flourish in great honour,
And poets' wits are had in peerless price: held
Religion hath lay power to rest upon her,   secular/to support
Advancing virtue and suppressing vice.
For end, all good, all grace there freely grows,   In conclusion
325 Had people grace it gratefully to use:
For God his gifts there plenteously bestows,
But graceless men them greatly do abuse.'
'But say on further,' then said Corylas,
'The rest of thine adventures that betided.'   happened
330   'Forth on our voyage we by land did pass,'
Quoth he, 'as that same shepherd still us guided,
Until that we to Cynthia's presence came:
Whose glory, greater than my simple thought,
I found much greater than the former fame.

335 Such greatness I cannot compare to ought:
But if I her like ought on earth might read,   describe
I would her liken to a crown of lillies   n. 15
Upon a virgin bride's adorned head,
With roses dight and golds and daffadillies;   adorned/daffodils
340 Or like the circlet of a turtle true,   turtle-dove/n. 16
In which all colours of the rainbow be;
Or like fair Phoebe's garland shining new,   moon-rainbow
In which all pure perfection one may see.
But vain it is to think by paragon   comparison
345 Of earthly things to judge of things divine:
Her power, her mercy, and her wisdom, none
Can deem but who the Godhead can define.   judge
Why then do I, base shepherd, bold and blind,   humble/in this
Presume the things so sacred to prophane?
350 More fit it is t'adore with humble mind
The image of the heavens in shape humane.'
        With that Alexis broke his tale asunder,
Saying: 'By wond'ring at thy Cynthia's praise,
Colin, thyself thou mak'st us more to wonder,
355 And her upraising, dost thyself upraise.
But let us hear what grace she showed thee,
And how that shepherd strange thy cause advanced.'
        'The Shepherd of the Ocean,' quoth he,   Ralegh
'Unto that Goddess's grace me first enhanced,   raised
360 And to mine oaten pipe enclined her ear
That she thenceforth therein gan take delight,
And it desired at timely hours to hear,   convenient
All were my notes but rude and roughly dight;*   although/homely
For not by measure of her own great mind   *composed
365 And wond'rous worth she mott my simple song,   judged
But joyed that country shepherd aught could find   devise
Worth harkening to, amongst the learned throng.'
        'Why,' said Alexis then, 'what needeth she
That is so great a shepherdess herself,
370 And hath so many shepherds in her fee,   service
To hear thee sing, a simple silly elf?   humble creature
Or be the shepherds which do serve her lazy,
That they list not their merry pipes apply?
Or be their pipes untunable and crazy,   cracked
375 That they cannot her honour worthily?'

'Ah, nay,' said Colin, 'neither so, nor so;
For better shepherds be not under sky,
Nor better able, when they list to blow
Their pipes aloud, her name to glorify.
380 There is good Harpalus, now waxen aged   Turberville?
In faithful service of fair Cynthia;
And there is Corydon, though meanly waged   Dyer?
Yet ablest wit of most I know this day;
And there is sad Alcyon bent to mourn,   Gorges
385 Though fit to frame an everlasting ditty,
Whose gentle spright for Daphne's death doth turn   spirit
Sweet lays of love to endless plaints of pity.
Ah, pensive boy, pursue that brave conceit,   conception
In thy sweet "Eglantine of Merifleure":
390 Lift up thy notes unto their wonted height,   customary
That may thy Muse and mates to mirth allure.
There eke is Palin worthy of great praise,   Peele?
Albe he envy at my rustic quill;   although
And there is pleasing Alcon – could he raise   Lodge?
395 His tunes from lays to matter of more skill!
And there is old Palemon, free from spite,   Churchyard?
Whose careful pipe may make the hearer rew;   full of care/rue
Yet he himself may rued be more right,   rightly
That sung so long until quite hoarse he grew.
400 And there is Alabaster throughly taught
In all this skill, though knowen yet to few: n. 17
Yet were he known to Cynthia as he ought,
His *Elisaeis* would be read anew.
Who lives that can match that heroic song,
405 Which he hath of that mighty Princess made?
O dreaded Dread, do not thyself that wrong,   n. 18
To let thy fame lie so in hidden shade,
But call it forth, O call him forth to thee,
To end thy glory which he hath begun: complete/praise
410 That, when he finished hath as it should be,
No braver poem can be under sun.
Nor Po nor Tiber's swans so much renowned,   Dante? & Virgil
Nor all the brood of Greece so highly praised,
Can match that Muse when it with bays is crowned,
415 And to the pitch of her perfection raised.
And there is a new shepherd late upsprung,

The which doth all afore him far surpass,
Appearing well in that well tuned song,
Which late he sung unto a scornful lass.
420 Yet doth his trembling Muse but lowly fly,
As daring not too rashly mount on height,
And doth her tender plumes as yet but try
In love's soft lays and looser thoughts' delight.
Then rouse thy feathers quickly, Daniel,
425 And to what course thou please thyself advance:
But most, me seems, thy accent will excel
In tragic plaints and passionate mischance.
And there that Shepherd of the Ocean is,
That spends his wit in love's consuming smart:
430 Full sweetly tempered is that Muse of his,   tuned
That can empierce a Prince's mighty heart.
There also is – ah no, he is not now;
But since I said he is, he quite is gone,   n. 19
Amyntas quite is gone and lies full low,   Stanley
435 Having his Amaryllis left to moan.
Help, O ye shepherds, help ye all in this,
Help Amaryllis this her loss to mourn:
Her loss is yours, your loss Amyntas is,
Amyntas, flower of shepherds' pride forlorn.   flower
440 He whilst he lived was the noblest swain,
That ever piped in an oaten quill:
Both did he other, which could pipe, maintain,
And eke could pipe himself with passing skill.   surpassing
And there, though last not least, is Aetion –   Drayton?
445 A gentler shepherd may no where be found –
Whose Muse, full of high thoughts' invention,
Doth like himself heroically sound.
All these and many others moe remain,
Now after Astrofell is dead and gone: Sidney
450 But while as Astrofell did live and reign,
Amongst all these was none his paragon.   equal
All these do flourish in their sundry kind,
And do their Cynthia immortal make:
Yet found I liking in her royal mind,
455 Not for my skill, but for that Shepherd's sake.'
      Then spake a lovely lass, hight Lucida: called
'Shepherd, enough of shepherds thou hast told,

Which favour thee and honour Cynthia:
But of so many nymphs which she doth hold
460 In her retinue, thou hast nothing said,
That seems with none of them thou favour foundest,
Or art ingrateful to each gentle maid,
That none of all their due deserts resoundest.'   proclaim
'Ah, far be it,' quoth Colin Clout, 'fro me,
465 That I of gentle maids should ill deserve;
For that myself I do profess to be
Vassal to one whom all my days I serve:
The beam of beauty sparkled from above,
The flower of virtue and pure chastity,
470 The blossom of sweet joy and perfect love,
The pearl of peerless grace and modesty;
To her my thoughts I daily dedicate,
To her my heart I nightly martyrize,   sacrifice
To her my love I lowly do prostrate,
475 To her my life I wholly sacrifice;
My thought, my heart, my love, my life is she,
And I hers ever only, ever one –
One ever I all vowed hers to be,   entirely/n. 20
One ever I, and others never none.'
480   Then thus Melissa said: 'Thrice happy maid
Whom thou dost so enforce to deify   strive
That woods, and hills, and valleys thou hast made
Her name to echo unto heaven high.
But say, who else vouchsafed thee of grace?'   granted
485   'They all,' quoth he, 'me graced goodly well,   n. 21
That all I praise, but in the highest place
Urania, sister unto Astrofell,   Herbert
In whose brave mind, as in a golden coffer,
All heavenly gifts and riches locked are –
490 More rich than pearls of Ind, or gold of Ophir,   India/n. 22
And in her sex more wonderful and rare.
Ne less praiseworthy I Theana read,   Russell/name
Whose goodly beams, though they be overdight   covered
With mourning stole of careful widowhead,   a long robe
495 Yet through that darksome vale do glister bright.
She is the well of bounty and brave mind,
Excelling most in glory and great light;
She is the ornament of womankind,

And Court's chief garland with all virtues dight.
500 Therefore great Cynthia her in chiefest grace
Doth hold, and next unto herself advance,
Well worthy of so honourable place
For her great worth and noble governance.   conduct of life
Ne less praiseworthy is her sister dear,
505 Fair Marian, the Muses' only darling,   M. Russell?
Whose beauty shineth as the morning clear,
With silver dew upon the roses pearling.
Ne less praiseworthy is Mansilia,   Snackenborg
Best known by bearing up great Cynthia's train:
510 That same is she to whom *Daphnaida*
Upon her niece's death I did complain.
She is the pattern of true womanhead   model
And only mirror of feminity,
Worthy next after Cynthia to tread,
515 As she is next her in nobility.
Ne less praiseworthy Galathea seems   Howard?
Than best of all that honourable crew,
Fair Galathea with bright shining beams,
Inflaming feeble eyes that her do view.
520 She there then waited upon Cynthia,
Yet there is not her won, but here with us   home
About the borders of our rich Coshma –
Now made of Maa, the nymph, delicious.   delightful
Ne less praiseworthy fair Neæra is,   Sheffield
525 Neæra ours, not theirs, though there she be;
For of the famous Shure the nymph she is,
For high desert advanced to that degree.
She is the blossom of grace and courtesy,
Adorned with all honourable parts;
530 She is the branch of true nobility,
Beloved of high and low with faithful hearts.
Ne less praiseworthy Stella do I read,   Walsingham/name
Though nought my praises of her needed are,
Whom verse of noblest shepherd lately dead
535 Hath praised and raised above each other star.
Ne less praiseworthy are the sisters three,
The honour of the noble family   glory
Of which I meanest boast myself to be
(And most that unto them I am so nigh) –   particularly since

540 Phyllis, Charillis, and sweet Amaryllis.   Spencers
    Phyllis, the fair, is eldest of the three;
    The next to her is bountiful Charillis;
    But th'youngest is the highest in degree.   n. 23
    Phyllis [is] the flower of rare perfection,   n. 24
545 Fair spreading forth her leaves with fresh delight,
    That with their beauties' amorous reflection
    Bereave of sense each rash beholder's sight.
    But sweet Charillis is the paragon   model
    Of peerless price, and ornament of praise,
550 Admired of all, yet envied of none,
    Through the mild temperance of her goodly rays.   n. 25
    Thrice happy do I hold thee, noble swain,   Sackville
    The which art of so rich a spoil possessed,   treasure
    And, it embracing dear without disdain,   cherishing
555 Hast sole possession in so chaste a breast.
    Of all the shepherds' daughters which there be
    (And yet there be the fairest under sky
    Or that elsewhere I ever yet did see),
    A fairer nymph yet never saw mine eye:
560 She is the pride and primrose of the rest,   best
    Made by the maker self to be admired,   himself
    And like a goodly beacon high addressed,   raised
    That is with sparks of heavenly beauty fired.
    But Amaryllis, whether fortunate
565 Or else unfortunate may I arede,   surmise
    That freed is from Cupid's yoke by fate,
    Since which she doth new bands' adventure dread –   marriage
    Shepherd, whatever thou hast heard to be
    In this or that praised diversely apart,   that nymph
570 In her thou mayst them all assembled see,
    And sealed up in the treasure of her heart.
    Ne thee less worthy, gentle Flavia,   n. 26
    For thy chaste life and virtue I esteem;
    Ne thee less worthy, courteous Candida,
575 For thy true love and loyalty I deem;
    Besides yet many moe that Cynthia serve,
    Right noble nymphs, and high to be commended:
    But if I all should praise as they deserve,
    This sun would fail me ere I half had ended.
580 Therefore, in closure of a thankful mind,   within the bounds

I deem it best to hold eternally
Their bounteous deeds and noble favours shrined,   enshrined
Than by discourse them to indignify.'   dishonour
    So having said, Aglaura him bespake:
585 'Colin, well worthy were those goodly favours
Bestowed on thee, that so of them dost make,   sing
And them requitest with thy thankful labours.
But, of great Cynthia's goodness and high grace,
Finish the story which thou hast begun.'
590   'More eath,' quoth he, 'it is in such a case   easy
How to begin, than know how to have done;
For every gift and every goodly meed   reward
Which she on me bestowed, demands a day,
And every day in which she did a deed,
595 Demands a year it duly to display.
Her words were like a stream of honey fleeting,   flowing/n.27
The which doth softly trickle from the hive,
Able to melt the hearer's heart unweeting,   unknowing
And eke to make the dead again alive.
600 Her deeds were like great clusters of ripe grapes,
Which load the bunches of the fruitful vine,
Off'ring to fall into each mouth that gapes,
And fill the same with store of timely wine.   n. 28
Her looks were like beams of the morning sun,
605 Forth looking through the windows of the East,
When first the fleecy cattle have begun
Upon the pearled grass to make their feast.
Her thoughts are like the fume of frankincense,
Which from a golden censer forth doth rise,
610 And throwing forth sweet odours mounts fro thence   from
In rolling globes up to the vaulted skies.
There she beholds with high aspiring thought,
The cradle of her own creation –
Amongst the seats of angels heavenly wrought,
615 Much like an angel in all form and fashion.'   behaviour
        'Colin,' said Cuddy then, 'thou hast forgot
Thyself, me seems, too much, to mount so high;   I think
Such lofty flight base shepherd seemeth not,   suits
From flocks and fields to angels and to sky.'
620   'True,' answered he, 'but her great excellence
Lifts me above the measure of my might,

That, being filled with furious insolence,   *inspiration*
I feel myself like one ywrapped in spright.   *enraptured/spirit*
For when I think of her, as oft I ought,
625 Then want I words to speak it fitly forth;   *lack*
And when I speak of her what I have thought,
I cannot think according to her worth.
Yet will I think of her, yet will I speak,
So long as life my limbs doth hold together,
630 And whenas death these vital bands shall break,   *bonds of life*
Her name recorded I will leave for ever.
Her name in every tree I will endoss,   *inscribe*
That, as the trees do grow, her name may grow;
And in the ground each-where will it engross,   *write large*
635 And fill with stones that all men may it know.
The speaking woods, and murmuring waters' fall,
Her name I'll teach in knowen terms to frame,
And eke my lambs when for their dams they call,
I'll teach to call for Cynthia by name.
640 And long while after I am dead and rotten,
Amongst the shepherd's daughters dancing round,
My lays made of her shall not be forgotten,
But sung by them with flowery garlands crowned.
And ye, whoso ye be, that shall survive,
645 Whenas ye hear her memory renewed,
Be witness of her bounty here alive,
Which she to Colin her poor shepherd shewed.'   *showed*
        Much was the whole assembly of those herds   *shepherds*
Moved at his speech, so feelingly he spake,
650 And stood awhile astonished at his words,
Till Thestylis at last their silence brake,   *broke*
Saying: 'Why Colin, since thou foundst such grace
With Cynthia and all her noble crew,
Why didst thou ever leave that happy place,
655 In which such wealth might unto thee accrue,
And back returnedst to this barren soil,
Where cold and care and penury do dwell,
Here to keep sheep with hunger and with toil?
Most wretched he, that is and cannot tell.'   *that does not know it*
660   'Happy indeed,' said Colin, 'I him hold,
That may that blessed presence still enjoy,
Of fortune and of envy uncontrolled,   *unhindered*

Which still are wont most happy states t'annoy.
But I, by that which little while I proved,   experienced
665 Some part of those enormities did see,   abuses
The which in court continually hoved,   lingered
And followed those which happy seemed to be.
Therefore I, silly man, whose former days   simple
Had in rude fields been altogether spent,
670 Durst not adventure such unknowen ways,
Nor trust the guile of fortune's blandishment: flattery
But rather chose back to my sheep to turn,
Whose utmost hardness I before had tried,   the worst of which life
Than, having learned repentance late, to mourn
675 Amongst those wretches which I there descried.'
        'Shepherd,' said Thestylis, 'it seems of spite   out of
Thou speakest thus gainst their felicity,
Which thou enviest, rather than of right
That aught in them blameworthy thou dost spy.'
680   'Cause have I none,' quoth he, 'of cankered will   poisoned
To quite them ill that me demeaned so well: repay/treated
But self-regard of private good or ill   what I saw of/personal
Moves me of each, so as I found, to tell –   just
And eke to warn young shepherds' wand'ring wit,
685 Which, through report of that life's painted bliss,
Abandon quiet home to seek for it,
And leave their lambs to loss, misled amiss.
For, sooth to say, it is no sort of life,   truth
For shepherd fit to lead in that same place,
690 Where each one seeks with malice and with strife
To thrust down other into foul disgrace,
Himself to raise: and he doth soonest rise
That best can handle his deceitful wit
In subtle shifts, and finest sleights devise –   n. 29
695 Either by sland'ring his well-deemed name   the other's
Through leasings lewd and feigned forgery;   lies/misleading tales
Or else by breeding him some blot of blame,   disgrace
By creeping close into his secrecy.   confidence
To which him needs a guileful hollow heart,   for which
700 Masked with fair dissembling courtesy,
A filed tongue furnished with terms of art –   smooth/the speaker's art
No art of school, but courtier's schoolery.
For arts of school have there small countenance,   value

Counted but toys to busy idle brains,
705 And there professors find small maintenance,
But to be instruments of others' gains.
Ne is there place for any gentle wit,
Unless, to please, itself it can apply:
But shouldered is, or out of door quite shit,   thrust aside/shut
710 As base, or blunt, unmeet for melody.   unsuitable
For each man's worth is measured by his weed,   dress
As harts by horns, or asses by their ears: antlers
Yet asses be not all whose ears exceed,
Nor yet all harts that horns the highest bears.
715 For highest looks have not the highest mind,
Nor haughty words most full of highest thoughts,
But are like bladders blowen up with wind,
That being pricked do vanish into noughts.
Even such is all their vaunted vanity
720 Nought else but smoke that fumeth soon away: rises and passes
Such is their glory that in simple eye   to the naive eye
Seem greatest, when their garments are most gay.
So they themselves for praise of fools do sell,
And all their wealth for painting on a wall;   on their appearance
725 With price whereof they buy a golden bell,   n. 30
And purchase highest rooms in bower and hall,   n. 31
Whiles single Truth and simple Honesty
Do wander up and down despised of all:
Their plain attire such glorious gallantry
730 Disdains so much that none them in doth call.'   overshadows
'Ah, Colin,' then said Hobbinol, 'the blame
Which thou imputest is too general,
As if not any gentle wit of name
Nor honest mind might there be found at all.
735 For well I wot, sith I myself was there   know
To wait on Lobbin (Lobbin well thou knewest),   Leicester
Full many worthy ones then waiting were,
As ever else in prince's court thou viewest.
Of which, among you, many yet remain,
740 Whose names I cannot readily now guess:
Those that poor suitors' papers do retain,   take care of
And those that skill of medicine profess,
And those that do to Cynthia expound
The ledden of strange languages in charge;   speech/as their responsibility

745 For Cynthia doth in sciences abound,   *disciplines*
     And gives to their professors stipends large.
     Therefore unjustly thou dost wite them all,   *blame*
     For that which thou mislikedst in a few.'
       'Blame is,' quoth he, 'more blameless general,   *n. 32*
750 Than that which private errors doth pursue.
     For well I wot that there amongst them be
     Full many persons of right worthy parts –
     Both for report of spotless honesty,
     And for profession of all learned arts –
755 Whose praise hereby no whit impaired is,
     Though blame do light on those that faulty be.   *alight*
     For all the rest do most-what far amiss,   *generally*
     And yet their own misfaring will not see: *wrongdoing*
     For either they be puffed up with pride,
760 Or fraught with envy that their galls do swell,   *gall-bladders*
     Or they their days to idleness divide,
     Or drowned lie in pleasure's wasteful well,
     In which like mouldwarps nousling still they lurk, *moles/burrowing*
     Unmindful of chief parts of manliness;
765 And do themselves, for want of other work,
     Vain votaries of lazy love profess,   *devotees*
     Whose service high so basely they ensue   *follow*
     That Cupid self of them ashamed is,
     And must'ring all his men in Venus' view,
770 Denies them quite for servitors of his.'
       'And is Love then,' said Corylas, 'once known
     In court, and his sweet lore professed there?   *creed*
     I weened sure he was our god alone,
     And only wonned in fields and forests here.'   *dwelt*
775   'Not so,' quoth he, 'love most aboundeth there;
     For all the walls and windows there are writ,   *engraved*
     All full of 'Love', and 'Love', and 'Love, my dear' –
     And all their talk and study is of it.   *see Elizabeth*
     Ne any there doth brave or valiant seem,
780 Unless that some gay mistress' badge he bears: *love-token*
     Ne anyone himself doth aught esteem
     Unless he swim in love up to the ears.
     But they of Love, and of his sacred lere   *lore*
     (As it should be), all otherwise devise
785 Than we poor shepherds are accustomed here,

And him do sue and serve all otherwise.   follow
For with lewd speeches and licentious deeds
His mighty mysteries they do prophane,
And use his idle name to other needs,   now meaningless
790 But as a compliment for courting vain.   only
So him they do not serve as they profess,
But make him serve to them for sordid uses –
Ah, my dread lord, that dost liege hearts possess,   true
Avenge thyself on them for their abuses!
795   'But we poor shepherds, whether rightly so,
Or through our rudeness into error led,   simplicity
Do make religion how we rashly go   take reverent care
To serve that god that is so greatly dread:
For him the greatest of the gods we deem,
800 Born without sire or couples of one kind;   nature
For Venus self doth solely couples seem,
Both male and female through commixture joined.
So, pure and spotless, Cupid forth she brought,
And in the gardens of Adonis nursed:
805 Where, growing, he his own perfection wrought,
And shortly was of all the gods the first.
Then got he bow and shafts of gold and lead,   n. 33
In which so fell and puissant* he grew,   with which/deadly
That Jove himself his power began to dread,   *powerful
810 And, taking up to heaven, him godded new.   deified
From thence he shoots his arrows everywhere
Into the world, at random as he will,
On us frail men, his wretched vassals here,
Like as himself us pleaseth, save or spill.   spoil
815 So we him worship, so we him adore
With humble hearts to heaven uplifted high,
That to true loves he may us evermore
Prefer, and of their grace us dignify.   advance
Ne is there shepherd, ne yet shepherd's swain,
820 What ever feeds in forest or in field,
That dare with evil deed or leasing vain   lying
Blaspheme his power, or terms unworthy yield.'   n. 34
        'Shepherd, it seems that some celestial rage   inspiration
Of love,' quoth Cuddy, 'is breathed into thy breast,
825 That poureth forth these oracles so sage
Of that high power wherewith thou art possessed.

But never wist I till this present day,   knew
Albe of Love I always humbly deemed,   with reverence
That he was such a one as thou dost say,
830 And so religiously to be esteemed.
Well may it seem, by this thy deep insight,
That of that god the priest thou shouldest be:
So well thou wot'st the mystery of his might,
As if his godhead thou didst present see.'
835   'Of Love's perfection perfectly to speak,   n. 35
Or of his nature rightly to define,
Indeed,' said Colin, 'passeth reason's reach,
And needs his priest t'express his power divine.
For long before the world he was y'bore,   born
840 And bred above in Venus' bosom dear:
For by his power the world was made of yore,
And all that therein wondrous doth appear.
For how should else things so far from attone,   concord
And so great enemies as of them be,   i.e. the elements
845 Be ever drawn together into one,
And taught in such accordance to agree?
Through him the cold began to covet heat,
And water fire; the light to mount on high,
And th'heavy down to peise; the hungry t'eat,   sink
850 And voidness to seek full satiety.
So, being former foes, they waxed friends,
And gan by little learn to love each other;
So, being knit, they brought forth other kinds
Out of the fruitful womb of their great mother.   chaos/n. 36
855 Then first gan heaven out of darkness dread
For to appear, and brought forth cheerful day:
Next gan the earth to show her naked head,
Out of deep waters which her drowned alway:
And, shortly after, every living wight   creature
860 Crept forth like worms out of her slimy nature.
Soon as on them the sun's life-giving light
Had poured kindly heat and formal feature,
Thenceforth they gan each one his like to love,
And like himself desire for to beget:
865 The lion chose his mate, the turtle dove
Her dear, the dolphin his own dolphinet;   female dolphin
But man, that had the spark of reason's might

More than the rest to rule his passion,
Chose for his love the fairest in his sight,
870 Like as himself was fairest by creation.
For beauty is the bait which with delight
Doth man allure for to enlarge his kind –   entice
Beauty, the burning lamp of heaven's light,
Darting her beams into each feeble mind;
875 Against whose power nor god nor man can find
Defense, ne ward the danger of the wound,
But, being hurt, seek to be medicined
Of her that first did stir that mortal stound.   hurt
Then do they cry and call to Love apace,   immediately
880 With prayers loud importuning the sky:
Whence he them hears and, when he list show grace,
Does grant them grace that otherwise would die.
So Love is lord of all the world by right,
And rules the creatures by his powerful saw: decree
885 All being made the vassalls of his might
Through secret sense which thereto doth them draw.
Thus ought all lovers of their Lord to deem,
And with chaste heart to honour him alway:
But whoso else doth otherwise esteem
890 Are outlaws, and his lore do disobey.
For their desire is base and doth not merit
The name of love, but of disloyal lust:
Ne 'mongst true lovers they shall place inherit,
But as exuls out of his court be thrust.'   exiles
895   So having said, Melissa spake at will:
'Colin, thou now full deeply hast divined
Of love and beauty, and with wondrous skill
Hast Cupid self depainted in his kind.   nature
To thee are all true lovers greatly bound,   indebted
900 That dost their cause so mightily defend:
But most, all women are thy debtors found,
That dost their bounty still so much commend.'   goodness
          'That ill,' said Hobbinol, 'they him requite;
For having loved ever one most dear,
905 He is repaid with scorn and foul despite
That irks each gentle heart which it doth hear.'
          'Indeed,' said Lucid, 'I have often heard
Fair Rosalind of divers foully blamed   a number

For being to that swain too cruel hard –
910 That her bright glory else hath much defamed.
But who can tell what cause had that fair maid
To use him so that used her so well?
Or who with blame can justly her upbraid,
For loving not? For who can love compel?
915 And sooth to say, it is foolhardy thing,
Rashly to witen creatures so divine,   blame
For demigods they be and first did spring
From heaven, though graft in frailness feminine.
And well I wot, that oft I heard it spoken,
920 How one that fairest Helen did revile,   Stesichorus
Through judgement of the gods to be ywroken,   punished
Lost both his eyes, and so remained long while,
Till he recanted had his wicked rhymes,
And made amends to her with treble praise.
925 Beware, therefore, ye grooms, I rede betimes,   advise/in time
How rashly blame of Rosalind you raise.'
        'Ah, shepherds,' then said Colin, 'ye ne weet   know
How great a guilt upon your heads ye draw
To make so bold a doom with words unmeet,   judgement
930 Of thing celestial which ye never saw.
For she is not like as the other crew
Of shepherds' daughters which amongst you be,
But of divine regard and heavenly hue,   appearance
Excelling all that ever ye did see.
935 Not then to her that scorned thing so base,
But to myself the blame that looked so high:
So high her thoughts as she herself have place,
And loathe each lowly thing with lofty eye.   n. 37
Yet so much grace let her vouchsafe to grant
940 To simple swain, sith her I may not love:
Yet that I may her honour paravant,   above all
And praise her worth, though far my wit above.
Such grace shall be some guerdon for the grief   reward
And long affliction which I have endured;
945 Such grace sometimes shall give me some relief,
And ease of pain which cannot be recured.   cured
And ye, my fellow shepherds, which do see
And hear the languors of my too long dying,   sorrows
Unto the world for ever witness be

950 That hers I die, nought to the world denying
      This simple trophy of her great conquest.'
          So having ended, he from ground did rise,
      And after him uprose eke all the rest,
      All loath to part, but that the glooming skies
955 Warned them to draw their bleating flocks to rest.

                    FINIS

AMORETTI AND EPITHALAMION

Written not long since
by Edmund Spenser

Printed for William Ponsonby 1595

To the Right Worshipful Sir Robert Needham,
Knight.

Sir, to gratulate your safe return from Ireland
I had nothing so ready, nor thought anything
so meet, as these sweet-conceited sonnets, the *witty*
deed of that well-deserving gentleman, Master
Edmund Spenser. Whose name sufficiently
warranting the worthiness of the work, I do
more confidently presume to publish it in his
absence under your name, to whom (in my
poor opinion) the patronage thereof doth in
some respects properly appertain. For, besides
your judgement and delight in learned poesy,
this gentle Muse – for her former perfection
long wished for in England – now at the length
crossing the seas in your happy company
(though to yourself unknown) seemeth to
make choice of you, as meetest to give her *fittest*
deserved countenance after her return. Enter- *support*
tain her, then, Right Worshipful, in sort best
beseeming your gentle mind and her merit, *suiting*
and take in worth my goodwill herein, who
seek no more but to show myself yours in all
dutiful affection.

                      W. P.   *Ponsonby*

G. W. Snr, to the Author   Whitney?

Dark is the day when Phoebus' face is shrouded,
    And weaker sights may wander soon astray: the weak-sighted
    But when they see his glorious rays unclouded,
4   With steady steps they keep the perfect way.
So while this Muse in foreign lands doth stay,
    Invention weeps, and pens are cast aside,
    The time like night, deprived of cheerful day,
8   And few do write but (ah!) too soon may slide.   err morally
Then hie thee home, that art our perfect guide,
    And with thy wit illustrate England's fame,
    Daunting thereby our neighbours' ancient pride
12   That do for poesy challenge chiefest name:
So we that live and ages that succeed,
    With great applause thy learned works shall read.

G. W. Jnr

Ah, Colin, whether on the lowly plain
    Piping to shepherds thy sweet roundelays;   short songs
    Or whether singing in some lofty vein
4   Heroic deeds of past or present days;   FQ
Or whether in thy lovely mistress' praise
    Thou list to exercise thy learned quill,   choose
    Thy Muse hath got such grace and power to please,
8   With rare invention beautified by skill,
As who therein can ever joy their fill?   have enough
    O therefore let that happy Muse proceed
    To climb the height of Virtue's sacred hill,
12   Where endless honour shall be made thy meed,   reward
Because no malice of succeeding days
    Can rase those records of thy lasting praise.

[1]   n. 1
Happy, ye leaves! whenas those lily hands –   pages/when
     Which hold my life in their dead-doing might –   murderous
     Shall handle you and hold in love's soft bands,
4   Like captives trembling at the victor's sight;
And happy lines, on which with starry light
     Those lamping eyes will deign sometimes to look,
     And read the sorrows of my dying spright,   spirit
8   Written with tears in heart's close bleeding book;   secret
And happy rhymes, bathed in the sacred brook
     Of Helicon (whence she derived is),
     When ye behold that angel's blessed look,
12   My soul's long-lacked food, my heaven's bliss:
Leaves, lines, and rhymes, seek her to please alone,   only
     Whom if ye please, I care for other none.

[2]

Unquiet thought, whom at the first I bred
    Of th'inward bale of my love-pined heart,   sorrow/tormented
    And sithence have with sighs and sorrows fed,   since
4   Till greater than my womb thou waxen art: grown
Break forth at length out of the inner part,
    In which thou lurkest like to viper's brood,
    And seek some succour both to ease my smart   help
8   And also to sustain thyself with food.
But if in presence of that fairest proud
    Thou chance to come, fall lowly at her feet,
    And, with meek humblesse and afflicted mood,   downcast
12   Pardon for thee, and grace for me, entreat:
Which if she grant, then live and my love cherish;
    If not, die soon, and I with thee will perish.

[3]

The sovereign beauty which I do admire,
    Witness the world how worthy to be praised!
    The light whereof hath kindled heavenly fire
4   In my frail spirit (by her from baseness raised);
That being now with her huge brightness dazed,
    Base thing I can no more endure to view,
    But, looking still on her, I stand amazed
8   At wondrous sight of so celestial hue.
So when my tongue would speak her praises due,
    It stopped is with thought's astonishment;
    And when my pen would write her titles true,
12   It ravished is with fancy's wonderment:
Yet in my heart I then both speak and write
    The wonder that my wit cannot indite.

[4]
New Year, forth looking out of Janus' gate,
   Doth seem to promise hope of new delight:
   And bidding th'Old 'adieu', his passed date
4   Bids all old thoughts to die in dumpish spright;   *mournful spirit*
And calling forth out of sad Winter's night
   Fresh Love, that long hath slept in cheerless bower,   *Cupid*
   Wills him awake and soon about him dight   *put on*
8   His wanton wings and darts of deadly power.
For lusty Spring, now in his timely hour,   *seasonable*
   Is ready to come forth him to receive,
   And warns the Earth with diverse-coloured flower
12   To deck herself, and her fair mantle weave: *dress/cloak*
Then you, fair flower, in whom fresh youth doth reign,
   Prepare yourself new love to entertain.

[5]
Rudely thou wrongest my dear heart's desire   *ignorantly*
   In finding fault with her too portly pride: *stately*
   The thing which I do most in her admire
4   Is of the world unworthy most envied;
For in those lofty looks is close implied   *secretly*
   Scorn of base things, and sdeign of foul dishonour,   *disdain*
   Threat'ning rash eyes which gaze on her so wide   *far & wide*
8   That loosely they ne dare to look upon her.   *lewdly/not*
Such pride is praise, such portliness is honour
   That boldened innocence bears in her eyes,
   And her fair countenance like a goodly banner
12   Spreads in defiance of all enemies:
Was never in this world aught worthy tried,   *proved*
   Without some spark of such self-pleasing pride.

[6]
Be nought dismayed that her unmoved mind
    Doth still persist in her rebellious pride:
    Such love, not like to lusts of baser kind,
4   The harder won, the firmer will abide.
The dureful oak, whose sap is not yet dried,   hard
    Is long ere it conceive the kindling fire;   before
    But when it once doth burn, it doth divide   provide
8   Great heat, and makes his flames to heaven aspire.
So hard it is to kindle new desire
    In gentle breast, that shall endure for ever:
    Deep is the wound that dints the parts entire impresses/internal
12   With chaste affects that naught but death can sever.
Then think not long in taking little pain
    To knit the knot that ever shall remain.

[7]
Fair eyes, the mirror of my mazed heart,   bewildered
    What wondrous virtue is contained in you,   power
    The which both life and death forth from you dart
4   Into the object of your mighty view?
For when ye mildly look with lovely hue,
    Then is my soul with life and love inspired;
    But when ye lour, or look on me askew,
8   Then do I die, as one with lightning fired.
But since that life is more than death desired,
    Look ever lovely, as becomes you best,
    That your bright beams, of my weak eyes admired,
12   May kindle living fire within my breast.
Such life should be the honour of your light,
    Such death the sad ensample of your might.   example

[8]
More than most fair, full of the living fire
    Kindled above unto the Maker near;
    No eyes, but joys in which all powers conspire   *sources of joy*
4   That to the world nought else be counted dear –
Through your bright beams doth not the blinded guest   *Cupid*
    Shoot out his darts to base affection's wound?   *n. 2*
    But angels come to lead frail minds to rest
8   In chaste desires on heavenly Beauty bound.   *focused*
You frame my thoughts and fashion me within,
    You stop my tongue and teach my heart to speak;
    You calm the storm that passion did begin,
12   Strong through your cause, but by your virtue weak:
Dark is the world where your light shined never;
    Well is he born that may behold you ever.

[9]
Long while I sought to what I might compare
    Those powerful eyes which lighten my dark spright,
    Yet find I nought on earth to which I dare
4   Resemble th'image of their goodly light:
Not to the sun, for they do shine by night;
    Nor to the moon, for they are changed never;
    Nor to the stars, for they have purer sight;
8   Nor to the fire, for they consume not ever;
Nor to the lightning, for they still persevere;
    Nor to the diamond, for they are more tender;
    Nor unto crystal, for nought may them sever;
12   Nor unto glass – such baseness mought offend her.   *might*
Then to the Maker's self they likest be,   *himself*
    Whose light doth lighten all that here we see.

[10]
Unrighteous Lord of love, what law is this,
    That me thou makest thus tormented be,
    The whiles she lordeth in licentious bliss
4   Of her freewill, scorning both thee and me?
See how the tyranness doth joy to see
    The huge massacres which her eyes do make;
    And humbled hearts brings captives unto thee,   as captives
8   That thou of them mayst mighty vengeance take.
But her proud heart do thou a little shake,
    And that high look (with which she doth control
    All this world's pride) bow to a baser make,   mate
12   And all her faults in thy black book enrol,
That I may laugh at her in equal sort
    As she doth laugh at me, and makes my pain her sport.

[11]
Daily – when I do seek and sue for peace,
    And hostages do offer for my truth –
    She, cruel warrior, doth herself address
4   To battle, and the weary war renew'th;
Ne will be moved, with reason or with ruth,   nor/pity
    To grant small respite to my restless toil,
    But greedily her fell intent pursu'th,
8   Of my poor life to make unpitied spoil.
Yet my poor life, all sorrows to assoil,   release from
    I would her yield, her wrath to pacify:
    But then she seeks, with torment and turmoil,
12   To force me live, and will not let me die.
All pain hath end, and every war hath peace,
    But mine no price nor prayer may surcease.   bring to a close

[12]
One day I sought with her heart-thrilling eyes
   To make a truce, and terms to entertain,
   All fearless then of so false enemies   such
4   Which sought me to entrap in treason's train.   web
So, as I then disarmed did remain,
   A wicked ambush, which lay hidden long
   In the close covert of her guileful eyen,   impenetrable/eyes
8   Thence breaking forth did thick about me throng.
Too feeble I t'abide the brunt so strong,   assault
   Was forced to yield myself into their hands,
   Who, me captiving straight with rigorous wrong, immediately
12   Have ever since me kept in cruel bands.
So, Lady, now to you I do complain
   Against your eyes, that justice I may gain.

[13]
In that proud port which her so goodly graceth,   bearing
   Whiles her fair face she rears up to the sky   n. 3
   And to the ground her eyelids low embaseth,   inclines
4   Most goodly temperature ye may descry –   character/discern
Mild humblesse mixed with awful majesty.   humbleness
   For, looking on the earth whence she was born,
   Her mind remembreth her mortality –
8   Whatso is fairest shall to earth return;   whatever
But that same lofty countenance seems to scorn
   Base thing, and think how she to heaven may climb,
   Treading down earth as loathsome and forlorn,   n. 4
12   That hinders heavenly thoughts with drossy slime.   impure
Yet lowly, still vouchsafe to look on me;   deign
   Such lowliness shall make you lofty be.   n. 5

[14]
Return again, my forces late dismayed,   defeated
   Unto the siege by you abandoned quite;
   Great shame it is to leave, like one afraid,
4   So fair a piece for one repulse so light.
Gainst such strong castles needeth greater might
   Than those small forts which ye were wont   used to
     belay;   besiege
   Such haughty minds, inured to hardy fight,
8   Disdain to yield unto the first assay.   attempt
Bring, therefore, all the forces that ye may,
   And lay incessant battery to her heart:
   Plaints, prayers, vows, ruth, sorrow, and dismay –   pity
12 Those engines can the proudest love convert. siege-engines, tricks
And if those fail, fall down and die before her;
   So dying live, and living do adore her.

[15]   n. 6
Ye tradeful merchants that with weary toil
   Do seek most precious things to make your gain,
   And both the Indias of their treasures spoil,
4   What needeth you to seek so far in vain?
For lo, my love doth in herself contain
   All this world's riches that may far be found:
   If sapphires, lo, her eyes be sapphires plain;
8   If rubies, lo, her lips be rubies sound;   perfect
If pearls, her teeth be pearls both pure and round;
   If ivory, her forehead ivory ween;   think
   If gold, her locks are finest gold on ground;   earth
12 If silver, her fair hands are silver sheen.   beautiful
But that which fairest is, but few behold:
   Her mind, adorned with virtues manifold.

[16]

One day, as I unwarily did gaze
    On those fair eyes, my love's immortal light –
    The whiles my 'stonished heart stood in amaze
4   Through sweet illusion of her look's delight –
I mote perceive how, in her glancing sight,   *I saw*
    Legions of loves with little wings did fly,   *amoretti*
    Darting their deadly arrows, fiery bright,
8   At every rash beholder passing by.
One of those archers closely I did spy   *covertly*
    Aiming his arrow at my very heart –
    When suddenly, with twinkle of her eye,   *blink*
12   The damsel broke his misintended dart.   *maliciously aimed*
Had she not so done, sure I had been slain:
    Yet as it was, I hardly 'scaped with pain.   *with difficulty*

[17]

The glorious portrait of that angel's face,   *n. 7*
    Made to amaze weak men's confused skill
    And this world's worthless glory to embase,   *humble*
4   What pen, what pencil can express her fill?   *brush/fully*
For though he colours could devise at will,
    And eke his learned hand at pleasure guide   *also*
    (Lest, trembling, it his workmanship should spill),   *ruin*
8   Yet many wondrous things there are beside:
The sweet eye-glances that like arrows glide,
    The charming smiles that rob sense from the heart,
    The lovely pleasance and the lofty pride,   *delight*
12   Cannot expressed be by any art.
A greater craftsman's hand thereto doth need,
    That can express the life of things indeed.

[18]
The rolling wheel that runneth often round,
    The hardest steel in tract of time doth tear;
    And drizzlng drops that often do redound,   fall
4   The firmest flint doth in continuance wear.
Yet cannot I, with many a dropping tear
    And long entreaty, soften her hard heart
    That she will once vouchsafe my plaint to hear,   grant
8   Or look with pity on my painful smart:
But when I plead, she bids me play my part,
    And when I weep, she says tears are but water;
    And when I sigh, she says I know the art,
12   And when I wail she turns herself to laughter.
So do I weep, and wail, and plead in vain,
    Whiles she as steel and flint doth still remain.   always

[19]
The merry cuckoo, messenger of spring,   n. 8
    His trumpet shrill hath thrice already sounded
    That warns all lovers wait upon their king,   Cupid
4   Who now is coming forth with garland crowned.
With noise whereof the choir of birds resounded
    Their anthems sweet devised of Love's praise,
    That all the woods their echoes back rebounded,
8   As if they knew the meaning of their lays.   songs
But 'mongst them all which did Love's honour raise,
    No word was heard of her that most it ought; from her/owed
    But she his precept proudly disobeys,   rule
12   And doth his idle message set at nought.
Therefore, O Love, unless she turn to thee
    Ere cuckoo end, let her a rebel be.   before

[20]

In vain I seek and sue to her for grace,   plead
   And do mine humbled heart before her pour,
   The whiles her foot she in my neck doth place,
4   And tread my life down in the lowly flour.   dust
And yet the lion, that is lord of power,
   And reigneth over every beast in field,
   In his most pride disdaineth to devour
8   The silly lamb that to his might doth yield.   helpless
But she, more cruel and more savage wild
   Than either lion or the lioness,
   Shames not to be with guiltless blood defiled,
12   But taketh glory in her cruelness.
Fairer than fairest, let none ever say
   That ye were blooded in a yielded prey.

[21]

Was it the work of Nature, or of Art,
   Which tempered so the feature of her face
   That pride and meekness, mixed by equal part,
4   Do both appear t'adorn her beauty's grace?
For with mild pleasance, which doth pride displace,   courtesy
   She to her Loves doth lookers' eyes allure,   cf. 16.6/attract
   And with stern countenance back again doth chase
8   Their looser looks that stir up lusts impure.
With such strange terms her eyes she doth inure   endow/n. 9
   That with one look she doth my life dismay,
   And with another doth it straight recure: at once remedy
12   Her smile me draws, her frown me drives away.
Thus doth she train and teach me with her looks:
   Such art of eyes I never read in books.

[22]

This holy season, fit to fast and pray,   n. 10
    Men to devotion ought to be inclined:
    Therefore, I likewise, on so holy day,
4   For my sweet saint some service fit will find.
Her temple fair is built within my mind,
    In which her glorious image placed is,
    On which my thoughts do day and night attend
8   Like sacred priests that never think amiss.
There I to her, as th'author of my bliss,
    Will build an altar to appease her ire,
    And on the same my heart will sacrifice,
12   Burning in flames of pure and chaste desire:
The which vouchsafe, O goddess, to accept,
    Amongst thy dearest relics to be kept.

[23]

Penelope, for her Ulysses' sake,   n. 11
    Devised a web her wooers to deceive,
    In which the work that she all day did make,
4   The same at night she did again unreave.   unravel
Such subtle craft my damsel doth conceive
    Th'importune suit of my desire to shun;   urgent
    For all that I in many days do weave,
8   In one short hour I find by her undone,
So when I think to end that I begun,   what
    I must begin and never bring to end:
    For with one look she spills that long I spun,   destroys/that which
12   And with one word my whole year's work doth rend.
Such labour like the spider's web I find,
    Whose fruitless work is broken with least wind.

[24]

When I behold that beauty's wonderment,
   And rare perfection of each goodly part –
   Of Nature's skill the only complement –   *full realization*
4   I honour and admire the maker's art.
But when I feel the bitter baleful smart
   Which her fair eyes unwares do work in me –   *unknowingly*
   That death out of their shiny beams do dart –
8   I think that I a new Pandora see,
Whom all the gods in council did agree
   Into this sinful world from heaven to send,
   That she to wicked men a scourge should be
12   For all their faults with which they did offend.
But since ye are my scourge, I will entreat
   That for my faults ye will me gently beat.

[25]

How long shall this like-dying life endure
   And know no end of her own misery,
   But waste and wear away in terms unsure,
4   'Twixt fear and hope depending doubtfully?   *hanging*
Yet better were at once to let me die,
   And show the last ensample of your pride,   *example*
   Than to torment me thus with cruelty
8   To prove your power, which I too well have tried.   *experienced*
But yet if in your hardened breast ye hide
   A close intent at last to show me grace,   *secret*
   Then all the woes and wrecks which I abide,   *endure*
12   As means of bliss, I gladly will embrace   *means to*
And wish that more and greater they might be,
   That greater meed at last may turn to me.   *reward*

[26]   n. 12

Sweet is the rose, but grows upon a briar;

    Sweet is the juniper, but sharp his bough;   n. 13

    Sweet is the eglantine, but pricketh near;   a wild rose/sharp

4   Sweet is the fir bloom, but his branches rough:

Sweet is the cypress, but his rind is tough;

    Sweet is the nut, but bitter is his pill;   shell

    Sweet is the broom flower, but yet sour enough;

8   Sweet is moly, but his root is ill.   n. 14

So every sweet with sour is tempered still,   always

    That maketh it be coveted the more:

    For easy things, that may be got at will,

12   Most sorts of men do set but little store.   care little for

Why then should I account of little pain   make much of

    That endless pleasure shall unto me gain?

[27]

Fair proud, now tell me why should fair be proud,

    Sith all world's glory is but dross unclean   since

    And in the shade of death itself shall shroud,   conceal

4   However now thereof ye little ween?

That goodly idol now so gay beseen,   looking

    Shall doff her flesh's borrowed fair attire   put off/dress

    And be forgot as it had never been,

8   That many now much worship and admire.

Ne any then shall after it enquire,

    Ne any mention shall thereof remain

    But what this verse, that never shall expire,

12   Shall to you purchase with her thankless pain.   unrewarded

Fair, be no lenger proud of that shall perish,   longer/what

    But that which shall you make immortal, cherish.

[28]
The laurel leaf which you this day do wear,   sign of a poet
    Gives me great hope of your relenting mind;
    For since it is the badge which I do bear,
4   Ye, bearing it, do seem to me inclined.
The power thereof, which oft in me I find,
    Let it likewise your gentle breast inspire
    With sweet infusion, and put you in mind
8   Of that proud maid whom now those leaves attire:
Proud Daphne, scorning Phoebus' lovely fire,   a nymph
    On the Thessalian shore from him did flee,
    For which the gods, in their revengeful ire,   anger
12   Did her transform into a laurel tree.   n. 15
Then fly no more, fair love, from Phoebus' chase,
    But in your breast his leaf and love embrace.

[29]
See how the stubborn damsel doth deprave
    My simple meaning with disdainful scorn,
    And by the bay which I unto her gave   bay = laurel
4   Accounts myself her captive quite forlorn:
'The bay,' quoth she, 'is of the victors borne,
    Yielded them by the vanquished as their meeds,   rewards
    And they therewith do poets' heads adorn,
8   To sing the glory of their famous deeds.'
But sith she will the conquest challenge needs,   claim victory
    Let her accept me as her faithful thrall,   servant
    That her great triumph – which my skill exceeds –
12   I may in trump of Fame blaze over all: n. 16
Then would I deck her head with glorious bays,   proclaim
    And fill the world with her victorious praise.

[30]
My Love is like to ice, and I to fire: n. 17
    How comes it then that this her cold so great
    Is not dissolved through my so hot desire,
4   But harder grows the more I her entreat?
Or how comes it that my exceeding heat
    Is not delayed by her heart frozen cold,   quenched
    But that I burn much more in boiling sweat,
8   And feel my flames augmented manifold?
What more miraculous thing may be told
    That fire, which all thing melts, should harden ice,
    And ice, which is congealed with senseless cold,
12   Should kindle fire by wonderful device?
Such is the power of Love in gentle mind   noble
    That it can alter all the course of kind.   nature

[31]
Ah, why hath Nature to so hard a heart
    Given so goodly gifts of beauty's grace –
    Whose pride depraves each other better part,   to a heart/spoils
4   And all those precious ornaments deface –
Sith to all other beasts of bloody race   nature
    A dreadful countenance she given hath,   appearance
    That with their terror all the rest may chase,   terrifying looks
8   And warn to shun the danger of their wrath?
But my proud one doth work the greater scathe   harm
    Through sweet allurement of her lovely hue,   attraction/form
    That she the better may, in bloody bath
12   Of such poor thralls, her cruel hands imbrue: soak
But did she know how ill these two accord,
    Such cruelty she would have soon abhorred.

[32]

The painful smith, with force of fervent heat,		careful/intense
	The hardest iron soon doth mollify,	soften
	That with his heavy sledge he can it beat	hammer
4	And fashion to what he it list apply.	wishes
	Yet cannot all these flames in which I fry,	
	Her heart more hard than iron soft a whit?	soften/a little
	Ne all the plaints and prayers with which I	
8	Do beat on th'anvil of her stubborn wit?	
	But still the more she fervent sees my fit,	n. 18
	The more she freezeth in her wilful pride,	
	And harder grows the harder she is smit	struck
12	With all the plaints which to her be applied.	
	What then remains but I to ashes burn,	
	And she to stones at length all frozen turn?	hailstones

[33]

Great wrong I do, I can it not deny,		
	To that most sacred Empress, my dear dread,	n. 19
	Not finishing her Queen of Faery,	n. 20
4	That mote enlarge her living praises dead.	might/when dead
	But Lodwick, this of grace to me arede:	Bryskett/tell
	Do ye not think th'accomplishment of it	
	Sufficient work for one man's simple head,	
8	All were it as the rest but rudely writ?	even/unskilfully
	How then should I, without another wit,	
	Think ever to endure so tedious toil,	
	Since that this one is tossed with troublous fit	one wit
12	Of a proud love that doth my spirit spoil?	
	Cease, then, till she vouchsafe to grant me rest,	
	Or lend you me another living breast.	

AMORETTI 147

[34]
Like as a ship that through the ocean wide
    By conduct of some star doth make her way,   guidance
    Whenas a storm hath dimmed her trusty guide,   when
4   Out of her course doth wander far astray:
So I, whose star (that wont with her bright ray   used
    Me to direct) with clouds is overcast,
    Do wander now in darkness and dismay
8   Through hidden perils round about me placed.
Yet hope I well, that when this storm is past
    My Helice, the loadstar of my life,   Ursa Major/n. 22
    Will shine again, and look on me at last
12   With lovely light to clear my cloudy grief.
Till then I wander careful, comfortless,   troubled
    In secret sorrow and sad pensiveness.

[35]
My hungry eyes, through greedy covetise   desire
    Still to behold the object of their pain,
    With no contentment can themselves suffice,
4   But having, pine, and having not, complain.
For lacking it, they cannot life sustain: the object
    And having it, they gaze on it the more;
    In their amazement like Narcissus vain,
8   Whose eyes him starved: so plenty makes me poor. n. 24
Yet are mine eyes so filled with the store
    Of that fair sight that nothing else they brook, tolerate
    But loathe the things which they did like before
12   And can no more endure on them to look:
All this world's glory seemeth vain to me,
    And all their shows but shadows, saving she.   except

[36]
Tell me, when shall these weary woes have end?
    Or shall their ruthless torment never cease,
    But all my days in pining languour spend   be spent
4   Without hope of assuagement or release?   relief
Is there no means for me to purchase peace,
    Or make agreement with her thrilling eyes,
    But that their cruelty doth still increase
8   And daily more augment my miseries?
But when ye have showed all extremities,   of passion
    Then think how little glory ye have gained
    By slaying him whose life, though ye despise,
12   Mote have your life in honour long maintained.   might
But by his death (which some, perhaps, will moan),
    Ye shall condemned be of many a one.

[37]
What guile is this, that those her golden tresses
    She doth attire under a net of gold,   arrange
    And with sly skill so cunningly them dresses
4   That which is gold or hair may scarce be told?
Is it that men's frail eyes, which gaze too bold,
    She may entangle in that golden snare,
    And, being caught, may craftily enfold
8   Their weaker hearts, which are not well aware?
Take heed, therefore, mine eyes, how ye do stare
    Henceforth too rashly on that guileful net
    In which, if ever ye entrapped are,
12   Out of her bands ye by no means shall get:
Fondness it were for any, being free,   foolishness
    To covet fetters, though they golden be.   chains

[38]
Arion, when through tempest's cruel wrack   force/n. 25
    He forth was thrown into the greedy seas,
    Through the sweet music which his harp did make,
4   Allured a dolphin him from death to ease.   attracted/save
But my rude music, which was wont to please   used
    Some dainty ears, cannot with any skill
    The dreadful tempest of her wrath appease,
8   Nor move the dolphin from her stubborn will.
But in her pride she doth persevere still,
    All careless how my life for her decays:
    Yet with one word she can it save or spill –   destroy
12   To spill were pity, but to save were praise.
Choose rather to be praised for doing good
    Than to be blamed for spilling guiltless blood.

[39]
Sweet smile, the daughter of the Queen of Love,   Venus
    Expressing all thy mother's powerful art,
    With which she wonts to temper angry Jove
4   When all the gods he threats with thund'ring dart:
Sweet is thy virtue as thyself sweet art;   power
    For when on me thou shinedst late in sadness,   lately
    A melting pleasance ran through every part,   delight
8   And me revived with heart-robbing gladness,
Whilst, rapt with joy resembling heavenly madness,
    My soul was ravished quite as in a trance
    And, feeling thence no more her sorrow's sadness,
12   Fed on the fulness of that cheerful glance:
More sweet than nectar or ambrosial meat   godly food
    Seemed every bit which thenceforth I did eat.

[40]
Mark when she smiles with amiable cheer,
    And tell me whereto can ye liken it,   to what
    When on each eyelid sweetly do appear
4   A hundred Graces as in shade to sit?
Likest it seemeth, in my simple wit,
    Unto the fair sunshine in summer's day
    That, when a dreadful storm away is flit,
8   Through the broad world doth spread his goodly ray;
At sight whereof each bird that sits on spray,
    And every beast that to his den was fled,
    Comes forth afresh out of their late dismay,   terror
12   And to the light lift up their drooping head:
So my storm-beaten heart likewise is cheered
    With that sunshine, when cloudy looks are cleared.

[41]
Is it her nature or is it her will,
    To be so cruel to a humbled foe?
    If nature, then she may it mend with skill;
4   If will, then she at will may will forego.   renounce
But if her nature and her will be so
    That she will plague the man that loves her most,
    And take delight t'increase a wretch's woe,
8   Then all her nature's goodly gifts are lost:
And that same glorious beauty's idle boast
    Is but a bait such wretches to beguile,
    As, being long in her love's tempest tossed,   as if
12   She means at last to make her piteous spoil.   satisfy
O fairest fair, let never it be named
    That so fair beauty was so foully shamed.

[42]
The love which me so cruelly tormenteth,
   So pleasing is in my extremest pain
   That, all the more my sorrow it augmenteth,
4   The more I love and do embrace my bane.   ruin
Ne do I wish (for wishing were but vain)
   To be acquit from my continual smart,   freed
   But joy her thrall forever to remain,   rejoice/servant
8   And yield for pledge my poor captived heart;
The which, that it from her may never start,   move
   Let her, if please her, bind with adamant chain, unbreakable
   And from all wand'ring loves which mote pervart* might
12   His safe assurance, strongly it restrain.   *undermine/pledge
Only let her abstain from cruelty,
   And do me not before my time to die.   make

[43]
Shall I then silent be, or shall I speak?
   And if I speak, her wrath renew I shall;
   And if I silent be, my heart will break,
4   Or choked be with overflowing gall.   n. 26
What tyranny is this, both my heart to thrall,   enslave
   And eke my tongue with proud restraint to tie,   also
   That neither I may speak nor think at all,
8   But like a stupid stock in silence die?   block of wood
Yet I my heart with silence secretly
   Will teach to speak, and my just cause to plead;
   And eke mine eyes, with meek humility,   also
12   Love-learned letters to her eyes to read;
Which her deep wit, that true heart's thought can spell, read
   Will soon conceive, and learn to construe well. interpret

[44]
When those renowned noble peers of Greece,   companions
   Through stubborn pride, amongst themselves did jar, quarrel
   Forgetful of the famous Golden Fleece,   see Argonauts
4   Then Orpheus with his harp their strife did bar.
But this continual cruel civil war
   (The which myself against myself do make
   Whilst my weak powers of passions warrayed are) by/attacked
8   No skill can stint nor reason can aslake.   ease
But when in hand my tuneless harp I take,
   Then do I more augment my foe's despite,   scorn
   And grief renew, and passions do awake
12   To battle fresh against myself to fight:
   'Mongst whom the more I seek to settle peace,
   The more I find their malice to increase.

[45]
Leave, lady, in your glass of crystal clean,   mirror/clear
   Your goodly self for evermore to view,   beautiful
   And in myself – my inward self, I mean –
4   Most lively-like behold your semblant true. life-like/likeness
Within my heart, though hardly it can shew   scarcely/show
   Thing so divine to view of earthly eye,
   The fair Idea of your celestial hue,   see Plato/appearance
8   And every part, remains immortally;
And were it not that, through your cruelty,
   With sorrow dimmed and deformed it were,
   The goodly image of your visnomy   face
12   Clearer than crystal would therein appear.
But if yourself in me ye plain will see,
   Remove the cause by which your fair beams darkened be.

[46]

When my abode's prefixed time is spent,   visit's
   My cruel fair straight bids me wend my way: at once/go on
   But then from heaven most hideous storms are sent,
4   As willing me against her will to stay.
Whom, then, shall I – or heaven or her – obey?   either ... or
   The heavens know best what is the best for me,
   But, as she will – whose will my life doth sway,
8   My lower heaven – so it perforce must be.   of necessity
But ye high heavens that all this sorrow see,
   Sith all your tempests cannot hold me back,
   Assuage your storms, or else both you and she   ease
12   Will both together me too sorely wrack: torment
Enough it is for one man to sustain
   The storms which she alone on me doth rain.

[47]

Trust not the treason of those smiling looks
   Until ye have their guileful trains well tried;   traps
   For they are like but unto golden hooks
4   That from the foolish fish their baits do hide.
So she with flatt'ring smiles weak hearts doth guide
   Unto her love, and tempt to their decay;   destruction
   Whom, being caught, she kills with cruel pride,
8   And feeds at pleasure on the wretched prey.
Yet, even whilst her bloody hands them slay,
   Her eyes look lovely and upon them smile
   That they take pleasure in her cruel play,
12   And, dying, do themselves of* pain beguile.   trick themselves
O mighty charm! which makes men love their bane,   *out of/ruin
   And think they die with pleasure, live with pain.

[48]
Innocent paper – whom too cruel hand
    Did make the matter to avenge her ire
    And, ere she could thy cause well understand,   *before*
4   Did sacrifice unto the greedy fire –
Well worthy thou to have found better hire   *payment*
    Than so bad end for heretics ordained:
    Yet heresy nor treason didst conspire,   *you did*
8   But pled thy master's cause unjustly pained,
Whom she, all careless of his grief, constrained
    To utter forth th'anguish of his heart,
    And would not hear when he to her complained
12   The piteous passion of his dying smart.   *suffering*
Yet live for ever, though against her will,
    And speak her good though she requite it ill.   *well of her/repay*

[49]
Fair cruel, why are ye so fierce and cruel?
    Is it because your eyes have power to kill?
    Then know that mercy is the Mighty's jewel,
4   And greater glory think to save than spill.
But if it be your pleasure and proud will
    To show the power of your imperious eyes,
    Then not on him that never thought you ill,
8   But bend your force against your enemies:
Let them feel th'utmost of your cruelties,
    And kill with looks, as cockatrices do;
    But him that at your foostool humbled lies,
12   With merciful regard give mercy to.
Such mercy shall you make admired to be,
    So shall you live by giving life to me.

[50]
Long languishing in double malady
    Of my heart's wound and of my body's grief,
    There came to me a leech that would apply   doctor
4   Fit medicines for my body's best relief.
'Vain man,' quod I, 'that hast but little prief   experience
    In deep discovery of the mind's disease,
    Is not the heart of all the body chief,
8   And rules the members as itself doth please?   n. 27
Then with some cordials seek first to appease   medicinal drink
    The inward languor of my wounded heart,   sickness
    And then my body shall have shortly ease:
12   But such sweet cordials pass physician's art.'
Then, my life's leech, do you your skill reveal,   his lady
    And with one salve both heart and body heal.   remedy

[51]
Do I not see that fairest images
    Of hardest marble are of purpose made,
    For that they should endure through many ages,
4   Ne let their famous monuments to fade?
Why then do I, untrained in lovers' trade,
    Her hardness blame, which I should more commend,
    Sith never aught was excellent assayed   tried
8   Which was not hard t'achieve and bring to end?
Ne aught so hard but he that would attend   attend to it
    Mote soften it and to his will allure:
    So do I hope her stubborn heart to bend,
12   And that it then more steadfast will endure.
Only my pains will be the more to get her,
    But, having her, my joy will be the greater.

[52]
So oft as homeward I from her depart,
    I go like one that, having lost the field,
    Is prisoner led away with heavy heart,
4   Despoiled of war-like arms and knowen shield.   shield of arms
So do I now myself a prisoner yield
    To sorrow and to solitary pain,
    From presence of my dearest dear exiled,
8   Long while alone in languor to remain.   sorrow
There let no thought of joy or pleasure vain
    Dare to approach that may my solace breed,
    But sudden dumps and dreary sad disdain   depressions
12   Of all world's gladness more my torment feed:
So I her absence will my penance make,
    That of her presence I my meed may take.

[53]
The panther, knowing that his spotted hide
    Doth please all beasts, but that his looks them fray, frighten
    Within a bush his dreadful head doth hide,
4   To let them gaze whilst he on them may prey.   until
Right so my cruel fair with me doth play;   just so
    For with the goodly semblant of her hue   likeness/form
    She doth allure me to mine own decay,   ruin
8   And then no mercy will unto me show.
Great shame it is, thing so divine in view,
    Made for to be the world's most ornament,   best
    To make the bait her gazers to imbrue:*   make herself
12   Good shames to be to ill an instrument, *stain with blood
But mercy doth with beauty best agree,
    As in their Maker ye them best may see.

[54]
Of this world's theatre in which we stay,   n. 28
    My love, like the spectator, idly sits
    Beholding me that all the pageants play,
4   Disguising diversely my troubled wits.
Sometimes I joy when glad occasion fits,
    And mask in mirth like to a comedy;
    Soon after, when my joy to sorrow flits,
8   I wail and make my woes a tragedy.
Yet she, beholding me with constant eye,
    Delights not in my mirth, nor rues my smart,   pities
    But when I laugh she mocks, and when I cry
12   She laughs, and hardens evermore her heart.   always
What then can move her? If nor mirth nor moan,   neither ... nor
    She is no woman, but a senseless stone.

[55]
So oft as I her beauty do behold,
    And therewith do her cruelty compare,
    I marvel of what substance was the mould   n. 29
4   The which her made at once so cruel fair:
Not earth, for her high thoughts more heavenly are;
    Not water, for her love doth burn like fire;
    Not air, for she is not so light or rare;
8   Not fire, for she doth freeze with faint desire.   n. 30
Then needs another element inquire   I need to seek
    Whereof she mote be made; that is the sky –   n. 31
    For to the heaven her haughty looks aspire,
12   And eke her mind is pure, immortal, high.
Then sith to heaven ye likened are the best,
    Be like in mercy as in all the rest.

[56]
Fair ye be sure, but cruel and unkind   certainly
   As is a tiger that with greediness
   Hunts after blood: when he by chance doth find
4   A feeble beast, doth felly him oppress.   cruelly
Fair be ye sure, but proud and pitiless
   As is a storm that all things doth prostrate: beat down
   Finding a tree alone all comfortless,
8   Beats on it strongly, it to ruinate.
Fair be ye sure, but hard and obstinate,
   As is a rock amidst the raging floods:
   Gainst which a ship of succour desolate   help
12   Doth suffer wreck both of herself and goods.
That ship, that tree, and that same beast am I,
   Whom ye do wreck, do ruin, and destroy.

[57]
Sweet warrior, when shall I have peace with you?
   High time it is this war now ended were,
   Which I no longer can endure to sue,   wage
4   Ne your incessant batt'ry more to bear;
So weak my powers, so sore my wounds appear,
   That wonder is how I should live a jot,
   Seeing my heart through-launched everywhere   pierced
8   With thousand arrows which your eyes have shot.
Yet shoot ye sharply still, and spare me not,   vigorously
   But glory think to make these cruel stours: assaults
   Ye cruel one, what glory can be got
12   In slaying him that would live gladly yours?
Make peace, therefore, and grant me timely grace   in time
   That all my wounds will heal in little space.   space of time

[58]
By her that is most assured to herself.   n. 32

Weak is th'assurance that weak flesh reposeth   n. 33
   In her own power, and scorneth others' aid:
   That soonest falls whenas she most supposeth   when
4   Herself assured, and is of nought afraid.
All flesh is frail, and all her strength unstaid,   uncertain
   Like a vain bubble blowen up with air:
   Devouring Time and changeful Chance have preyed   preyed on
8   Her glory's pride, that none may it repair.
Ne none so rich or wise, so strong or fair,   no one is
   But faileth trusting on his own assurance;
   And he that standeth on the highest stair
12 Falls lowest, for on earth nought hath endurance.
Why then do ye, proud fair, misdeem so far   misjudge
   That to yourself ye most assured are?

[59]
Thrice happy she, that is so well assured
   Unto herself, and settled so in heart,
   That neither will for better be allured,
4   Ne feared with worse to any chance to start,   n. 34
But, like a steady ship, doth strongly part
   The raging waves and keeps her course aright:
   Ne aught for tempest doth from it depart,
8   Ne aught for fairer weather's false delight.
Such self-assurance need not fear the spite
   Of grudging foes, ne favour seek of friends,
   But in the stay of her own steadfast might   support
12 Neither to one herself nor other bends.
Most happy she that most assured doth rest;
   But he most happy who such one loves best.

[60]
They that in course of heavenly spheres are skilled,
    To every planet point his sundry year   appoint/distinct period
    In which her circle's voyage is fulfilled,
4   As Mars in threescore years doth run his sphere.
So, since the winged god his planet clear   Cupid/distinctly
    Began in me to move, one year is spent,
    The which doth longer unto me appear
8   Than all those forty which my life outwent.   passed
Then by that count, which lovers' books invent,
    The sphere of Cupid forty years contains,
    Which I have wasted in long languishment
12   That seemed the longer for my greater pains.
But let my love's fair planet short her ways   shorten
    This year ensuing, or else short my days.   following

[61]
The glorious image of the Maker's beauty,
    My sovereign saint, the idol of my thought,
    Dare not henceforth above the bounds of duty   n. 35
4   T'accuse of pride, or rashly blame for aught.
For being, as she is, divinely wrought,
    And of the brood of angels heavenly born,
    And with the crew of blessed saints upbrought,   brought up
8   Each of which did her with their gifts adorn –   cf. Pandora
The bud of joy, the blossom of the morn,
    The beam of light whom mortal eyes admire –
    What reason is it, then, but she should scorn   but reason
12   Base things that to her love too bold aspire?
Such heavenly forms ought rather worshipped be
    Than dare be loved by men of mean degree.

[62]
The weary year his race now having run,
    The new begins his compassed course anew: circular
    With show of morning mild he hath begun,
4   Betokening peace and plenty to ensue.   see n. 10
So let us, which this change of weather view,   who
    Change eke our minds, and former lives amend;
    The old year's sins forepassed let us eschew,   gone past
8   And fly the faults with which we did offend.
Then shall the new year's joy forth freshly send
    Into the glooming world his gladsome ray,   dark
    And all these storms which now his beauty blend,   blemish
12   Shall turn to calms and timely clear away.
So likewise, love, cheer you your heavy spright,
    And change old year's annoy to new delight.

[63]   cf. *Am* 34
After long storms' and tempests' sad assay –   violent/trial
    Which hardly I endured heretofore   scarcely
    In dread of death and dangerous dismay –   loss of spirit
4   With which my silly bark was tossed sore,   helpless ship
I do at length descry the happy shore   glimpse
    In which I hope ere long for to arrive: before
    Fair soil it seems from far, and fraught with store   filled
8   Of all that dear and dainty is alive.   delightful
Most happy he that can at last achieve
    The joyous safety of so sweet a rest,   n. 36
    Whose least delight sufficeth to deprive
12   Remembrance of all pains which him oppressed:
All pains are nothing in respect of this,
    All sorrows short that gain eternal bliss.

[64]   cf. *Am* 15, 26

Coming to kiss her lips, such grace I found,
    Me seemed I smelled a garden of sweet flowers
    That dainty odours from them threw around   scents
4   For damzels fit to deck their lovers' bowers:
Her lips did smell like unto gillyflowers;   clove-pinks
    Her ruddy cheeks like unto roses red;
    Her snowy brows like budded bellamours;   n. 37
8   Her lovely eyes like pinks but newly spread;   carnations
Her goodly bosom like a strawberry bed;
    Her neck like to a bunch of columbines;
    Her breast like lilies ere their leaves be shed;
12   Her nipples like young-blossomed jessamines: jasmines
Such fragrant flowers do give most odorous smell,
    But her sweet odour did them all excel.

[65]

The doubt which ye misdeem, fair love, is vain,   worry over
    That fondly fear to loose your liberty   foolishly
    When, losing one, two liberties ye gain,
4   And make him bond that bondage erst did fly.   bound/before
Sweet be the bands, the which true love doth tie
    Without constraint or dread of any ill:
    The gentle bird feels no captivity   noble
8   Within her cage, but sings and feeds her fill.
There Pride dare not approach, nor Discord spill
    The league 'twixt them that loyal love hath bound;   alliance
    But simple Truth and mutual Goodwill
12   Seeks with sweet Peace to salve each other's wound: heal
There Faith doth fearless dwell in brazen tower,
    And spotless Pleasure builds her sacred bower.

[66]
To all those happy blessings which ye have,
    With plenteous hand by heaven upon you thrown,
    This one disparagement they to you gave,
4   That ye your love lent to so mean a one.   *humble*
Ye – whose high worths, surpassing paragon,   *comparison*
    Could not on earth have found one fit for mate,
    Ne but in heaven matchable to none –   *nor even*
8   Why did ye stoop unto so lowly state?   *one of my rank*
But ye thereby much greater glory gate   *got*
    Than had ye sorted with a prince's peer,   *matched/equal*
    For now your light doth more itself dilate,
12   And in my darkness greater doth appear.
Yet, since your light hath once enlumined me,   *illumined*
    With my reflex yours shall increased be.   *reflection*

[67]   n. 38
Like as a huntsman after weary chase,   *tiring/n. 39*
    Seeing the game from him escaped away,
    Sits down to rest him in some shady place,
4   With panting hounds beguiled of their prey –   *cheated*
So, after long pursuit and vain assay,
    When I, all weary, had the chase forsook,   *abandoned*
    The gentle deer returned the selfsame way,
8   Thinking to quench her thirst at the next brook.
There she, beholding me with milder look,
    Sought not to fly, but fearless still did bide   *stay*
    Till I in hand her (yet half-trembling) took,
12   And with her own goodwill her firmly tied.
Strange thing, me seemed, to see a beast so wild
    So goodly won, with her own will beguiled.   *easily*

[68]   see n. 10

Most glorious Lord of life, that on this day   Easter Day
 Didst make Thy triumph over death and sin,
 And, having harrowed hell, didst bring away   subdued/n. 40
4   Captivity thence captive, us to win: n. 41
This joyous day, dear Lord, with joy begin,
 And grant that we, for whom Thou didest die,   did
 Being with Thy dear blood clean washed from sin,   precious
8   May live for ever in felicity;   happiness
And that, Thy love we weighing worthily,   at its worth
 May likewise love Thee for the same again,
 And for Thy sake, that all like dear didst buy,   alike
12   With love may one another entertain.
So let us love, dear love, like as we ought;
 Love is the lesson which the Lord us taught.

[69]
The famous warriors of the antique world
 Used trophies to erect in stately wise,   manner
 In which they would the records have enrolled
4   Of their great deeds and valorous emprise.   enterprise
What trophy, then, shall I most fit devise
 In which I may record the memory
 Of my love's conquest, peerless beauty's prize,   she who is
8   Adorned with honour, love and chastity?
Even this verse, vowed to eternity,
 Shall be thereof immortal monument,
 And tell her praise to all posterity,
12   That may admire such world's rare wonderment –   marvel
The happy purchase of my glorious spoil,   plunder
 Gotten at last with labour and long toil.

[70]
Fresh Spring, the herald of love's mighty king,   Cupid
  In whose coat-armour richly are displayed   heraldic tunic
  All sorts of flowers, the which on earth do spring
4 In goodly colours gloriously arrayed –
Go to my love where she is careless laid,   lies untroubled
  Yet in her winter's bower not well awake;
  Tell her the joyous time will not be stayed
8 Unless she do him by the forelock take;   n. 42
Bid her therefore herself soon ready make
  To wait on Love amongst his lovely crew,
  Where everyone that misseth then her make   partner
12 Shall be by him amerced with penance due.   punished
Make haste therefore, sweet love, whilst it is prime,   n. 43
  For none can call again the passed time.

[71]   cf. *Am* 23
I joy to see how, in your drawen work,   tapestry
  Yourself unto the bee ye do compare,
  And me unto the spider that doth lurk
4 In close await to catch her unaware;   secret ambush
Right so yourself were caught in cunning snare   just so
  Of a dear foe, and thralled to his love,   enslaved
  In whose strait bands ye now captived are   tight
8 So firmly that ye never may remove.
But as your work is woven all about
  With woodbine flowers and fragrant eglantine,   honeysuckle
  So sweet your prison you in time shall prove,   find
12 With many dear delights bedecked fine:
And all, thenceforth, eternal peace shall see
  Between the spider and the gentle bee.

[72]
Oft when my spirit doth spread her bolder wings
    In mind to mount up to the purest sky,
    It down is weighed with thought of earthly things,
4   And clogged with burden of mortality;   *encumbered*
Where, when that sovereign beauty it doth spy,
    Resembling heaven's glory in her light,
    Drawn with sweet pleasure's bait it back doth fly
8   And unto heaven forgets her former flight.
There my frail fancy, fed with full delight,
    Doth bathe in bliss and mantleth most at ease;   *relaxes*
    Ne thinks of other heaven, but how it might
12   Her heart's desire with most contentment please.
Heart need not wish none other happiness
    But here on earth to have such heaven's bliss.

[73]
Being myself captived here in care,   *sorrow*
    My heart – whom none with servile bands can tie,
    But the fair tresses of your golden hair –
4   Breaking his prison, forth to you doth fly;
Like as a bird that in one's hand doth spy
    Desired food, to it doth make his flight,
    Even so my heart that wont on your fair eye
8   To feed his fill, flies back unto your sight.
Do you him take, and in your bosom bright
    Gently encage, that he may be your thrall: *cage him*
    Perhaps he there may learn with rare delight
12   To sing your name and praises over all,   *above*
That it hereafter may you not repent,   *regret*
    Him lodging in your bosom to have lent.

[74]
Most happy letters, framed by skilful trade,   formed/n. 44
   With which that happy name was first designed,
   The which three times thrice happy hath me made,
4   With gifts of body, fortune, and of mind:
The first my being to me gave by kind,   nature
   From mother's womb derived by due descent;
   The second is my sovereign Queen most kind,
8   That honour and large richesse to me lent;   granted
The third my love, my life's last ornament,
   By whom my spirit out of dust was raised
   To speak her praise and glory excellent –
12   Of all alive most worthy to be praised.
Ye three Elizabeths, for ever live,
   That three such graces did unto me give.

[75]
One day I wrote her name upon the strand,   beach
   But came the waves and washed it away;
   Again I wrote it with a second hand,
4   But came the tide, and made my pains his prey.
'Vain man,' said she, 'that dost in vain assay   his lady/try
   A mortal thing so to immortalize;
   For I myself shall like to this decay,
8   And eke my name be wiped out likewise.'
'Not so,' quod I, 'let baser things devise
   To die in dust, but you shall live by fame:
   My verse your virtues rare shall eternize,
12   And in the heavens write your glorious name
Where – whenas death shall all the world subdue –
   Our love shall live, and later life renew.'

[76]

Fair bosom fraught with virtue's richest treasure,   filled
   The nest of love, the lodging of delight,
   The bower of bliss, the paradise of pleasure,
4   The sacred harbour of that heavenly spright –
How was I ravished with your lovely sight,
   And my frail thoughts too rashly led astray!
   Whiles diving deep through amorous insight,   while
8   On the sweet spoil of beauty they did prey,   treasure/the thoughts
And 'twixt her paps (like early fruit in May   nipples
   Whose harvest seemed to hasten now apace).
   They loosely did their wanton wings display,
12   And there to rest themselves did boldly place:
Sweet thoughts, I envy your so happy rest,
   Which oft I wished, yet never was so blessed.

[77]

Was it a dream, or did I see it plain? –
   A goodly table of pure ivory,
   All spread with junkets, fit to entertain   delicacies
4   The greatest prince with pompous royalty;   magnificent splendour
'Mongst which there in a silver dish did lie
   Two golden apples of unvalued price,   invaluable
   Far passing those which Hercules came by,   surpassing
8   Or those which Atalanta did entice: n. 45
Exceeding sweet, yet void of sinful vice,   free
   That many sought, yet none could ever taste;
   Sweet fruit of pleasure brought from paradise
12   By Love himself, and in his garden placed.
Her breast that table was, so richly spread;
   My thoughts the guest which would thereon have fed.

[78]
Lacking my love, I go from place to place
    Like a young fawn that late hath lost the hind,
    And seek each-where where last I saw her face,
4   Whose image yet I carry fresh in mind:
I seek the fields with her late footing signed,
    I seek her bower with her late presence decked;
    Yet nor in field nor bower I her can find,
8   Yet field and bower are full of her aspect.   _presence_
But when mine eyes I thereunto direct,
    They idly back return to me again,   _profitlessly_
    And when I hope to see their true object,
12   I find myself but fed with fancies vain:
Cease then, mine eyes, to seek herself to see,
    And let my thoughts behold herself in me.

[79]
Men call you fair, and you do credit it,   _believe_
    For that yourself ye daily such do see;
    But the true fair, that is the gentle wit
4   And virtuous mind, is much more praised of me.
For all the rest, however fair it be,
    Shall turn to nought and loose that glorious hue;
    But only that is permanent and free
8   From frail corruption that doth flesh ensue.   _follow_
That is true beauty: that doth argue you
    To be divine and born of heavenly seed,
    Derived from that fair Spirit from whom all true   _God_
12   And perfect beauty did at first proceed.
He only fair, and what He fair hath made;
    All other fair like flowers untimely fade.   _n. 46_

[80]
After so long a race as I have run
    Through faery land, which those six books compile,   comprise
    Give leave to rest me, being half fordone,   exhausted
4   And gather to myself new breath awhile.   n. 47
Then, as a steed refreshed after toil,
    Out of my prison I will break anew,
    And stoutly will that second work assoil   discharge
8   With strong endeavour and attention due.
Till then, give leave to me in pleasant mew   confinement
    To sport my Muse and sing my Love's sweet praise,   divert
    The contemplation of whose heavenly hue,
12   My spirit to an higher pitch will raise: see Plato
But let her praises yet be low and mean,   modest
    Fit for the handmaid of the Faery Queen.

[81]
Fair is my Love, when her fair golden hairs
    With the loose wind ye waving chance to mark;
    Fair when the rose in her red cheeks appears,
4   Or in her eyes the fire of love does spark;
Fair when her breast, like a rich laden bark   boat
    With precious merchandise, she forth doth lay;
    Fair when that cloud of pride, which oft doth dark
8   Her goodly light, with smiles she drives away;
But fairest she, when so she doth display
    The gate, with pearls and rubies richly dight,   adorned
    Through which her words so wise do make their way
12   To bear the message of her gentle spright.
The rest be works of Nature's wonderment,
    But this the work of heart's astonishment.

[82]

Joy of my life, full oft for loving you
   I bless my lot, that was so lucky placed:
   But then the more your own mishap I rue,
4   That are so much by so mean love embased.   *humbled*
For had the equal heavens so much you graced   *equitable*
   In this as in the rest, ye mote invent   *discover*
   Some heavenly wit, whose verse could have enchased   *set*
8   Your glorious name in golden monument.
But since ye deigned so goodly to relent   *nobly*
   To me, your thrall, in whom is little worth,
   That little that I am shall all be spent
12   In setting your immortal praises forth:
Whose lofty argument, uplifting me,
   Shall lift you up unto a high degree.

[83]

My hungry eyes, through greedy covetise   *desire*
   Still to behold the object of their pain,
   With no contentment can themselves suffice,
4   But having, pine, and having not, complain:
For lacking it, they cannot life sustain;   *the object*
   And seeing it, they gaze on it the more,   *n. 48*
   In their amazement like Narcissus vain,
8   Whose eyes him starved: so plenty makes me poor.
Yet are mine eyes so filled with the store
   Of that fair sight that nothing else they brook,   *tolerate*
   But loathe the things which they did like before
12   And can no more endure on them to look:
All this world's glory seemeth vain to me,
   And all their shows but shadows, saving she.   *except*

[84]
Let not one spark of filthy lustful fire
    Break out that may her sacred peace molest,
    Ne one light glance of sensual desire   *wanton*
4   Attempt to work her gentle mind's unrest;
But pure affections bred in spotless breast,
    And modest thoughts breathed from well-tempered sprites*
    Go visit her in her chaste bower of rest,   *spirits
8   Accompanied with angelic delights.
There fill yourself with those most joyous sights
    (The which myself could never yet attain),
    But speak no word to her of these sad plights   *moods*
12   Which her too constant stiffness doth constrain:* *resolution*
Only behold her rare perfection,   *produce
    And bless your fortune's fair election.

[85]   cf. *Am* 19
The world, that cannot deem of worthy things,   *judge*
    When I do praise her, say I do but flatter:
    So does the cuckoo, when the mavis sings,   *thrush*
4   Begin his witless note apace to clatter.   *quickly*
But they that skill not of so heavenly matter,   *understand*
    All that they know not, envy or admire:
    Rather than envy, let them wonder at her,
8   But not to deem of her desert aspire.
Deep in the closet of my parts entire   n. 49
    Her worth is written with a golden quill,
    That me with heavenly fury doth inspire,   n. 50
12   And my glad mouth with her sweet praises fill:
Which whenas Fame in her shrill trump shall thunder, *trumpet*
    Let the world choose to envy or to wonder.

[86]
Venomous tongue, tipped with vile adder's sting,
    Of that self kind with which the Furies fell   same/terrible
    Their snaky heads do comb, from which a spring
4   Of poisoned words and spiteful speeches well –
Let all the plagues and horrid pains of hell
    Upon thee fall for thine accursed hire,   as thine/reward
    That with false forged lies, which thou didst tell,
8   In my true love did stir up coals of ire:
The sparks whereof let kindle thine own fire,
    And catching hold on thine own wicked head
    Consume thee quite, that didst with guile conspire
12   In my sweet peace such breaches to have bred.
Shame be thy meed, and mischief thy reward,   wages
    Due to thyself that it for me prepared.

[87]
Since I did leave the presence of my love,
    Many long weary days I have outworn,
    And many nights, that slowly seemed to move
4   Their sad protract from evening until morn.   span
For whenas day the heaven doth adorn,
    I wish that night the noyous day would end;   vexatious
    And whenas night hath us of light forlorn,   deprived
8   I wish that day would shortly reascend.
Thus I the time with expectation spend,   in
    And feign my grief with changes to beguile,   try
    That further seems his term still to extend,   with the result
12   And maketh every minute seem a mile.
So sorrow still doth seem too long to last,
    But joyous hours do fly away too fast.

[88]
Since I have lacked the comfort of that light   the lady
  (The which was wont to lead my thoughts astray),
  I wander as in darkness of the night,
4   Afraid of every danger's least dismay.   terror
Ne aught I see, though in the clearest day
  When others gaze upon their shadows vain,   see Plato
  But th'only image of that heavenly ray,
8   Whereof some glance doth in mine eye remain;
Of which beholding th'Idea plain,
  Through contemplation of my purest part,
  With light thereof I do myself sustain,
12   And thereon feed my love-affamished heart:
But with such brightness whilst I fill my mind,
  I starve my body and mine eyes do blind.

[89]
Like as the culver on the bared bough   dove/n. 51
  Sits mourning for the absence of her mate,
  And in her songs sends many a wishful vow
4   For his return that seems to linger late,
So I alone now left disconsolate,
  Mourn to myself the absence of my love,
  And wand'ring here and there all desolate,
8   Seek with my plaints to match that mournful dove.
Ne joy of aught that under heaven doth hove   dwell
  Can comfort me, but her own joyous sight,
  Whose sweet aspect both God and man can move
12   In her unspotted pleasance to delight.   charm
Dark is my day, whiles her fair light I miss,
  And dead my life that wants such lively bliss.   lacks

Anacreontics

[1]

In youth, before I waxed old,
    The blind boy, Venus' baby,
For want of cunning, made me bold
    In bitter hive to grope for honey:
5   But when he saw me stung and cry,
        He took his wings and away did fly.

n. 52
grew

lack

[2]

As Dian hunted on a day,
She chanced to come where Cupid lay,
    His quiver by his head:
One of his shafts she stole away,
5 And one of hers did close convey
    Into the other's stead.
        With that Love wounded my love's heart
        But Dian beasts with Cupid's dart.

place

n. 53

[3]

I saw in secret to my dame
    How little Cupid humbly came
    And said to her, 'All hail, my mother.'
But when he saw me laugh, for shame
5 His face with bashful blood did flame,
    Not knowing Venus from the other.
'Then never blush, Cupid,' quoth I,
    'For many have erred in this beauty.'

n. 54

the dame

[4]

Upon a day, as Love lay sweetly slumb'ring
    All in his mother's lap,
A gentle bee, with his loud trumpet murm'ring,
    About him flew by hap.
5 Whereof, when he was awakened with the noise,
    And saw the beast so small,
'What's this,' quoth he, 'that gives so great a voice
    That wakens men withal?
In angry-wise he flies about,
10   And threatens all with courage stout.'

chance

manner

To whom his mother, closely smiling, said
    ('Twixt earnest and 'twixt game):
'See, thou thyself likewise art little made,
    If thou regard the same;
15 And yet thou suff'rest neither gods in sky   allow
    Nor men in earth to rest,
But when thou art disposed cruelly,
    Their sleep thou dost molest:
Then either change thy cruelty,
20   Or give like leave unto the fly.'

Natheless, the cruel boy, not so content,   nevertheless
    Would needs the fly pursue,
And in his hand with heedless hardiment   thoughtless boldness
    Him caught for to subdue.
25 But when on it he hasty hand did lay,
    The bee him stung therefore:
'Now out, alas!' he cried, 'and wellaway!
    I wounded am full sore;
The fly that I so much did scorn,
30   Hath hurt me with his little horn.'

Unto his mother straight he weeping came,
    And of his grief complained;
Who could not choose but laugh at his fond game,   foolish
    Though sad to see him pained.
35 'Think now,' quod she, 'my son, how great the smart
    Of those whom thou dost wound;
Full many thou hast pricked to the heart,
    That pity never found:
Therefore henceforth some pity take,
40   When thou dost spoil of lovers make.'

She took him straight, full piteously lamenting,
    And wrapped him in her smock;
She wrapped him softly, all the while repenting
    That he the fly did mock.
45 She dressed his wound and it embalmed well,
    With salve of sovereign might,
And then she bathed him in a dainty well,
    The well of dear delight.

Who would not oft be stung as this,
50   To be so bathed in Venus' bliss?

The wanton boy was shortly well-recured   recovered
    Of that his malady;
But he soon after fresh again enured   began
    His former cruelty.
55 And since that time he wounded hath myself
    With his sharp dart of love,
And now forgets, the cruel careless elf,
    His mother's hest to prove: bidding/obey
So now I languish till he please
60   My pining anguish to appease.

FINIS

[1]
Ye learned Sisters, which have oftentimes   Muses
Been to me aiding, others to adorn   celebrate
Whom ye thought worthy of your graceful rhymes,
That even the greatest did not greatly scorn   so that
5 To hear their names sung in your simple lays,   songs
But joyed in their praise;   delighted
And, when ye list your own mishaps to mourn,   wish
Which death, or love, or fortune's wreck did raise,
Your string could soon to sadder tenor turn,   mood/n. 56
10 And teach the woods and waters to lament
Your doleful dreariment: melancholy
Now lay those sorrowful complaints aside,
And, having all your heads with garland crowned,
Help me mine own love's praises to resound –
15 Ne let the same of any be envied.
So Orpheus did for his own bride;
So I unto myself alone will sing –
The woods shall to me answer and my echo ring.

[2]
Early, before the world's light-giving lamp
20 His golden beam upon the hills doth spread,
Having dispersed the night's uncheerful damp,   dismal
Do ye awake, and with fresh lustihead   the Muses/delight
Go to the bower of my beloved love,   bedchamber
My truest turtle dove;
25 Bid her awake; for Hymen is awake,
And long since ready forth his masque to move,   procession
With his bright tede that flames with many a flake,   torch
And many a bachelor to wait on him
In their fresh garments trim.
30 Bid her awake therefore, and soon her dight,   dress
For, lo! the wished day is come at last
That shall for all the pains and sorrows passed
Pay to her usury of long delight: the interest

And whilst she doth her dight,
35 Do ye to her of joy and solace sing,   pleasure
That all the woods may answer and your echo ring.

[3]
Bring with you all the nymphs that you can hear,   can hear you
Both of the rivers and the forests green,
And of the sea that neighbours to her near,   the bride
40 All with gay garlands goodly well-beseen;   n. 57
And let them also with them bring in hand
Another gay garland
For my fair love, of lilies and of roses,
Bound true-love wise with a blue silk ribband;
45 And let them make great store of bridal posies,
And let them eke bring store of other flowers
To deck the bridal bowers;
And let the ground whereas her foot shall tread,
For fear the stones her tender foot should wrong,
50 Be strewed with fragrant flowers all along,
And diapered like the discoloured mead.*   patterned/many-coloured
Which done, do at her chamber door await,   * meadow
For she will waken straight:
The whiles do ye this song unto her sing,
55 The woods shall to you answer and your echo ring.

[4]
Ye Nymphs of Mulla, which with careful heed
The silver scaly trouts do tend full well,
And greedy pikes which use therein to feed   in the river
(Those trouts and pikes all others do excel);
60 And ye likewise which keep the rushy lake   guard/Kilcolman
Where none do fishes take –
Bind up the locks the which hang scattered light,   loosely
And in his waters, which your mirror make,
Behold your faces as the crystal bright,
65 That when you come whereas my love doth lie,
No blemish she may spy.
And eke ye lightfoot maids which keep the deer
That on the hoary mountain use to tower,   roam
And the wild wolves which seek them to devour
70 With your steel darts do chase from coming near,
Be also present here,

To help to deck her and to help to sing,
That all the woods may answer and your echo ring.

[5]

75 Wake now, my love, awake, for it is time:
The rosy Morn long since left Tithon's bed,
All ready to her silver coach to climb,
And Phoebus gins to show his glorious head.
Hark how the cheerful birds do chant their lays
And carol of love's praise:
80 The merry lark her matins sings aloft,   morning prayers
The thrush replies, the mavis descant plays,   song-thrush
The ouzel shrills, the ruddock warbles soft –   blackbird/robin
So goodly all agree with sweet consent   harmony
To this day's merriment.
85 Ah my dear love, why do ye sleep thus long,
When meeter were that ye should now awake   fitter
T'await the coming of your joyous make,   husband
And hearken to the birds' love-learned song,
The dewy leaves among?
90 For they of joy and pleasance to you sing,
That all the woods them answer and their echo ring.

[6]

My love is now awake out of her dream,
And her fair eyes, like stars that dimmed were
With darksome cloud, now show their goodly beams
95 More bright than Hesperus his head doth rear.
Come now, ye damsels, daughters of delight,
Help quickly her to dight;
But first come ye fair Hours – which were begot,
In Jove's sweet paradise, of Day and Night –   by
100 Which do the seasons of the year allot,
And all that ever in this world is fair
Do make and still repair.
And ye three handmaids of the Cyprian Queen,   the Graces/Venus
The which do still adorn her beauty's pride,   splendour
105 Help to adorn my beautifullest bride:
And as ye her array, still throw between
Some graces to be seen;
And as ye use to Venus, to her sing,   do
The whiles the woods shall answer and your echo ring.

[7]

110 Now is my love all ready forth to come:
Let all the virgins therefore well await,   be ready
And ye fresh boys that tend upon her groom
Prepare yourselves, for he is coming straight.
Set all your things in seemly good array,
115 Fit for so joyful day,
The joyfull'st day that ever sun did see.
Fair sun, show forth thy favourable ray,
And let thy lifeful heat not fervent be,   life-giving/fierce
For fear of burning her sunshiny face,
120 Her beauty to disgrace.   mar
O fairest Phoebus, father of the Muse,
If ever I did honour thee aright,
Or sing the thing that mote thy mind delight,
Do not thy servant's simple boon refuse,   prayer
125 But let this day, let this one day be mine –
Let all the rest be thine.
Then I thy sovereign praises loud will sing,
That all the woods shall answer and their echo ring.

[8]

Hark! how the minstrels gin to shrill aloud   begin
130 Their merry music that resounds from far,
The pipe, the tabor, and the trembling croud,   small drum/fiddle
That well agree withouten breach or jar.   discord
But most of all the damsels do delight
When they their timbrels smite,   tambourine
135 And thereunto do dance and carol sweet,
That all the senses they do ravish quite –
The whiles the boys run up and down the street,
Crying aloud with strong confused noise   united
As if it were one voice.
140 'Hymen *io* Hymen, Hymen', they do shout,
That even to the heavens their shouting shrill
Doth reach, and all the firmament doth fill;   skies
To which the people standing all about,
As in approvance, do thereto applaud
145 And loud advance her laud;   praise
And evermore they 'Hymen, Hymen' sing,
That all the woods them answer and their echo ring.

[9]
Lo, where she comes along with portly pace,   stately
Like Phoebe, from her chamber of the East,
150 Arising forth to run her mighty race,
Clad all in white, that seems a virgin best: suits
So well it her beseems that ye would ween
Some angel she had been.
Her long loose yellow locks like golden wire,
155 Sprinkled with pearl, and pearling flowers atween,   lacework
Do like a golden mantle her attire,   dress
And, being crowned with a garland green,
Seem like some maiden queen.   she seems
Her modest eyes abashed to behold
160 So many gazers as on her do stare,
Upon the lowly ground affixed are;
Ne dare lift up her countenance too bold,   she lift/face
But blush to hear her praises sung so loud,
So far from being proud.
165 Nathless, do ye still loud her praises sing,   nevertheless
That all the woods may answer and your echo ring.

[10]
Tell me, ye merchants' daughters, did ye see
So fair a creature in your town before –   n. 58
So sweet, so lovely, and so mild as she,
170 Adorned with beauty's grace and virtue's store?
Her goodly eyes like sapphires shining bright,
Her forehead ivory white,
Her cheeks like apples which the sun hath rudded,   reddened
Her lips like cherries charming men to bite,
175 Her breast like to a bowl of cream uncrudded,   uncurdled
Her paps like lilies budded,   breasts
Her snowy neck like to a marble tower,
And all her body like a palace fair,
Ascending up with many a stately stair,
180 To honour's seat and chastity's sweet bower.   the head
Why stand ye still, ye virgins, in amaze
Upon her so to gaze,
Whiles ye forget your former lay to sing,
To which the woods did answer and your echo ring?

[11]
185 But if ye saw that which no eyes can see –
     The inward beauty of her lively spright,
     Garnished with heavenly gifts of high degree –
     Much more then would ye wonder at that sight,
     And stand astonished like to those which read   saw
190 Medusa's mazeful head.   Gorgon/bewildering
     There dwells sweet love and constant chastity,
     Unspotted faith and comely womanhood,   proper
     Regard of honour and mild modesty;
     There virtue reigns as queen in royal throne,
195 And giveth laws alone,
     The which the base affections do obey,   simple desires
     And yield their services unto her will;
     Ne thought of thing uncomely ever may
     Thereto approach to tempt her mind to ill.
200 Had ye once seen these her celestial treasures
     And unrevealed pleasures,
     Then would ye wonder and her praises sing,
     That all the woods should answer and your echo ring.

     [12]
     Open the temple gates unto my love,   n. 59
205 Open them wide that she may enter in;
     And all the posts adorn as doth behove,   as is proper
     And all the pillars deck with garlands trim,   n. 60
     For to receive this saint with honour due,   n. 61
     That cometh in to you.
210 With trembling steps and humble reverence
     She cometh in before th' Almighty's view:
     Of her, ye virgins, learn obedience,
     When so ye come into those holy places,
     To humble your proud faces.
215 Bring her up to th' high altar, that she may
     The sacred ceremonies there partake
     The which do endless matrimony make;   [central line]
     And let the roaring organs loudly play
     The praises of the Lord in lively notes,
220 The whiles, with hollow throats,
     The choristers the joyous anthem sing,
     That all the woods may answer and their echo ring.

[13]
Behold, whiles she before the altar stands,
Hearing the holy priest that to her speaks
225 And blesseth her with his two happy hands,
How the red roses flush up in her cheeks
And the pure snow with goodly vermeil stain   bright scarlet
Like crimson dyed in grain: dyed fast
That even th'angels, which continually
230 About the sacred altar do remain,
Forget their service and about her fly,   duty
Oft peeping in her face that seems more fair
The more they on it stare.
But her sad eyes, still fastened on the ground,   serious
235 Are governed with goodly modesty
That suffers not one look to glance awry
Which may let in a little thought unsound.   inappropriate
Why blush ye, love, to give to me your hand,
The pledge of all our band?   bond
240 Sing, ye sweet angels, 'alleluia' sing,
That all the woods may answer and your echo ring.

[14]
Now all is done: bring home the bride again;
Bring home the triumph of our victory;
Bring home with you the glory of her gain,
245 With joyance bring her and with jollity.
Never had man more joyful day than this,
Whom heaven would heap with bliss.
Make feast, therefore, now all this live-long day –
This day forever to me holy is.
250 Pour out the wine without restraint or stay,
Pour not by cups but by the belly-ful,
Pour out to all that wull,   will
And sprinkle all the posts and walls with wine,
That they may sweat, and drunken be withal.
255 Crown ye god Bacchus with a coronal,   garland
And Hymen also crown with wreaths of vine,
And let the Graces dance unto the rest –
For they can do it best –
The whiles the maidens do their carol sing,
260 To which the woods shall answer and their echo ring.

[15]
Ring ye the bells, ye young men of the town,
And leave your wonted labours for this day: usual
This day is holy – do ye write it down,
That ye for ever it remember may.
265 This day the sun is in his chiefest height,   n. 62
With Barnaby the bright;
From whence declining daily by degrees,
He somewhat loseth of his heat and light
When once the Crab behind his back he sees.   Cancer
270 But for this time it ill ordained was
To chose the longest day in all the year,
And shortest night, when longest fitter were:
Yet never day so long, but late would pass.
Ring ye the bells to make it wear away,
275 And bonfires make all day,
And dance about them, and about them sing,
That all the woods may answer and your echo ring.

[16]
Ah, when will this long weary day have end,
And lend me leave to come unto my love?
280 How slowly do the hours their numbers spend!
How slowly does sad Time his feathers move!   n. 63
Haste thee, O fairest planet, to thy home   the sun
Within the western foam:
Thy tired steeds long since have need of rest.
285 Long though it be, at last I see it gloom,   darken
And the bright Evening-star with golden crest
Appear out of the East.   n. 64
Fair child of beauty, glorious lamp of love,
That all the host of heaven in ranks dost lead,
290 And guidest lovers through the night's dread,
How cheerfully thou lookest from above,
And seem'st to laugh atween thy twinkling light   among
As joying in the sight
Of these glad many which for joy do sing,
295 That all the woods them answer and their echo ring.

[17]
Now cease, ye damsels, your delights forepassed;
Enough is it that all the day was yours.

Now day is done, and night is nighing fast,
Now bring the bride into the bridal bowers.
300 Now night is come, now soon her disarray,   undress
And in her bed her lay:
Lay her in lilies and in violets,
And silken curtains over her display,
And odoured sheets, and arras coverlets.   tapestry
305 Behold how goodly my fair love does lie
In proud humility,
Like unto Maia, whenas Jove her took   n. 65
In Tempe, lying on the flowery grass,   n. 66
'Twixt sleep and wake, after she weary was
310 With bathing in the Acidalian brook.
Now it is night, ye damsels may be gone
And leave my love alone,
And leave likewise your former lay to sing:
The woods no more shall answer, nor your echo ring.

[18]
315 Now welcome, Night, thou night so long expected
That long day's labour dost at last defray,   repay
And all my cares, which cruel Love collected,
Hast summed in one, and cancelled for aye: gathered
Spread thy broad wing over my love and me,
320 That no man may us see,
And in thy sable mantle us enwrap,   black
From fear of peril and foul horror free.
Let no false treason seek us to entrap,
Nor any dread disquiet once annoy
325 The safety of our joy;
But let the night be calm and quietsome,
Without tempestuous storms or sad affray,   disturbance
Like as when Jove with fair Alcmena lay,
When he begot the great Tirynthian groom;
330 Or like as when he with thyself did lie,
And begot Majesty.   n. 67
And let the maids and young men cease to sing;
Ne let the woods them answer, nor their echo ring.

[19]
Let no lamenting cries nor doleful tears
335 Be heard all night within nor yet without;

Ne let false whispers, breeding hidden fears,
Break gentle sleep with misconceived doubt.
Let no deluding dreams, nor dreadful sights
Make sudden sad affrights;
340 Ne let house fires, nor lightning's helpless harms,   unavoidable
Ne let the Puck, nor other evil sprights,
Ne let mischievous witches with their charms,   wicked
Ne let hobgoblins, names whose sense we see not,
Fray us with things that be not.   frighten
345 Let not the screech owl nor the stork be heard,   ill omens
Nor the night raven that still deadly yells;
Nor damned ghosts called up with mighty spells,
Nor grisly vultures make us once affeared;
Ne let th'unpleasant choir of frogs still croaking
350 Make us to wish their choking.
Let none of these their dreary accents sing,
Ne let the woods them answer, nor their echo ring.

[20]
But let still Silence true night-watches keep,
That sacred Peace may in assurance reign,
355 And timely Sleep, when it is time to sleep,
May pour his limbs forth on your pleasant plain,   complaint
The whiles an hundred little winged loves,   cupids
Like diverse-feathered doves,
Shall fly and flutter round about your bed,
360 And in the secret dark that none reproves,
Their pretty stealths shall work, and snares shall spread
To filch away sweet snatches of delight,
Concealed through covert night.   sheltering
Ye sons of Venus, play your sports at will,
365 For greedy Pleasure, careless of your toys,   games
Thinks more upon her paradise of joys
Than what ye do, albeit good or ill.
All night, therefore, attend your merry play,
For it will soon be day:
370 Now none doth hinder you that say or sing;
Ne will the woods now answer, nor your echo ring.

[21]
Who is the same which at my window peeps?   is that
Or whose is that fair face that shines so bright?

Is it not Cynthia, she that never sleeps,
375 But walks about high heaven all the night?
O fairest goddess, do thou not envy
My love with me to spy:
For thou likewise didst love, though now unthought,   unthought of
And for a fleece of wool, which privily   secretly
380 The Latmian shepherd once unto thee brought,   Endymion
His pleasures with thee wrought.
Therefore to us be favourable now;
And sith of women's labours thou hast charge,
And generation goodly dost enlarge,   grant
385 Incline thy will t'effect our wishful vow,
And the chaste womb inform with timely seed   fruitful
That may our comfort breed:
Till which we cease our hopeful hap to sing;   lot
Ne let the woods us answer, nor our echo ring.

[22]

390 And thou, great Juno, which with awful might   awe-inspiring
The laws of wedlock still dost patronize,
And the religion of the faith first plight
With sacred rites hast taught to solemnize;
And eke for comfort often called art
395 Of women in their smart –   pain
Eternally bind thou this lovely band,   loving/bond
And all thy blessings unto us impart.
And thou, glad Genius, in whose gentle hand
The bridal bower and genial bed remain   begetting
400 Without blemish or stain,
And the sweet pleasures of their love's delight
With secret aid dost succour and supply
Till they bring forth the fruitful progeny –
Send us the timely fruit of this same night.
405 And thou, fair Hebe, and thou, Hymen free,
Grant that it may so be.
Till which we cease your further praise to sing,
Ne any woods shall answer, nor your echo ring.

[23]
And ye high heavens, the temple of the gods,
410 In which a thousand torches flaming bright
Do burn, that to us wretched earthly clods

In dreadful darkness lend desired light;
And all ye powers which in the same remain,
More than we men can feign,   imagine
415 Pour out your blessing on us plenteously,
And happy influence upon us rain
That we may raise a large posterity
Which from the earth, which they may long possess
With lasting happiness,
420 Up to your haughty palaces may mount;   high
And, for the guerdon of their glorious merit,   reward
May heavenly tabernacles there inherit,   dwellings
Of blessed saints for to increase the count.
So let us rest, sweet love, in hope of this,
425 And cease till then our timely joys to sing:
The woods no more us answer, nor our echo ring.

[24]
Song made in lieu of many ornaments
With which my love should duly have been decked,
Which, cutting off through hasty accidents,
430 Ye would not stay your due time to expect,   await
But promised both to recompense: n. 68
Be unto her a goodly ornament,
And for short time an endless monument.

FINIS

PROTHALAMION: OR,
A SPOUSAL VERSE *marriage*

made by Edm. Spenser

In honour of the double marriage of the
two honourable & virtuous ladies, the
Lady Elizabeth and the Lady Katherine
Somerset, daughters to the Right
Honourable the Earl of Worcester
and espoused to the two worthy *engaged*
gentlemen, Master Henry Guildford and
Master William Petre, Esquires.

At London. Printed for William Ponsonby. 1596

[1]
Calm was the day, and through the trembling air
Sweet-breathing Zephyrus did softly play, *West Wind*
A gentle spirit that lightly did delay *cool*
Hot Titan's beams, which then did glister fair; *Hyperion/glitter*
5 When I (whom sullen care,
Through discontent of my long fruitless stay
In Prince's court and expectation vain
Of idle hopes – which still do fly away *constantly*
Like empty shadows – did afflict my brain)
10 Walked forth to ease my pain
Along the shore of silver streaming Thames,
Whose rutty bank, the which his river hems, *rooty*
Was painted all with variable flowers, *various*
And all the meads adorned with dainty gems *meadows*
15 Fit to deck maidens' bowers, *chambers*
And crown their paramours *lovers*
Against the bridal day, which is not long: *in anticipation of*
Sweet Thames run softly till I end my song.

[2]
There, in a meadow, by the river's side,
A flock of nymphs I chanced to espy –
20 All lovely daughters of the flood thereby, *nearby river*
With goodly greenish locks all loose untied

As each had been a bride;
And each one had a little wicker basket
Made of fine twigs entrailed curiously,   *woven finely*
25 In which they gathered flowers to fill their flasket,   *shallow basket*
And with fine fingers cropped full feateously   *nimbly*
The tender stalks on hie.   *quickly*
Of every sort which in that meadow grew,
30 They gathered some – the violet pallid blue,   *pale*
The little daisy that at evening closes,
The virgin lily and the primrose true,
With store of vermeil roses,   *many vermilion*
To deck their bridegrooms' posies   *bouquets*
35 Against the bridal day, which was not long: *in anticipation of*
  Sweet Thames run softly till I end my song.

[3]
With that I saw two swans of goodly hue   *appearance/n. 1*
Come softly swimming down along the Lea;   *n. 2*
Two fairer birds I yet did never see:
40 The snow which doth the top of Pindus strew
Did never whiter show;
Nor Jove himself, when he a swan would be
For love of Leda, whiter did appear;
Yet Leda was (they say) as white as he,
45 Yet not so white as these, nor nothing near:
So purely white they were
That even the gentle stream, the which them bare,
Seemed foul to them, and bade his billows spare   *compared to*
To wet their silken feathers, lest they might
50 Soil their fair plumes with water not so fair,   *dirty*
And mar their beauties bright
That shone as heaven's light
Against their bridal day, which was not long:
  Sweet Thames run softly till I end my song.

[4]
55 Eftsoons the nymphs, which now had flowers their fill,   *presently*
Ran all in haste to see that silver brood   *the swans*
As they came floating on the crystal flood:
Whom when they saw, they stood amazed still
Their wond'ring eyes to fill.
60 Them seemed they never saw a sight so fair   *it seemed to*

Of fowls so lovely, that they sure did deem   judge
Them heavenly born, or to be that same pair   n. 3
Which through the sky draw Venus' silver team;   chariot
For sure they did not seem
65 To be begot of any earthly seed,
But rather of angels or of angels' breed.
Yet were they bred of summer's-heat, they say,   n. 4
In sweetest season, when each flower and weed   plant
The earth did fresh array;
70 So fresh they seemed as day,
Even as their bridal day, which was not long:
    Sweet Thames run softly till I end my song.

[5]
Then forth they all out of their baskets drew
Great store of flowers, the honour of the field,
75 That to the sense did fragrant odours yield,
All which upon those goodly birds they threw,
And all the waves did strew:
That like old Peneus' waters they did seem,
When down along by pleasant Tempe's shore,   n. 5
80 Scattered with flowers, through Thessaly they stream;
That they appear, through lilies' plenteous store,
Like a bride's chamber floor.
Two of those nymphs, meanwhile, two garlands bound
Of freshest flowers which in that mead they found,   meadow
85 The which presenting all in trim array,
Their snowy foreheads therewithal they crowned,   the swans
Whilst one did sing this lay,   song
Prepared against that day,
Against their bridal day, which was not long:
90   Sweet Thames run softly till I end my song.

[6]
'Ye gentle birds, the world's fair ornament
And heaven's glory, whom this happy hour
Doth lead unto your lovers' blissful bower,
Joy may you have and gentle heart's content   noble
95 Of your love's couplement;   union
And let fair Venus that is queen of love,
With her heart-quelling son upon you smile –   Cupid
Whose smile, they say, hath virtue to remove

All love's dislike, and friendship's faulty guile
100 For ever to assoil.   *remove*
Let endless Peace your steadfast hearts accord,   *attune*
And blessed Plenty wait upon your board,   *table*
And let your bed with pleasures chaste abound,
That fruitful issue may to you afford,   *supply*
105 Which may your foes confound,
And make your joys redound   *overflow*
Upon your bridal day, which is not long:
    Sweet Thames run softly till I end my song.'

[7]
So ended she, and all the rest around
110 To her redoubled that her undersong
Which said their bridal day should not be long;
And gentle Echo from the neighbour ground
Their accents did resound.   *words*
So forth those joyous birds did pass along,
115 Adown the Lea that to them murmured low
As he would speak, but that he lacked a tongue –
Yet did by signs his glad affection show,
Making his stream run slow.
And all the fowl which in his flood did dwell
120 Gan flock about these twain, that did excel
The rest so far as Cynthia doth shend   *shame*
The lesser stars. So they, enranged well,   *in good order*
Did on those two attend,
And their best service lend
125 Against their wedding day, which was not long:
    Sweet Thames run softly till I end my song.

[8]
At length they all to merry London came,
To merry London, my most kindly nurse,
That to me gave this life's first native source,
130 Though from another place I take my name,
A house of ancient fame.   *see Spencers*
There when they came, whereas those bricky towers   *where*
The which on Thames's broad aged back do ride,   *n. 6*
Where now the studious lawyers have their bowers,   *chambers*
135 There whilom wont the Templar Knights to bide,   *formerly used*
Till they decayed through pride;

Next whereunto there stands a stately place,
Where oft I gained gifts and goodly grace
Of that great lord which therein wont to dwell,   Leicester
140 Whose want too well now feels my friendless case –   lack/state
But, ah! here fits not well
Old woes, but joys to tell
Against the bridal day, which is not long:
    Sweet Thames run softly till I end my song.

[9]
145 Yet therein now doth lodge a noble peer,   Essex
Great England's glory and the world's wide wonder,
Whose dreadful name late through all Spain did thunder, recently
And Hercules' two pillars standing near   n. 7
Did make to quake and fear.
150 Fair branch of honour, flower of chivalry,
That fillest England with thy triumph's fame,
Joy have thou of thy noble victory,
And endless happiness of thine own name
That promiseth the same: n. 8
155 That through thy prowess and victorious arms
Thy country may be freed from foreign harms,
And great Elisa's glorious name may ring
Through all the world, filled with thy wide alarms,   calls to arms
Which some brave Muse may sing
160 To ages following
Upon the bridal day, which is not long:
    Sweet Thames run softly till I end my song.

[10]
From those high towers, this noble lord issuing –
Like radiant Hesper when his golden hair
165 In th' Ocean billows he hath bathed fair –
Descended to the river's open viewing,
With a great train ensuing.   retinue
Above the rest were goodly to be seen
Two gentle knights of lovely face and feature,   the grooms
170 Beseeming well the bower of any queen,   befitting
With gifts of wit and ornaments of nature
Fit for so goodly stature,   notable
That like the twins of Jove they seemed in sight,   Leda
Which deck the baldric of the heavens bright.   zodiac

175 They two, forth pacing to the river's side,
       Received those two fair brides, their love's delight,
       Which, at th'appointed tide,
       Each one did make his bride
       Against their bridal day, which is not long:
180   Sweet Thames run softly till I end my song.

FINIS

NOTES

The Shepherds' Calendar

Epistle

n. 1 The original spelling of the title – 'Shepheardes' – does not distinguish whether this is the calendar of *the* shepherd or of *the* shepherds. This doubleness neatly captures the personal and public aspects of the poem.

n. 2 For proper names see 'Glossary of Names'.

n. 3 See Chaucer, *Troilus and Criseyde* 5.1786.

n. 4 'Patronage' – 'hopes he will be the patron of'.

n. 5 Chaucer, *Troilus and Criseyde* 1.809.

n. 6 Lydgate, *The Fall of Princes* l.252.

n. 7 'Decorum' – the matching of style to content.

n. 8 Cicero, *De Oratore* 2.14.60.

n. 9 Cicero, *De Oratore* 3.38.153; *Orator* 23.80.

n. 10 Perhaps Cicero, *De Natura Deorum* 1.28.79. Little of Alcaeus' work has survived.

n. 11 'For, not marking ... his cast' – 'Without understanding what he aims at, he will judge what has been achieved'.

n. 12 For Evander's mother see Aulus Gellius, *Noctes Atticae* 1.10.2.

n. 13 EK here refers to the very loose syntax of some earlier verse, which made extensive alterations to the usual syntax and rhythms of English in order to make lines fit metre.

n. 14 'For so ... to hunt the letter' – 'To use the alliteration they love'.

n. 15 Virgil, *Aeneid* 6.80, a line which describes the raging of a prophetess which precedes her inspiration by Apollo; literally, 'taming her raving mouth, her wild heart'.

n. 16 *SC*, 'June' ll.65 & 79.

n. 17 The name is 'old' as it is similar to *The Calendar of Shepherds*, a frequently reprinted English translation of a French almanac – *Le Compost et Calendrier des Bergiers* (1493).

n. 18 These works, if they existed, are lost or renamed.

n. 19 Harvey published some of his best poems in English in *Four Letters and Certain Sonnets* (1592).

n. 20 EK, pointing out that he has already traced the literary genealogy of eclogues, now turns to the etymology of the term, and explains why 'Aeglogue' (elsewhere modernized) is his preferred spelling. The term 'eclogue' in fact comes from the Greek for 'a selection'.

n. 21 'This specially . . . deriving' – 'who derives from Theocritus'.

n. 22 'Pleasance' – 'pleasure giving quality (of the earth)'.

n. 23 See *Exodus* 12 & 13.

n. 24 An intercalary day is one added to adapt the lunar to the solar reckoning of time; the reason for calling this day a bissextile is bound up with the Roman calendar.

n. 25 See *Leviticus* 23:34.

'January'

n. 1 'January' is printed as closely as is here possible to the way in which it originally appeared. Its format – a woodcut, the argument, the poem, and then EK's notes – was repeated for the other 11 eclogues. Where a line of the poem is commented on in EK's notes, an 'EK' has been placed in the margin.

n. 2 The poem's woodcuts were probably carried out under Spenser's direction. With their incorporation of the appropriate signs of the zodiac (in 'January' Aquarius can be seen at the top left), they indicate on a visual level the calendrical concerns of the poem. Individually, the woodcuts also often illustrate the eclogue they precede. Sometimes this illustration takes the form of the depiction of an activity relevant to the month; in the February woodcut, a tree is being cut down in the background, a feature which alerts the reader to the calendrical appropriateness of the eclogue's fable of the Oak and the Brier. 'January', by contrast, does not have such a seasonal activity; instead it shows a shepherd's boy with his back turned to his sheep and looking towards a town. This may be the town that Colin rues visiting in the eclogue; or perhaps Colin is looking away from the pastoral poetry of his past, represented by his sheep, and towards a more elevated future of epic poetry, represented by the classical buildings of the town. At Colin's feet lies the broken pipe of his poetry: in the woodcut this is a bagpipe (it is an 'oaten pipe' in the eclogue), a symbol of male desire, and here a symbol of frustrated desire as it is broken. In the woodcut's pipe, the relationship between Colin's personal love and his poetic activity is thus signalled. There are also, however, details in the woodcuts that seem not to agree with their respective eclogues; in the January woodcut the sheep appear well fed and healthy, though the eclogue describes them as feeble and weak. Perhaps, then, Spenser gave directions concerning significant details of the woodcuts, and the craftsmen 'filled in' what remained unstated.

n. 3   'Daffadillies' are 'daffodils', a group of flowers which, in the Elizabethan period, included what are now called asphodels. Given that the flowers are summer's dress, asphodels are probably being referred to here.

n. 4   I.e., the name 'Tityrus' would look out of place in an English pastoral.

n. 5   Sir Thomas Smith, *De Republica Anglorum* (written 1556, pubd 1581).

n. 6   'Corydon, you're a yokel; Alexis scorns your gifts.' Virgil, *Ecl.* 2.56.

n. 7   EK names the friend as Harvey in his notes to 'September'.

n. 8   'Paederastice' – the love of a man for a boy, sodomy.

n. 9   Plato, *Alcibiades* 1.131; Xenophon, *Symposium* 8; Maximus, *Dissertationes* 21.8.

n. 10   Statius, *Epithalamium Stellae et Violentillae* in his *Silvae* (92 AD onwards) 2.ll.197–8.

n. 11   Madonna Celia, *Lettre Amorose* (1562).

'February'

n. 1   See EK's discussion in the General Argument (p. 12) of whether the year should be taken to begin in January or March.

n. 2   'It avails' – that habit is broken ('dropped', in fact, like the cows' tales).

n. 3   'Fall' here has the sense of 'condition'; it suggests decay through association with the earlier fall of Adam and Eve.

n. 4   Good Friday commemorates the day of Christ's crucifixion; the sun was held to have darkened, and so the sky to have 'frowned', as Christ died. See *Luke* 23:44–5.

n. 5   'So, loit'ring ... and misery' – these lines expand Mantuan, *Ecl* 6.19–24, while paraphrasing Chaucer, *House of Fame* ll.1224–6.

n. 6   'Broom' is a yellow-flowering shrub.

n. 7   'Lords of the Year' – Lords of Misrule who were crowned at summer (and other) festivals. The reign of these mock kings was one way of marking the freedom from normal order that distinguished periods of festivity. See Hutton (1994).

n. 8   A 'dewlap' is a fold of skin hanging from the throat.

n. 9   I.e., you have no head in your hood; you are empty-headed.

n. 10   See *Romans* 6:23.

n. 11   A 'stoop-gallant' is something that humbles 'gallants' (gentlemen of fashion); originally it was a contagious fever.

n. 12   EK points out that this tale is more 'like to Aesop's fables' than Chaucer. (See the fable of the Reed and the Olive Tree.)

n. 13   EK glosses 'trees of state' as 'taller trees fit for timber'.

n. 14   A 'liege lord' is a lord entitled to feudal allegiance.

'March'

n. 1   Willye suggests Thomalin has broken Love's slumber by enjoying 'wanton pleasures' [EK].

n. 2   An imitation of Virgil, *Ecl* 3.33 [EK].

n. 3   The mid-point of the poem, dividing past from future. The tale of
Cupid that follows is based on Bion's *Idyll* 4.

n. 4   There are 'pumice' stones as this is (in part) a Mediterranean
landscape.

n. 5   EK notes that commentators had taken Achilles' being wounded
in the heel to symbolize 'lustful love'. EK also offers a medical
account: 'from the heel . . . to the privy parts there pass certain
veins and slender sinews.'

'*April*'
n. 1   EK: 'In all this song is not to be respected what the worthiness of
Her Majesty deserveth, nor what to the highness of a prince is
agreeable, but what is most comely [fitting] for the meanness of a
shepherd's wit.'

n. 2   Pan had no daughter by Syrinx, but Hobbinol can think of no
greater parentage for Elisa than making her the daughter of the
god of shepherds [EK]. Such a parentage, since Pan can also be
taken to be God, gives to Elisa/Elizabeth a measure of divinity,
and casts her in a Christ-like role. Through this messianic aspect,
'April' recalls Virgil's *Ecl* 4 where the coming birth of a child who
will bring peace and unity to the world is described. Within 'April',
Elisa is also associated with the Virgin Mary through the phrase
'withouten spot'.
     Such suggestions of divinity were standard Tudor propaganda,
and a part of their version of sixteenth-century history, which held
the Tudors to have been divinely ordained to rule and bring peace.
Hobbinol goes on to invoke this history with his description of the
two roses 'meddled' in Elisa's cheeks, and EK makes sure the point
is not missed: 'By the mingling of the red rose and the white is
meant the uniting of the two principal houses of Lancaster and
York, by whose long discord and deadly debate this realm many
years was sore travailed and almost clean decayed, till the famous
Henry the Seventh, of the line of Lancaster, taking to wife the
most virtuous Princess Elizabeth, daughter to the fourth Edward
of the House of York, begat the most royal Henry the Eighth
aforesaid, in whom was the first union of the white rose and the
red.'
     The relationship between Elisa and Elizabeth is, then, not the
direct equivalence of simple allegory, but rather a part of the

ongoing creation of a symbolic persona of considerable political power, through which the Queen ruled and lived.

n. 3   EK notes that bay branches 'be the sign of honour and victory, and [are] therefore of mighty conquerors worn in their triumphs, and eke of famous poets'.

n. 4   By alluding to Arthurian legend (with 'Ladies of the Lake'), Hobbinol weaves yet another strand of Tudor historiography into our reading of Elisa/Elizabeth; Henry VII and subsequent Tudor monarchs claimed their rule fulfilled Merlin's prophecy for the coming of a second Arthur who would reunite the kingdom of Britain.

n. 5   I.e., the establishment or maintenance of peace is one of the most important responsibilities of those who rule. Elizabeth was officially celebrated at this time for the peace she had brought to England.

n. 6   Certainty about which flowers are being referred to in the list that follows is elusive. For instance, the OED2 notes that 'gillyflower' was used to refer both to varieties of 'the pink' and to 'coronations'. Similarly 'the pink' might refer to the 'clove-pink', another name for which is 'sops-in-wine'. The 'chevisance' is not a known plant, but possibly a Spenserism, intended to suggest chivalric qualities.

n. 7   'Flower-de-lys': OED2 notes as a 'fanciful etymology' the sixteenth-century belief that fleur-de-lys came from the Latin flos deliciae, flowers of delight.

n. 8   EK notes these lines come from Virgil's Aeneid (ll.327–8); they are spoken by Aeneas as he meets his mother, Venus, who is disguised as one of Diana's followers. Again, this stresses Elisa/Elizabeth's divinity. More subtly, as DBD points out, the figure of Venus-as-Diana is particularly appropriate to Elizabeth, 'as an affirmation of the Virgin Queen's betrothal to her realm'.

'May'

n. 1   The Argument for 'May' is misleadingly reductive in its suggestion that Piers and Palinode may be seen as representatives of Protestant and Catholic positions respectively; it is rather that the two represent antithetical positions within the Elizabethan, Protestant Church of England. Piers puts forward a view in line with the reforming, progressive and radical current of Protestantism; hence his quoting of 'Algrind' at l.75. Palinode puts forward a far more conservative stance, emotionally defending the (bad) practices of the pre-Reformation English Church.

Their names reflect this debate. 'Piers' recalls Langland's *Piers Plowman*, an association strengthened by the use of 'dream' on l.16. A 'palinode' is a recantation (usually in song or verse). Palinode recants some of the consequences of the reformation of the English Church.

n. 2   A hornpipe is a wind instrument. The taborer would play it with one hand while drumming with the other.

n. 3   'May' is the Lord of the May-day festival. See 'February', n. 7.

n. 4   Piers is here describing the practices of pluralism and absenteeism. 'Pluralism' occurs when one clergyman is in charge of, and so receiving the income from, several parishes. It generates 'absenteeism' – the absence of the clergyman from his parish.

n. 5   EK notes this is rather like the epitaph of the Earl of Devonshire:

> Ho, ho, who lies here?
> I, the good Earl of Devonshire,
> And Maulde my wife, that was full dear,
> We lived together 55 year.
> That we spent, we had;
> That we gave, we have;
> That we left, we lost.

n. 6   'In sufferance' is a legal term; here it may refer to the income from an area of land, the claim to which income was originally held quite legally, but which continues to be held without the express permission of the actual owner of the land.

n. 7   'Greedy governance' is government for self-enrichment. EK sees this as a reference to the Pope and the Roman Catholic Church.

n. 8   EK argues that the Kid stands for faithful but foolish Christians, his Dam for Christ, and the Fox for deceitful Papists.

n. 9   EK explains that this refers to the hairs which begin to grow under a goat's chin 'when lustful heat beginneth to kindle'.

n. 10 'Lustihead' has a range of meaning that centres on 'physical vitality'; it refers (non-pejoratively) to the enjoyment of one's strength, courage, and virility. For synonyms one has to go outside English, to the French *joie de vivre*, or the German *Leberslust*.

n. 11 EK notes that these are meant to suggest the relics and rags of popish superstition.

n. 12 'Me' is an indirect object of interest, a grammatical form that flourished in Elizabethan and Jacobean drama. Here it expresses the narrator's sense of vexation at the behaviour of the Fox.

n. 13 A wicket was a small door cut into a larger door. EK claims that 'clink' means 'key-hole', and suggests that Chaucer's 'clicket', meaning 'key', is derived from it. The OED2 finds no authority for this.

n. 14 'Travail' may mean 'work', 'travel', or 'trouble'.

n. 15 'Made him good glee' – 'entertained him well'.

n. 16 'After his cheer' – 'in response to Kiddie's mood'.

n. 17 EK suggests that 'Sir John' is a name for a 'popish priest'.

n. 18 Source unknown.

'June'

n. 1 EK: 'a paradise in Greek signifies a *garden of pleasure* or *place of delights*. So [Colin] compareth the soil wherein Hobbinol made his abode to that earthly paradise in scripture called Eden.'

n. 2 EK believes this refers to Spenser's having to move south in order to advance his career.

n. 3 EK notes that night-ravens are symbols of misfortune.

n. 4 'Queen-apples' – an early variety of apple. EK notes this line as an imitation of Virgil, *Ecl* 2.51.

n. 5 'Presume to Parnass hill' – 'compete with the gods'.

n. 6 EK contrasts this emblem with that of 'January'.

'July'

n. 1 The Argument is again misleading. In the eclogue, Thomalin is not simply good and Morell simply bad; in the shepherds' debate on the relative merits of hills and valleys, neither has the monopoly on right.

Morell's sense of the hills being closer to God may be naive, and part of a tendency to give too much credence to (Roman Catholic) external matters of religion (as in his belief in the shrine of Our Lady at Loretto, l.74). Yet Thomalin's refusal to leave the lowlands is a refusal to speak out for his beliefs. Hills may not, in themselves, be sacred, but they are where one talks with God or teaches others; Algrind, Thomalin's hero, was on a hill when he was struck down.

Morell and Thomalin are a pair rather like Palinode and Piers. The arguments of Thomalin and Piers, who stand clearly in the reforming, progressive tradition of Protestantism, are given more weight; however, Morell's and Palinode's arguments cannot be dismissed.

n. 2 The sun enters Leo in July. The Cup and Diadem are the constellations of Crater and Corona Borealis.

n. 3 EK: 'a promontory in the west part of England [near Penzance]'.

n. 4 The 'bloody sweat' refers to Christ's anguish in the Garden of Gethsemane; there, knowing that he is about to be betrayed to the authorities, Christ 'prayed more earnestly: and his sweat was as it were great drops of blood falling down' (*Luke* 22:44). Through prayer, Christ finds the strength to accept his sacrificial role and so 'save' humankind.

n. 5 EK notes that Morell seems confused, thinking that Adam was one among many shepherds in paradise. Adam's (and Eve's) 'folly' was in eating the forbidden fruit; this led to their expulsion from Paradise and rendered humankind mortal.

n. 6 Perhaps the shrine of the Virgin Mary at Loretto, Italy, mentioned in Mantuan, *Ecl* 8.52.

n. 7 The first two editions of *SC* read 'resourse'; this edition follows subsequent Elizabethan editions in emending to 'recourse'.

n. 8 According to EK, lightning strikes hills more frequently than the lowlands; and as lightning takes the quickest route from heaven to earth, so hills are nearer heaven – Q.E.D.

n. 9   EK explains these were the twelve sons of Jacob, who supported themselves only from their sheep. See *Genesis* 46.

n. 10   See Chaucer, *Squire's Tale* l.81 [DBD].

n. 11   See *Exodus* 33.11.

n. 12   EK explains that Aaron was 'not so true' since, while Moses was on Mt Sinai receiving the ten commandments, Aaron fashioned a golden calf for the Israelites to worship, and so 'committed idolatry'. See *Exodus* 32.

n. 13   Thomalin may be unsure if Rome is Rome because the corruption of the present-day city divorces it from the noble city that it had been in the classical past.

n. 14   The same fate befalls Aeschylus, the Greek tragedian. The eagle may be taken to be Elizabeth; see 'Grindal' in the 'Glossary of Names'.

n. 15   EK sees the two emblems (and so the poem) as being part of the same argument – as distinct but complementary positions, each being reasonable: '[Thomalin] taketh occasion to praise the mean [. . .] according to the saying of old philosophers that virtue dwelleth in the midst [middle way . . .]. Whereto Morrell replieth with continuance of the same philosopher's opinion that, albeit all bounty dwelleth in mediocrity, yet perfect felicity dwelleth in supremacy.'

'August'

n. 1   Theocritus, *Idylls* 5 & 6.

n. 2   'Having ended their cause' – 'having brought their contest to a conclusion'.

n. 3   EK: Virgil, *Ecl* 3.3.

n. 4   EK: Theocritus, *Idylls* 5.20–30; Virgil, *Ecl* 3.28–51.

n. 5   DBD notes that the 'holy eve' could be that of 'the Assumption of the Blessed Virgin, 15 August or, under the auspices of Virgo, the Nativity of the Blessed Virgin, 8 September, on the eve of which Queen Elizabeth was born'.

n. 6   A 'roundelay' is a simple song with refrain.

n. 7 Possibly a *double entendre*: Willye may be suggesting that the bonny lass is very ready to trip, that is to 'fall' down on her back as the first movement of sexual intercourse. Such a suggestion would suit the mocking vein in which Willye opens the roundelay.

n. 8 Green is fitting for virgins as it suggests that they are unripe.

n. 9 Most editions emend 'careless' to 'cureless'. However, though 'cureless' is obviously suitable, 'careless' (meaning 'untended') also makes sense.

n. 10 EK: Virgil, *Ecl* 3.109.

n. 11 EK: 'The meaning hereof is very ambiguous, for Perigot by his poesy claiming the conquest, and Willye not yielding, Cuddie (the arbiter of their cause and patron of his own) seemeth to challenge it [claim victory] as his due, saying that he is happy which can – so abruptly ending. But he meaneth either him that can win the best, or moderate himself being best, and leave off with the best.'

'September'

n. 1 The first quarter of the eclogue draws heavily on Mantuan, *Ecl* 9.

n. 2 The suggestion here – reinforced below by 'foreign coasts' and 'tho[se] countries' – is that it is not England that is being described, but (presumably) Rome. However, at times the corrupt practices that Diggon describes can be seen to be applicable to the Church of England.

n. 3 They sell their good name by selling benefices (ecclesiastical livings).

n. 4 These 'baits' probably refer to the way in which, in the Church of England, powerful bishops were able to manipulate the lower clergy. One particular source of complaint was the practice of ejecting clergy from a rich benefice to make way for a nominee of the Queen or one of her favourites [Variorum].

n. 5 Bulls could be an image of proud, powerful and cruel men; see the 'bulls of Bashan' in *Psalms* 22:12–13.

n. 6 EK: Horace, *Odes* 1.14.15–16.

n. 7 Diggon alludes to the dog on a bridge who dropped the meat he had in order to pick up the meat he saw in his reflection in the stream.

n. 8   EK: Mantuan, *Ecl* 7.8–9.

n. 9   EK: 'That is, their souls, which – by popish exorcisms and practices – they damn to hell.'

n. 10   The 'bad . . . best' are the clergy, who are corrupt.

n. 11   I.e., they have sold the ox, and the money now lies in their purse.

n. 12   The 'other[s]' being those above the clergy – their patrons and the great landowners. For 'bulls of Bashan' see n. 5.

n. 13   Most editions, following the Folio edition of 1611, emend 'yield' to 'yede' (meaning 'go'). But 'yield' (meaning 'submit') makes sense.

n. 14   EK notes that King Edgar (959–75) is said to have rid England of wolves.

n. 15   EK explains that this phrase is proverbial; in the reign of King Ethelbert (860–66), Kent was the only part of England that had not become Christianized, and so was not in the 'Christendom' of England.

n. 16   EK glosses 'the great hunt' as the 'executing of laws and justice' against Roman Catholics.

n. 17   EK notes that Roffy is the name of a shepherd in Marot, *Ecl* 1.42 (*Mme Louise de Savoie*).

n. 18   EK at this point declares that Colin represents Spenser, and that Hobbinol represents Spenser's 'especial good friend' Gabriel Harvey. EK goes on to praise Harvey's talents and achievements in poetry and rhetoric.

n. 19   EK: Ovid, *Heroides* 4.89.

n. 20   EK notes this emblem is spoken by Narcissus in Ovid, *Meta* 3.466. Though the episode was extremely well known, EK thinks there is no allusion intended. Spenser also uses an English version of the emblem in *Am* 35 & 85.

'October'

n. 1   If *The English Poet* existed, it is now lost.

n. 2   The first 79 lines are closely modelled on Mantuan, *Ecl* 5.

n. 3   'Bidding base' may refer either to a children's game or to a singing match: both meanings involve the challenging of an opponent, and the phrase suggests the playful nature of pastoral singing (as seen in the first half of 'August').

n. 4   According to the fable, in the summer the ant provides for winter while the grasshopper sings, and in the winter the grasshopper starves.

n. 5   The sense of music's and language's power stemmed from (and gave rise to) a voluntarist psychology, which EK explains:

'What the secret working of music is in the minds of men [. . .] well appeareth hereby, that some of the ancient philosophers [. . .] held for opinion that the mind was made of certain harmony and musical numbers, for the great compassion and likeness of affection in the one and in the other; as [is shown] also by that memorable history of Alexander. To whom, whenas Timotheus, the great musician, played the Phrygian melody, it is said that he was distraught with such unwonted fury that, straight away rising from the table, in great rage he caused himself to be armed as ready to go to war (for that music is very war-like); and immediately whenas the musician changed his stroke to the Lydian and Ionic harmony, he was so far from warring that he sat as still as if he had been in matters of council. Such might is in music [. . .] So that it is not incredible which the poet here saith, that music can bereave the soul of sense.' See also *Col* ll.6–9.

n. 6   Orpheus' rescue of Eurydice recalls the rescue of man's soul by Christ (as Pan) in 'September' ll.96–7. The very large claims here being made for the importance of poetry and language were commonplace during the English Renaissance.

n. 7   I.e., give up writing about rustics and rustic subjects.

n. 8   Piers argues that Cuddie can only display a small part of his poetic ability within pastoral. A heroic genre – such as an epic of 'bloody Mars' – would allow him 'to stretch his wings' and demonstrate the true extent of his abilities.

n. 9   EK: 'In these three verses are the three several works of Virgil intended: for in teaching his flocks to feed is meant his *Eclogues*; in labouring of lands is his Bucolics [*Georgics*]; in singing of wars and deadly dread is his divine *Aeneid* figured.'

n. 10 'To put in press among the learned troop' – 'to put in competition with poets of classical times'.

n. 11 EK notes that swans were said to sing beautifully before their death.

n. 12 The neo-Platonism of this stanza is particularly explicit: Elisa's beauty is an 'immortal mirror' because, within neo-Platonic theory, human beauty is seen as a reflection of divine beauty; so the worship of Elisa (or another beauty) is at the same time the worship of divinity; and so love ennobles, as the lover's desire is led from mortal to divine concerns.

n. 13 EK: Horace, *Epistles* 1.5.19.

n. 14 A 'buskin' was the boot worn by actors in ancient Greek tragedy.

n. 15 Part of a line from Ovid's *Fasti* 6.5. In full it runs: 'There is a god in us and when he stirs we glow.' EK comments, 'Hereby is meant (as also is the whole course of this eclogue) that poetry is a divine instinct and unnatural rage passing the reach of common reason.'

'November'

n. 1   Few commentators have been satisfied with EK's assertion that 'the personage is secret'. Recently, many have identified Dido with Elizabeth (see n. 4 and 'Dido' in the 'Glossary of Names'). Such an identification reads 'November' as another warning to Elizabeth concerning the Duc d'Alençon: personal disaster lies in their proposed marriage, which will render Elizabeth, in effect, dead to her Protestant realm, and to her favourite, Leicester (Lobbin).

n. 2   Marot's first eclogue, *Mme Louise de Savoie*, is itself in a tradition of pastoral elegy, one history of which can be seen descending from Theocritus, *Idylls* 1; to Virgil, *Ecl* 5; and on (after Spenser) to Milton, *Lycidas*.

n. 3   There has been a great deal of learned debate over the precise meaning of 'fishes' hask', stimulated by EK's astrologically incorrect gloss: 'the sun reigneth [. . .] in the sign Pisces all November.'

(The sun is in Pisces in February.) This editor wonders whether EK's reference to Pisces may not be one of his many misleading or erroneous suggestions, and whether this suggestion has in turn become a red herring for commentators; could not Colin simply be referring to the fact that the sun has set, as opposed to indicating the sun's position within the zodiac?

In Greek myth the sun was personified as a charioteer who drove daily from east to west across the sky, floating back to the east during the night in a huge cup on the Ocean. This seems to be what Colin describes: Phoebus stables his horses and then takes up his dwelling in the 'fishes' hask [basket]' – the ocean.

Colin takes this time of day as descriptive of the time of year; he says it is a 'sullen season'. This image of a dismal, twilight time (a time that winter has 'welked' or withered), and from which the sun is absent, complements the image that Colin goes on to establish when he suggests that Dido's death has taken the light from the world: 'the earth now lacks her wonted light/And all we dwell in deadly night.' Similarly, in 'December' Colin notes, 'No sun now shines.'

Such a sense of twilight suits many details of the 'November' eclogue; it makes Thenot's analogy of Colin as a nightingale apt (though out of season); it makes visually accurate Colin's sense that 'the blue in black, the green in grey is tinct', for as dusk falls, so these colours change tone and leech; it is the right time for animal cries, and for wolves to be chasing sheep; it renders more vivid the idea that Dido has broken the bound of 'eternal night', and is now installed in 'heaven's hight' where Colin may 'see thee, blessed soul', perhaps imagining her as a star; and it makes it clear why 'mizzle', not the fading of the light, draws the eclogue to a close. Moreover, such an attention to the interplay between light and the time of day is very Spenserian (see particularly *Epithalamion*).

Against this interpretation needs to be set the use of 'inn', and 'fishes' hask'. 'Inn' may be problematic in that it does have a specifically astronomical range of reference (though this is not mentioned in the *OED*2). However, 'to take up one's inn' was a common phrase meaning 'to take up one's abode' (*OED*2); and Spenser uses this phrase in this sense elsewhere. 'Fishes' hask' may pose a problem as some readers may find the image of the ocean as a fishes' basket either un-Spenserian, or unsatisfactory, or both. The image does have a rather old-fashioned, kenning-like aspect.

This may, however, be thought to be in keeping with *SC*'s neo-archaisms and, at times, northern dialect words; it is also possible that Spenser knew Anglo-Saxon.

n. 4   EK dismisses suggestions that the 'great shepherd' is 'God Pan', arguing that 'some man of high degree' is meant. If one wanted to see Dido as Elizabeth, however, one would recall that Elisa was the daughter of 'Great Pan' in the April eclogue.

n. 5   'Nosegays' are bunches of sweet-smelling flowers.

n. 6   Rosemary is a symbol of remembrance.

n. 7   EK: 'For the sundry flowers are like a mantle or coverlet wrought with many colours.'

n. 8   Turtle-doves symbolize faithfulness in love.

n. 9   Olive branches are a symbol of peace, cypress a symbol of mourning; the laurel ('green bays') is associated with Apollo, and so its leaves are suitable to be made into crowns for Apollo's followers, the Muses; and elder is associated with death and grief: all of which make a much sadder list than the list of flowers in 'April'.

n. 10 The sense of these lines is difficult. One possible paraphrase is: 'For her body, now buried, held in it the full, realized potential of earthly mankind; yet I watched when the body was brought on the bier . . .'

n. 11 EK: 'Nectar and ambrosia be feigned to be the drink and food of the gods; ambrosia they liken to manna in scripture, and nectar to be white like cream.'

'December'

n. 1   As EK observes, 'December' rounds off *SC* with an ending that recalls its beginning. This is not only the result of the eclogue having the same speaker as, and similar concerns to, 'January', but also of its having the same stanza form. Also, 'December' has twice as many lines as 'January' (156 to 78), a relationship taken to symbolize the poem's wholeness and completion [DBD].

n. 2   The opening imitates Marot, *Ecl* 3 (*au Roi*), which itself imitates Virgil, *Ecl* 1.

n. 3   EK: Virgil, *Ecl* 2.33.

n. 4   The hare was an emblem of Venus and lust [DBD].

n. 5   A 'bit' is the mouthpiece of a horse's bridle: Colin is pictured as a horse being ridden by his own imagination.

n. 6   EK glosses 'flowers' as: 'sundry studies and laudable parts of learning'. Poems were often referred to as flowers; 'anthology' derives from the Greek for 'a collection of flowers'.

n. 7   'Cockle' is the name given to a weed which grows in cornfields, particularly among wheat. 'Chaff' is the inedible matter, such as the husk, which surrounds the grain. A 'fan' is an instrument for winnowing corn; to 'winnow' is to expose the corn and chaff to a light wind so that the chaff is blown off.

n. 8   The emblem is missing, though EK provides a gloss. Working back from this gloss, Hughes in his edition of 1715 suggested that the emblem should have been *Vivitur ingenio, caetera mortis erunt*: 'He lives in his works, the rest was mortal.' This comes from the pseudo-Virgilian, *Elegiae in Maecenalum* ll.37–8 [Variorum].

n. 9   The epilogue is a 'square poem', as it has 12 lines of 12 syllables (12 being an appropriate number for an epilogue to a calendar). Such poems were seen to symbolize steadiness and constancy.

n. 10   EK quotes similar claims for permanence from Horace, *Odes* 3.30.1–3; and Ovid, *Meta* 15.871–2.

n. 11   The 'pilgrim' may be William Langland, the author of *Piers Plowman*; or the line may refer to the author of the pseudo-Chaucerian *The Plowman's Tale*.

n. 12   This is a difficult emblem to translate. For the translation given here, and others, see SE.

Muiopotmos

n. 1   *Muiopotmos* was published in 1591 as one of the nine poems in *Complaints*. Most of these poems were written considerably earlier; *Muiopotmos*, usually on the grounds of its complexity, is argued to have been written reasonably close to the date of publication.

n. 2   Spenser's request for a 'mild construction' ('judicious interpretation') can be taken either to discourage or encourage allegorical interpretations.

n. 3   The poem opens as if it were an epic by recalling the openings of both Homer's *Iliad* and Virgil's *Aeneid*, and by prefacing the narrative with epic's traditional *principium* (a statement of the scope of the poem's action) and *invocatio* (invocation of the Muse).

n. 4   When it is realized that the hero is a butterfly, the poem begins to appear to be more of a mock epic. (For a similar example see Pope, *The Rape of the Lock*.) This mock-epic perspective continues through such stock epic scenes as the arming of the hero. Cf. Homer, *Iliad* 11.15–46.

n. 5   'Muscaroll' derives from the Latin 'musca', a fly; 'Clarion' from the Latin 'clarus', bright, shining.

n. 6   'Bilbo' (Bilbao, Spain) was famous for the quality of its swords, Corinth for its brass. 'Orichalc', strictly 'mountain-copper', was often regarded as a very precious metal, known only by report.

n. 7   'So many a changeful token' – 'such a many-coloured emblem (or pattern)'.

n. 8   The 'grace' of a lady could be her favour or her love.

n. 9   'Astery' derives from the Latin and Greek 'aster', a star.

n. 10   'Orpine' is a herb used to treat wounds, noted for its longevity; 'balm' is a herb often used in infusions; 'galingale' is a sedge, the root of which was used to treat dyspepsia; 'costmary' is an aromatic perennial, used medicinally and for its flavour; 'camomile' is used as an expectorant; 'savory' is used for cooking; 'basil' was thought good for the heart; 'perseline' is a low succulent herb, comforting to the stomach.

n. 11   A 'diaper' is a linen, woven with a simple pattern, and 'damask' is a rich silk, woven with elaborate designs, often in various colours.

n. 12   'Aragnoll' may derive from the Latin 'aranea', a spider.

n. 13   This ending recalls that of Virgil's *Aeneid*.

Colin Clout's Come Home Again

n. 1   'Stanneries' – tin mines in Devon and Cornwall.

n. 2   See 'Introduction', p. xxxiii.

n. 3   I.e., to retell the 'good passed' is to recreate the experience of the good fortune, and so to enjoy the event and the remembering of the event. 'Angel' continues the banking imagery, as an 'angel' was also an Elizabethan coin.

n. 4   'Thy ready course restrain' – 'upset your story's order'.

n. 5   I.e., love had abandoned me, I having abandoned love.

n. 6   No poem of Ralegh's has been convincingly identified as the 'lamentable lay'. These lines may allude to Ralegh's fall from favour when Elizabeth discovered his secret marriage to Elizabeth Throckmorton, the Queen's maid of honour. As this occurred in 1592, these lines would seem to be an addition to the poem as it existed in its first, 1591 edition. Other similar additions may be found in the lines involving Amaryllis, Charillis, and Amyntas.

n. 7   I.e., arguing that the place was not suitable for a man who possessed any quality worthy of regard.

n. 8   See Ovid, *Meta* 1.330–42.

n. 9   See Homer, *Odyssey* 4.384ff.

n. 10   'Porc-pisces' points out the etymology of 'porpoise' from the Latin for 'hog-fish'.

n. 11   'Cornu' is the Latin for 'horn'.

n. 12   Probably St Michael's Mount, near Penzance [Norton].

n. 13   I.e., no civil disturbances; the image is of the nation as a body (the 'body politic'), in which rebellions are seen as discharging wounds and diseases.

n. 14   A 'hue and cry' is the shout raised by a victim or constable for the pursuit of a criminal.

n. 15   'Lillies' are symbols of purity, roses of love. The 'golds' are probably marigolds, the flower of the Virgin Mary, and so suitable for Elizabeth in her role as the Protestant, imperial virgin. The whites, reds, and yellows also make an attractive picture.

n. 16 Turtle-doves are, as before, symbols of true love; the 'circlet' refers to the iridescent band around their necks.

n. 17 The way in which Colin names Alabaster ('knowen yet to few') and Daniel ('late upsprung') suggests that Spenser's audience would have recognized all the other poets from their shepherd's pseudonyms – as we cannot.

n. 18 Elizabeth is 'Dread', as she should be reverenced, held in awe, and feared.

n. 19 This passage would seem to have been added to an earlier version of the poem.

n. 20 'Ever one' may be a translation of Elizabeth's motto, *semper eadem* (see Cheney). If so, then at the poem's centre Colin declares his love for and obedience to the one maid beyond all others – Elizabeth.

n. 21 As with the 12 shepherd-poets, not all the identifications of the 12 nymphs are certain.

n. 22 Ophir is mentioned in the Old Testament as an exotic land which produced fine gold; its location has not been agreed on.

n. 23 Alice Spencer was the only Countess amongst her sisters at this time.

n. 24 'Phyllis' is Greek for 'foliage'.

n. 25 Women's beauty was often represented emblematically by showing beams of light streaming from their eyes. This is connected to the image of lovers as moths circling the candle of a woman's beauty.

n. 26 Flavia and Candida have not been identified. Perhaps they were not meant to be; instead, any lady who felt that she should be in Colin's catalogue might identify herself, if unmarried, with Flavia, if married, with Candida. Thus Spenser would avoid giving offence [Variorum].

n. 27 These lines (down to l.615) combine biblical and Platonic imagery.

n. 28 'Timely' may mean either 'good' or 'earthly'.

n. 29 The missing rhyme and difficulties of sense may indicate a missing line [Variorum].

n. 30 Golden bells were associated with the caps of court jesters, and were also given as the prizes in contests, as well as being used to mark out the leading cow or sheep of a herd or flock. All these meanings may be suggested here. The general sense of the passage is that the magnificent courtiers purchase their positions, while plain-dressed Truth passes unnoticed.

Colin's sense of the courtier's vast and ruinous expenditure on dress is accurate; however, such expenditure was necessary for the courtier, whose success depended on being seen. (See Loades, 1986.)

n. 31 Within a large house, a 'bower' is a private room (a bedroom), while a 'hall' is a much larger public room (a reception room).

n. 32 I.e., when criticizing, it is better to attack general vices than particular people.

n. 33 Gold arrows were held to cause love or happy love, and lead arrows to cause hate or unhappy love.

n. 34 I.e., speak slightingly of him.

n. 35 This particularly neo-Platonic passage (ll.835–94) draws on classical and biblical treatments of chaos and creation.

n. 36 See Milton, PL 2.890–920.

n. 37 I.e., her thoughts are beyond criticism, being matched to her high place. He and his thoughts, by contrast, are loathsome as they go beyond their proper station.

Amoretti and Epithalamion

n. 1 In the first edition (1595), the sonnets were printed one to a page, the first sonnet appearing on the right. On occasion, this was used to create 'pairs' of sonnets, where the right-hand sonnet mirrors or contrasts the left-hand sonnet's concerns. This edition prints each pair on a single page. (See Fukuda, 1989.)

n. 2 I.e., to create base desires.

n. 3   Mankind's 'proud port' or erect bearing, with head raised towards the stars, was often used as an image of his innate superiority to the ground-viewing beasts.

n. 4   Earth, in a Christian context, has been 'loathsome and forlorn' ever since Adam and Eve ate the forbidden fruit and were expelled from Paradise. Mankind is made out of, and returns to, its 'dust'. See *Genesis* 1-3.

n. 5   I.e., by comparison and by his poetry.

n. 6   This sonnet is an example of a *blazon* (French for 'coat-of-arms'), a group of verses which list the various parts of the beloved's body. Shakespeare plays with the convention, common within the Petrarchan tradition of love poetry, in his Sonnet 130, 'My mistress's eyes are nothing like the sun.' See also the *Song of Songs*.

n. 7   The painting described here seems to be the intimate, and gentle-manly, art of miniature painting, one of whose aims was to catch the fleeting glance of character. See Nicholas Hilliard, *A Treatise Concerning the Art of Limning*.

n. 8   The cuckoo was also the bird of wanton, adulterous love. The poet has a quite different attitude by sonnet 85.

n. 9   'Terms' is a word which has a large range of meaning in this context; a roughly equivalent modern usage would be 'terms of endearment'.

n. 10   This sonnet seems to celebrate Ash Wednesday, the 'so holy day' that begins the period of Lent, a period which culminates 47 days later with Easter Day. This temporal period is reflected structurally within the sequence, as in 47 sonnets' time comes the Easter Day sonnet 68. (See 'Numerology' in the Glossary of Names.)
        A Renaissance tradition of calendrical patterning had as chief poetic example the *Canzionere* of Petrarch. Psalm 90:12 was also taken as an authority ('Teach me to number my days'). The calendrical patterning of *Amoretti and Epithalamion* not only ties the sonnets into the timeless cycle of the endlessly repeated story of the love of God for man, but also locates the sequence in a specific time. Before the Easter Day sonnet has come the New Year's day sonnet 62. The year was still at this time commonly reckoned by the liturgical year, which began on 25 March, which places Easter Day, coming, as it does, six sonnets later, on 31 March. Easter

Day fell on the 31 March in 1594, the year of Spenser's courtship and the year that *Amoretti and Epithalamion* was entered in the Stationers' Register. Thus the sequence opens up a double vision, locating itself both in linear and cyclical time. This double vision reaches its magnificent culmination in *Epithalamion*.

The structure also has architectural qualities. The Lent sonnets are at the centre of the sonnet sequence, with 21 sonnets preceding and following. They lie at the heart of the sequence, as the lover's distress is at the heart of the sonnets' emotional world (see 'Spenser and his Critics', p. 263). For further discussion of numerology, and of the sonnets' place within the larger structure of the 1595 edition, see the entry 'number symbolism' in SE.

n. 11 See Homer, *Odyssey* 2.75-128.

n. 12 This sonnet, coming four sonnets after the Ash Wednesday sonnet, may be compared and contrasted with the sonnet which comes four sonnets before the Easter Day sonnet [Yale].

n. 13 'Juniper' may refer not only to juniper berries, but also to the tree's wood, which is aromatic, giving off a sweet smell when burnt. It was believed to purify the air. 'Fir' refers to Scotch Pine, a tree which used to cover large areas of northern Britain and Ireland. It has purple flowers. 'Cypress' seems to refer to the Sweet Cyperus or Galingale, a plant with aromatic roots, used both for its perfume and medicinal qualities. Yet the Cypress tree, associated with mourning, is also invoked. (This ambivalence replays the sweet and sour motif in a different register.) 'Broom' is a thorny shrub with attractive yellow flowers; the flowers were used in a similar fashion to capers. The first quatrain, then, focuses predominantly on sight, the second on taste.

n. 14 According to Homer, a god gave Odysseus the herb moly to protect him from Circe's sorcery. Moly had a white flower and black ('ill') root. It was often taken as either a symbol of eloquence or of temperance. See *Odyssey* 10.290-306.

n. 15 See, for example, Ovid, *Meta* 1.452-567. In Ovid's version the transformation is at Daphne's request.

n. 16 I.e., with Fame's trumpet.

n. 17 See Petrarch, *Rime* 202. The contrast between the lover's fire and lady's ice became one of the most common Petrarchan conventions.

n. 18 'Fit' here may refer both to a fit of love and to a fit (i.e. a part) of a poem.

n. 19 Elizabeth (his 'Empress') is 'dear dread', as she should be reverenced, held in awe, and feared.

n. 20 At this time, only Books 1–3 of *The Faerie Queene* had been published. Books 4–6 would appear in 1596.

n. 21 See Petrarch, *Rime* 189, and Wyatt, 'My galley'.

n. 22 Ursa Major revolves around the pole-star, hence its poetic name of Helice, Greek for 'winding'. The pole-star gives roughly the direction of the north pole and so is the star to which compasses (loadstones) point and by which ships may steer. Elise/Eliza would also be heard within Helice at this time, so casting Elizabeth as Spenser's loadstar.

n. 23 This sonnet is reprinted, almost verbatim, as sonnet 83. See n. 48.

n. 24 See Ovid, *Meta* 3.339–510.

n. 25 See Herodotus, 1.23–4.

n. 26 In medieval physiology, one's mental and physical constitution were governed by the mixture of the chief fluids of the body, the four cardinal humours – blood, phlegm, choler (bile) and melancholy.

n. 27 I.e., rules the parts of the body as it pleases.

n. 28 A Renaissance commonplace, perhaps reflecting an aspect of the age's sense of itself.

n. 29 'Mould' refers to the material out of which the material of the human body is made (*OED*2).

n. 30 According to some ancient and medieval philosophy, the world was thought to be constituted out of four elements: earth, water, air and fire.

n. 31 The heavenly bodies were thought to be composed of a fifth element, or quintessence. This was held to be latent in all things, its extraction being one of the great aims of alchemy.

n. 32 'By' may mean either 'written by' or 'concerning'. If the former meaning is chosen, then the attribution ironically undercuts all that follows; in effect, the lady writes three quatrains warning against various forms of self-assurance, and the lover's response is to note that she is the most self-assured person that he knows. In this reading, the attribution pre-empts the couplet, which gives the lover's response within the sonnet. If, however, the latter meaning of 'by' is chosen, then the sonnet is one more reprimand to the lady; yet the title-line would seem rather redundant in this case.

n. 33 The warnings that follow are to a large extent proverbial, often having a biblical cast. See *Isaiah* 40: 6–7.

n. 34 I.e., nor frightened by any mischance to leave her usual path.

n. 35 'Dare' is an imperative verb (i.e. it gives a command).

n. 36 There may be a pun on Elizabeth here; the name was commonly, if mistakenly, held to derive from the Hebrew 'Eli sabbath', i.e., 'Lord's rest' [Norton].

n. 37 This flower is not identified; the name comes from the French *bel amour*, that is 'fair love'.

n. 38 See Petrarch *Rime* 190, and Wyatt, 'Whoso list to hunt'. In both the lover is unable to catch the deer.

n. 39 The deer, water, and voluntary submission place the sonnet in the context of the medieval liturgy for Easter (see Prescott).

n. 40 According to the Apocryphal Gospel of Nicodemus (2nd–3rdC AD), after Christ was crucified he descended to Hell, burst open its gates, bound Satan, and took away the souls of the saved. For a magnificent treatment of this series of actions, known as the Harrowing of Hell, see *The Vision of Piers Plowman*, XVIII.260–434. For the many biblical phrases in this sonnet see Variorum.

n. 41 See *Ephesians* 4:8.

n. 42 Opportunity is proverbially bald behind; miss the chance of catching the tuft of hair on his forehead and you have missed your chance of catching his attention.

n. 43 'Prime' may refer either to the spring season, or the early hour of the morning.

n. 44 According to George Puttenham (*c.* 1529–90), author of the first critical survey of English Literature, Elizabeth enjoyed 'deciphering' (i.e. making anagrams of) names. Puttenham makes *Multa regnabis ense gloria* ('By thy sword shalt thou reign in great renown') and *Multa regnabis sene gloria* ('Aged in much glory shall ye reign') out of *Elissabet Anglorum Regina* ('Elizabeth, Queen of the English'). (See also n. 36 for Elizabeth as 'Eli sabbath'.) Puttenham describes such deciphering in a light spirit, but suggests it may be taken as a good omen and a small, confirmatory sign that Elizabeth is a blessing from God sent to the English people. In this way, then, the letters of her name might be thought to be happy and well chosen ('framed by skilful trade').

n. 45 See Ovid, *Meta* 10.560–707.

n. 46 I.e., like flowers that are out of season or which have bloomed too soon.

n. 47 These lines suggest that Spenser had finished at least the first version of Books 4–6 of *FQ* by 1594, and at that time intended that there should be six more books.

n. 48 Sonnet 83 repeats sonnet 35 verbatim, except that 'seeing it' replaces sonnet 35's 'having it'. (There are also some small differences in the original punctuation of the two sonnets.) If its printing is not an error, the repetition raises interesting questions about the importance of context to meaning, a relationship which is here particularly bound up with the narrative sequence of the sonnets. For, while the quality of the pain the lover feels is the same as before, the recognition of the value of the pain, and the realization of the implications and consequences of human mortality, are by now quite different.

n. 49 I.e., deep in my heart of hearts.

n. 50 I.e., that fills me with poetic inspiration.

n. 51 Turtle-doves, as ever, symbolize married fidelity.

n. 52 These four slight poems, distinct in form from the sonnets which precede them and the epithalamium which follows them, have generated much critical puzzlement. However, as John Kerrigan shows in his edition of *Shakespeare's Sonnets*, Samuel Daniel's *Delia* (1592) had established in England the convention of a tripartite structure: a sonnet sequence is followed by a lyric interlude – made up of a short poem or poems in the manner of Anacreon – which is followed by a long poem.

Spenser's audience, then, would expect to find a short lyric interlude of 'Cupidic comedy' (in Kerrigan's phrase) between the *Amoretti* and *Epithalamion*. They would also expect this interlude to be meaningfully related to the previous and subsequent sections. Spencer's anacreontics return the reader to traditional and mythic accounts of the narrator's love. Doing so, they set up a dialogue between such traditional accounts and the more complex exploration of love in the sonnet sequence. For the mythic account has forgotten what the lover has learnt: his recognition of what love should be, who his beloved is, and of what gives love value. In this way, the cupidic comedy of these poems throws into relief the various movements of the sonnets. Having done so, the lovers, in all their particularity, will return in *Epithalamion*; a marriage ode which celebrates the complexities of a human love which is properly God-like in its interrelationship with the divine.

n. 53 So Cupid unintentionally makes the poet's beloved chaste (since he is shooting one of Diana's arrows), while Diana, equally unintentionally, makes beasts lustful.

n. 54 See Marot, *Epigrams* 3.24.

n. 55 An epithalamium is a wedding song. *Epithalamion*'s structure, like that of the *Amoretti* (see n. 10), locates the poem in linear and cyclical time. See 'Spenser and his Critics', p. 263.

n. 56 Perhaps the string's tension is here being slackened [DBD].

n. 57 Either the nymphs may look attractively dressed with the garlands, or the garlands may look attractive.

n. 58 See *Song of Solomon*.

n. 59 See *Isaiah* 26:2.

n. 60   An ancient Roman custom, which had Elizabethan parallels; see *SC*, 'May' l.11.

n. 61   A 'saint', within Protestant terminology, was one of the elect; that is, a person who had been chosen for salvation.

n. 62   St Barnabas's Day, 11 June, was the longest day of the year.

n. 63   Time was sometimes depicted with wings.

n. 64   DBD emends 'East' to 'West', pointing out that Venus appears in the West at sunset. However, the problem of how Venus can be thought to be guiding lovers through the whole night remains, as the planet itself sets – and, being a planet, Venus should not 'twinkle'.

n. 65   The allusion to Maia is problematic, as Spenser is not here following any recognized account. Perhaps Maia is here to be seen as a figure of modesty in particularly immodest circumstances [Variorum].

n. 66   See Catullus, *Odes* 64.285-6.

n. 67   This is another account that appears to be Spenser's own. Jove is not recorded as having slept with Night; and Ovid gives Honour and Reverence as Majesty's parents. Jove was, however, associated with Majesty in the Renaissance [DBD].

n. 68   The sense of this envoy (a concluding stanza) is very difficult, particularly in its middle lines, and the openness of the grammatical relationships between the clauses precludes any one satisfactory paraphrase. One such, finally unsatisfactory, paraphrase might run: 'Song, made in place of the ornaments which should have adorned my bride – you song which, ending abruptly because of events, would not stay for the needed amount of time, but are still promised to stand in place of the ornaments and recompense my bride – be unto her a goodly ornament, and for the short time (of mortal life or our lives or this day) be an endless monument.' The biographical details suggested by 'hasty accidents' have not been identified.

Prothalamion

n. 1 Swans are famous both for their beauty and monogamy; they were also used as an emblem of the poet.

n. 2 The 'Lea' is a tributary of the Thames at Greenwich. 'Lea' may also mean 'riverbank' or 'meadow'.

n. 3 Venus' chariot was often depicted as drawn by swans. See Ovid, *Meta* 10.718.

n. 4 'Summer's-heat' (in the original spelling 'Somers-heat') puns on 'Somerset', the brides' surname (see Worcester).

n. 5 See Catullus, *Odes* 64.285–6.

n. 6 The Inner and Middle Temple, originally owned by the Knights Templar.

n. 7 The Straits of Gibraltar.

n. 8 Essex's surname may be read as promising happiness in French: 'Devereux' was seen as deriving from the French *devenir heureux* – 'to become happy'.

GLOSSARY OF WORDS

The meanings listed are in addition to the words' usual meanings.

albe	although
all	just
als	also
arede	to explain, declare
avail	to hang down
aye	always
bale(ful)	sorrow(ful), pain(ful)
bane	sorrow, harm
base	humble
borrow	security, pledge
but	unless
care(ful)	troubled, woeful
cast	to decide, consider, purpose
colour	(*v*) to disguise, (*n*) semblance
compass	(*n*) measure, proper proportion
con	to know, be able, learn
couth	could
deem	to judge, think
discourse	to discuss
dole	grief, sorrow
eft	afterwards
eke	also
eld	(old) age
ere	before
fain	(*adj*) happy
fon, fond	fool, foolish, foolishly
for-thy	for this reason, therefore
gin, gan	begin, began
hem	them
hent	seized, grasped
her	their

hight	called
inly	inwardly
ken(st)	to know
lay	(*n*) song
list	to wish, desire
lust	vigour, desire
mantle	cloak
meed	reward
meet	suitable
moe	more
mought	might or must
ne	(*adv*) not, (*conj*) nor
n'is	is not
nould	would not
or . . . or	either . . . or
plain	to (com)plain, lament
pleasance	pleasure-giving quality, delight
plight	condition
privy (to)	private (intimate with)
rede	to advise
rude	rustic, homely
ruthful	piteous
seely	(too) simple, innocent, helpless
sere	withered
sicker	(*adv*) certainly
sike	such
sith(ence)	since, since that time
sithes	times
sooth	truth
spill	to destroy, waste
still	always
stour	time of turmoil or stress
swain	a country lover, labourer, servant or boy
thilk	this, these, the same
tho	(*conj*) then
travail	travel or trouble
trow	to believe, trust
vouchsafe	to grant, deign
wan	unhealthily pale, sickly
wasteful	desolate(ing), uninhabited
wax	to grow

ween	think, believe
welkin	sky
wend	to go
whenas	when, since
whilom	once, formerly
wit	intelligence
wont, wonned	used to, habituated
wot	to know
yode	went

GLOSSARY OF NAMES

Abel, younger brother of Cain, son of Adam and Eve.

Achilles, Greek hero who fought at Troy. EK recounts that Achilles' mother dipped him into the river Styx when a baby, so rendering him invulnerable, except where she had held on to his heel. It was there Paris shot him with a poisoned arrow when he was getting married.

Adonis, a beautiful youth whom Venus fell in love with. He was killed while hunting a wild boar.

Aeolus (Aeole), god of the winds.

Aesop, (early C6th BC), traditionally held to be the author of a stock of Greek fables.

Alabaster, William (1567–1640), an Elizabethan divine and neo-Latin poet. He wrote a small number of sonnets in English and the first book of a Latin epic, on the trials of Elizabeth's pre-coronation life, the *Elisaeis*.

Alcaeus (fl. 620–580 BC), Greek lyric poet.

Alcibiades (*c.* 450–404 BC), Athenian general and statesman, pupil of Socrates.

Alcmena, in Greek myth, she was a mortal whom Zeus fell in love with. Disguised as her husband, he visited her one night. She gave birth to twins: Iphicles, the child of her true husband, and Hercules, the child of Zeus.

Alençon, Duc d' (1554–84; after 1576 Duc d'Anjou), moderate French Catholic, who negotiated, but never concluded, a marriage contract with Elizabeth I.

Algrind, see **Grindal**.

Allo, Spenser's name for river Broadwater.

Anacreon (C6th BC), a Greek poet. What were thought to be his poems, 60 short odes, were discovered in 1549, initiating a Europe-wide vogue of imitation, particularly intense in England. During the mid-C19th the poems were recognized to have been composed by a number of poets over several centuries (see Mason, 1990).

Andalo (Andalo di Negro, fl. 1330), taught Boccaccio astronomy.

Arachne (Greek 'spider'), in Greek myth, a woman who challenged Athene to a weaving contest. Arachne's work was perfect, and mocked Athene in depicting the loves of the gods. The furious goddess destroyed Arachne's work and loom; Arachne, in despair, tried to hang herself but was turned to a spider. See Ovid, *Meta* 6.1–145. Spenser significantly alters the story in *Mui.*

Arcadia, bleak and mountainous area of the central Peloponnese. In the Renaissance, writers, following Virgil's example, made it the location of an idealized pastoral world.

Aretino, Pietro (1492–1556), Italian poet, prose writer and drama-tist, some of whose poetry was famously licentious.

Argonauts, in Greek myth, the heroes who sailed on the Argo to find the Golden Fleece. They were led by Jason, and included Orpheus.

Argus, had a hundred eyes in his head, and never went to sleep with more than two of them at a time. When he was slain (while guarding one of Jove's lovers for Juno), his eyes were placed by the goddess in the peacock's tail.

Arion (fl. 628–625 BC), Greek lyric poet and legendary figure. Returning from Italy, he was thrown overboard by sailors who wished to take his money. A dolphin, charmed by the song that Arion had sung, carried him to land.

Armulla, the 'Mulla' valley.

Atalanta, in Greek myth, a fierce and beautiful huntress, who refused to marry any man who could not beat her in a running race; those men who tried and failed were put to death. Hippomenes succeeded (on the advice of the goddess Aphrodite) by dropping three golden apples; Atalanta could not resist stopping to pick them up. After-wards, according to Ovid, Hippomenes not only did not thank

Aphrodite, but made love to Atalanta in a temple; for their sacrilege the pair were turned into lions.

Athene, patron goddess of Athens, daughter of Zeus, from whose head she sprang fully formed. According to one account this happened on the banks of the river Triton, and hence her epithet Tritogeneia ('Trito-born') or Tritonian. Typically, she was depicted as a war goddess, and sometimes carrying an aegis – a skin-covered shield decorated with snakes around the outside and a Gorgon's head in the centre. This shield had the power to disperse her enemies and protect her friends. She was also patroness of urban arts and crafts, particularly spinning and weaving.

Athens, pre-eminent city in ancient Greece.

Atlas, in Greek myth a Titan who held up the sky.

Augustus (Gaius Octavius 63 BC–14 AD), the first emperor of Rome.

Bacchus, Roman god of wine and revelry.

Bellona, Roman goddess of war. EK identifies her with the Greek goddess Athene, who was 'strange' in being born, fully formed, out of the head of her father, Zeus.

Boccaccio, Giovanni (1313–75), Italian writer of poetry and prose, and humanist. He wrote Latin eclogues, and was a friend of Petrarch.

Boreas, 'the northern wind, that brings the most stormy weather' (EK).

Boyle, Elizabeth (?1574–1622), Spenser's second wife, their marriage taking place on 11 June 1594. There was one son. She was the cousin of Richard Boyle, who became the richest man in Ireland c. 1610.

Bregog (Erse for 'deceitful'), tributary of Awbeg, which ran through Spenser's Kilcolman estate.

Broadwater, Elizabethan name for river now known as Blackwater.

Bryskett, Lodowick, see Thestylis.

Burghley, Lord (William Cecil, 1520–98), Elizabeth's Lord Treasurer, said not to value poetry (though he was a literary patron). Burghley, with Leicester, was at the centre of Elizabethan policy-making. Given his power, Spenser's satirical depiction of him in *MHT* (not in this selection) is surprising.

Buttevant, a town on the Cork–Limerick road. Here there were ruins of a friary and, near by, of an abbey. Now once more called Kilnemullah.

Caesar (Gaius Julius 100–44 BC), accomplished general, prose writer and man of vision; he gained imperial control over the Roman republic, an achievement which eventually led to his assassination.

Calliope, muse of epic poetry.

Canaan, land where the Israelites settled after the Exodus from Egypt. See *Numbers* 34.

Carey, Lady Elizabeth (1557–1618), Lady Carey was a patroness of Nashe and Dowland, and translated Petrarch. See **Spencers.**

Cerberus, in Greek myth, the three-headed dog who guarded the underworld.

Charon, in Greek myth, the ferry-man who carried the dead across the river Styx to the underworld.

Chaucer, Geoffrey (?1343–1400), most famous English poet of the fourteenth century, particularly for his *The Book of the Duchess* (c. 1370), *Troilus and Criseyde* (c. 1384), and *The Canterbury Tales* (c. 1388–1400).

Cheke, Sir John (1514–57), Professor of Greek at Cambridge, who criticized Sallust's use of archaic terms.

Chloris, nymph with whom Zephyrus, the western wind, fell in love.

Churchyard, Thomas (?1520–1604), a soldier, (lowly) courtier, writer and poet. His works spanned much of the century, by the end of which – as a poet – he was a respected figure, though his poetry was old-fashioned in style.

Cicero (Marcus Tullius Cicero, 106–43 BC), influential Roman prose writer, orator, and theorist of rhetoric.

Circe, in Homer's *Odyssey*, a sorceress who turned Odysseus' men into swine.

Cockatrice, in fable, a serpent whose glance could kill. Identified with the Basilisk.

Colin Clout, pre-eminent poet within Spenser's poems, at times identified with aspects of Spenser himself. In *SC*, appears in 'Jan', 'June', 'Nov' and 'Dec', and is mentioned or referred to in 'April', 'Aug', and 'Sep'. EK argues that Colin simply is Spenser (in 'Sep'); he also notes that a Colin appears in both Marot's *Ecl 1* (*Sur le Trespas de ma Dame Loyse de Savoye*) and in Skelton's *Colin Clout*.

Cornwall, the south-west tip of England.

Coshma, a division of county Kildare, Ireland, through which runs the river Maigue ('Maa').

Cuddie, appears in *SC* 'Feb', 'Aug', and 'Oct', and in *Col*.

Cupid, Roman boy-god of love and the (unfathered) son of Venus. Anyone, god or mortal, shot by one of Cupid's arrows would fall in love. Behind Cupid stands the Greek Eros, whose ability to conquer all led him to be imagined as a cosmic force, uniting the sensible and ideal worlds (see Plato, *Symposium*).

Cynthia, see Diana.

Daniel, Samuel (1562–1619), a poet (as well as secret agent, tutor, courtier, and gentleman farmer) unique in achieving life-long patronage. One of his publications was the sonnet and complaint sequence *Delia* (1592, but printed in a pirate version earlier).

Dante (Dante Alighieri, 1265–1321), Italian poet, born in Florence (through which city the river Po flows). His masterpiece, the epic *Divina Commedia*, influenced English writers from Chaucer onwards.

Delphi, most important oracle in the ancient world, situated on the lower slopes of Mount Parnassus, and supposedly presided over by Apollo (see **Phoebus**).

Diana, Spenser follows the tradition of conflating the Roman Diana with the Greek Artemis (and Phoebe). As Spenser uses this tradition, Diana is the virgin goddess of the moon and of the hunt, sister of Phoebus Apollo. Elizabeth I, the virgin Queen, was frequently identified with Diana or, to use yet another of her names, Cynthia.

(Mt Cynthus was on the island of Delos, on which Artemis and Apollo were born.)

Dido, legendary Queen of Carthage, who threw herself on to a pyre to avoid marriage to a local king. Virgil adapts the story in his *Aeneid*; there, Dido falls in love with Aeneas and, when he leaves her, she takes her own life. 'Dido' was also one of the names of Queen Elizabeth (before Dido founded Carthage, she lived in Tyre, where she was known as Elissa – see *SC* 'April' for Elizabeth as 'Elisa').

Diggon Davie, probably meant to recall Richard Davies, Bishop of St David's 1561–81, and supporter of Grindal. Such an association places Diggon in the reforming Protestant tradition.

Drayton, Michael (1563–1631), devoted his life to the profession of poet and dramatist, and saw himself as Spenser's chief heir. A sober man, he wrote copiously and was well respected, but achieved limited financial success.

Du Bellay, Joachim (1522–60), French poet who published the first French sonnet sequence and wrote the manifesto of the Pléiade, a group of seven poets who sought to make the French language the equal of classical languages. Spenser translated his sonnet sequence addressed to Rome (perhaps the first sonnet sequence not addressed to a lady) – *Les Antiquitez de Rome* (1558).

Dyer, Sir Edward (?1543–1607), a court poet, to whom Sidney left part of his library in his will, and a friend of Leicester and Burghley. He was also an MP and secret agent. Spenser met him when working for Leicester.

Echo, according to Ovid, Echo was a nymph whose chattering to Hera prevented that goddess from spying on Zeus' affairs with other nymphs. As a punishment, Hera allowed Echo only to repeat the words of others. When rejected by Narcissus, Echo wasted away until all that was left of her was her voice.

EK, perhaps Edward Kirke (1533–1613), a friend of Spenser's from Pembroke Hall, Cambridge. Now more usually regarded as either Spenser or Gabriel Harvey, or both.

Elisa, Queen Elizabeth I.

Elizabeth I (1533–1603), daughter of Henry VIII, Queen of England and Wales 1558–1603. She came to the throne at a moment of religious turmoil in an age which thought a Queen both unnatural and impractical. As her reign endured and she remained unmarried, she was increasingly represented through a variety of mythopoetic cults. She was identified with various figures: with the national heroines of the Old Testament (Judith, Esther, and Deborah); with the Virgin Mary; with the lyric poet's or knight's adored but unachieveable mistress; and with various Greek and Roman goddesses (see **Diana**). She was also seen as Arthur's heir, and as perpetually young. Above all she was Gloriana, the semi-divine Virgin Queen who held the diversity – of her kingdom, its subjects, and their aspirations – in unity.

In literary criticism prior to the 1980s, these cults of praise (which shaped the day to day interaction between the Queen and her courtiers) were seen as evidence of the period's deep desire for order and conservative support of the status quo. During the 1980s New Historicist critics inverted this picture, seeing the cults as evidence of the enforced complicity of the Elizabethan subject in a theatre of cruelty with the Queen as supreme dominatrix. At present a new picture is emerging, in which the cults are understood as languages in which both the praised and praisee seek advancement, and in which the Queen is merely a powerful contestant. (See McCoy, 1995).

Elysium, in classical myth, the delightful land where those favoured by the gods go after their life on earth: EK describes it as 'like paradise'.

Endymion, as EK notes, Phoebe so loved Endymion that she kept him asleep in a cave on Mt Latmus for 30 years, to enjoy his company. Another version tells that this sleep was Zeus' punishment of the shepherd for making love to Phoebe.

Essex, Second Earl of (Robert Devereux, 1566–1601), rose from relative obscurity in the 1580s to become the Queen's favourite at the beginning of the 1590s. He was praised similarly to Sidney (whose widow he married) as the ideal patron and heroic soldier; the height of his military fame came when he was one of the leaders of the 1596 expedition which plundered Cadiz (in Spain). His stepfather was the Earl of Leicester, whose place at court (after Leicester's death) he was seen to fill.

In 1599, a military campaign in Ireland going badly, he abandoned his command and forces, and returned impetuously to his Queen. His questionable behaviour and speeches at this time led to the Queen's refusal to review his monopolies; bankrupt, he attempted to raise a rebellion against the Queen and was executed for treason on 25 February 1601. Tradition has it that he sent Spenser £20 on his death bed (which Spenser refused), and paid for his funeral.

Europa, in Greek myth, a princess whom Zeus loved. He, in the form of a beautiful white bull, came to where Europa and her handmaidens were playing on the sea shore. Europa was delighted with the gentle bull, and climbed on its back. The bull charged into the water and swam to Crete, where Europa bore Zeus three sons.

Evander, in Roman myth, Evander left Arcadia, came to Italy, and settled on the site of the future Rome. He provides a connection between Greece and Rome.

Faerie Queene, The (Books 1–3, pubd 1590; Books 4–6, pubd 1596), Spenser's unfinished epic poem. Elizabeth, as Gloriana, is the never quite present yet everywhere celebrated heroine; hence in *Am* 33 *FQ* is mentioned as 'her' book.

Fates, Fatal Sisters, three sisters who spin (and eventually cut off) the thread of each person's life.

Fauns (and sylvans), mischievous gods of the woods.

Flora, Roman goddess of flowering plants.

Fortune, the blind (or if sighted, fickle) goddess.

Funcheon, a river running parallel to the Awbeg (see **Bregog**).

Furies, in Greek myth, three goddesses who punished crimes with a terrible severity, insisting on the letter of the law. In Aeschylus' *Eumenides*, they may be seen as representatives of Old Testament justice, which is incorporated, through Athene's intercession, into a more merciful New Testament conception of justice. 'The authors of all evil and mischief' (EK).

Genius, the spirit on whom procreation depends.

Gorges, Sir Arthur (?1557–1625), soldier, courtier, poet, relative and friend of Ralegh. The death of his first wife (she died in 1590) is commemorated in Spenser's *Daph*. Gorges translated Lucan's *Pharsalia* and left a considerable collection of poetry in manuscript.

Gorgons, three sisters, one of whom, Medusa, had a head of so terrible an appearance that anyone who saw it was turned to stone. She had coiled snakes for hair.

Graces, The Three, daughters of Zeus, the personification of everything that contributed to human happiness and human civility; their Greek names mean beauty, abundance and mirth. Spenser also talks of more generally of nymphs as 'Graces'.

Grindal, Edmund (?1519–1583), Protestant churchman who held many high offices, and was Master of Pembroke Hall, Cambridge. He referred to the district of Cumberland in which he was raised as 'the ignorantest part in religion, and most oppressed of covetous landlords of any one part of this realm'. During Mary's reign (see **Reformation**) he had to flee the country. In 1576 he was appointed Archbishop of Canterbury for his sympathies with radical Protestantism; the same led him to be suspended (by the Queen's order) from exercise of his office from 1577 to 1582.

Guildford, Sir Henry (of Hemstead Place, Kent), married Elizabeth Somerset, the Earl of Worcester's daughter, on 8 November 1596. It was a double wedding; Elizabeth's sister, Katherine, married William Petre.

Hades, in Greek myth, the king of the underworld.

Harvey, Gabriel (1550–?1631), friend (and possibly university tutor) of Spenser, fellow at Pembroke Hall, Cambridge, and University Professor of Rhetoric. Sidney was a friend and member of the 'Areopagus', a scholarly group led by Harvey which sought to promote neo-classical theories and metrification in English Poetry. In his career, he was supported by Leicester and Burghley. EK identifies Hobbinol with Harvey in *SC* 'Sep'.

Hebe, in Greek myth, the daughter of Zeus and Hera, and personification of youth.

Helen, see **Paris**.

Helicon, highest mountain in Boeotia, below whose summit was the

Hippocrene spring, in Greek myth held to be the inspiration of poets. The muses were often to be found here.

Helios, in Greek myth, the son of Hyperion, and god of the sun. See Phoebus.

Hera, Queen of the Greek gods, wife of Zeus, often identified with the Roman Juno.

Herbert, Mary (Countess of Pembroke, 1561–1621), poet, translator, and influential literary patron; perhaps the greatest literary lady of her time. After the death of her brother, Philip Sidney, she oversaw the publication of his works and completed his translation of the psalms. These roles of poet, patroness and executrix are bound up in Spenser's identification of her as Urania, Muse of astronomy and Christian poetry.

Hercules (properly Heracles), Greek hero who killed his wife and children in a fit of madness. As punishment, the Delphic Oracle commanded him to go to Tiryns, in Argos, and serve its king. Thus Hercules came to perform the 12 labours for which he was particularly famous, the first of which was to kill the Nemean Lion, an invulnerable monster. (He strangled it.) His penultimate labour was to gain the Golden Apples of the Hesperides, wedding gifts of Hera, Queen of the Greek gods. The apples were in a garden on the edge of the world, guarded by a dragon.

Hesperus, the morning star (as Spenser uses it).

Hippocrene, see Helicon.

Hobbinol, appears in SC 'Apr', 'Jun', and 'Sep', and in Col. See Harvey.

Homer (C8th? BC), the most famous Greek epic poet, to whom is assigned the authorship of the Iliad and the Odyssey.

Hours, the three seasons of spring, summer, and winter, who often attend on Venus in company with the Graces. According to Spenser, they are the daughters of Day and Night; more usually they were considered the daughters of Zeus and Themis (a Greek goddess).

Howard, Frances (d. 1628), wife of Henry Fitzgerald, Earl of Kildare, Ireland.

Hydra, in Greek myth, a poisonous, many-headed water-snake; when one head was cut off, another grew in its place. Often used as a (derogatory) image of the people.

Hymen, a deity, usually pictured as a handsome young man, who presided over weddings.

Hyperion, god of the sun, and a Titan.

Ida, range of mountains in Phrygia (Turkey) which formed the southern boundary of the lands of Priam, King of Troy.

Iris, Greek goddess of the rainbow.

Janus, one of the principal Roman gods, he was often described as having two heads, one looking forward and to the future, and the other looking backwards and to the past. He was, in particular, the god of beginnings.

Jesuits, members of the Society of Jesus, founded in Rome in 1540. The society became the Roman Catholic Church's main instrument for education, propaganda and missionary activity.

Jove, King of the Roman gods.

Juno, Queen of the Roman gods. See **Argus.**

Kilcolman Castle (built *c.* 1420), a castle of the tower-house type, designed to be secure against marauding bands, halfway between Limerick and Cork in the Republic of Ireland. There was a small lake near by. The property passed into Spenser's possession in 1590. It was burned in the 1598 uprising.

Kirke, Edward (1553–1613), clergyman who began his university education as a sizar in Pembroke Hall, Cambridge, there becoming a friend of Spenser and Harvey.

Latona, Greek goddess, the mother (by Jove) of Phoebus Apollo and Diana. Niobe, Queen of Thebes, once claimed that she was more worthy of worship than Latona; she had fourteen children to Latona's two. Phoebus and Diana immediately killed all her children, after which Niobe was turned to stone. (See Ovid, *Meta* 6.146–312).

Leda, in Greek myth, the wife of the King of Sparta. Zeus made love to her in the form of a swan. Helen of Troy was sometimes held to have been their offspring, as were the twins Castor and Pollux (who became Gemini in the zodiac).

Leicester, Earl of (Robert Dudley, ?1532–88), a favourite of Queen Elizabeth. When Spenser was employed by him in 1579, Leicester was a militant advocate of the Protestant cause (along with Burghley and Sir Francis Walsingham among others). His emblem was a white bear chained to an uprooted tree trunk. See also **Lettice**.

Lethe, in Latin poetry, a river in the underworld, whose waters, when drunk, induced forgetfulness of one's former life.

Lettice, 'the name of some country lass' (EK). Perhaps an anglicized version of the Latin *laetitia,* 'joy'; perhaps also an allusion to Lettice Knolles, whom Leicester had secretly married in 1578. When Queen Elizabeth learnt about the marriage (over a year later) she was displeased.

Livy (Titus Livius 59 BC–17 AD), Roman historian.

Lobbin, possibly the Earl of Leicester.

Lodge, Thomas (?1558–1625), Roman-Catholic, naval adventurer, critic, playwright, writer of prose-verse romances. Disillusioned with his literary achievements, he ceased writing (*c.* 1595), turned to medicine, and left England.

Lucian (*c.* 115–after 180 AD), Greek writer, mainly of prose satires.

Lydgate, John (?1370–1449), poet of immense output (over 100,000 lines). Many of his poems are in a Chaucerian vein.

Macrobius (Ambrosius Aurelius Theodosius fl. 400 AD), late Latin author from whose *Saturnalia* EK borrows some observations on the calendar.

Maecenas (Gaius d. 8 BC), the most famous Roman patron of the arts and, for most of his life, a confidant of Augustus. He supported Horace and Virgil liberally, and was seen as the type of generous patronage in the Renaissance.

Maia, Roman nature goddess of increase and fertility, after whom May is probably named.

Mantuan (Johannes Baptista Spagnolo 1448–1516), Carmelite friar, born in Mantua, who wrote eclogues in Latin.

Marot, Clément (1496–1544), French poet who introduced many new poetic forms into his native tongue, one of which was the eclogue, as well as translating Petrarch. He was a Protestant.

Marsyas, satyr who played the pipes so well that those listening declared his skill greater than Apollo's. Marsyas did not contradict them and later took part in a competition with Apollo – the victor to do what he liked with the loser. Apollo won, tied Marsyas to a pine tree, and flayed him alive.

Medway, river in Kent which, running by Rochester, meets with the Thames.

Melpomene, Muse of tragedy.

Menalcas, shepherd who stole Colin's Rosalind. EK: 'The name of a shepherd in Virgil; but here [in *SC* 'June'] is meant a person unknown and secret.' See Virgil, *Ecl* 3.5.

Minerva, in Roman myth, goddess of trade and crafts; came to be associated with Athene.

Mole, the Ballahoura hills, to the north of Kilcolman, Spenser's Irish home.

Moses, leader and law-giver of Israelites at the time of the Exodus from Egypt; brother of Aaron.

Mulla, river Awbeg (a tributary of the Blackwater), which formed the east and south boundary of Spenser's Irish estate.

Muses, in Greek myth nine sisters, the daughters of Zeus and Mnemosyne (memory), they were personifications of the highest aspirations of artistic and intellectual minds. In Roman myth each Muse was given a particular area of interest. They lived on Mount Helicon; in *SC* they are placed on Parnassus and said to be daughters of Jove, and in *Am&Ep* they are the daughters of Phoebus.

Narcissus, in Greek myth, a beautiful youth who rejected the nymph Echo's love. Aphrodite punished him by making him fall in love with his reflection in the water; doting on this, he wasted away.

Needham, Sir Robert (no dates), having been recently knighted in Ireland, he returned to England on 25 September 1594, seemingly on the same boat as the manuscript of *Am&Ep*.

Nemesis, in Greek myth the personification of righteous anger or retribution, particularly that of the gods at human presumption or wrongdoing.

Neptune, Roman god of the seas.

Numa Pompilius, the legendary second King of Rome (715–673 BC).

Numerology, composition by numerical pattern was a widespread practice in the Renaissance. It was an accepted part of poetic craft, and reflected the belief that the world itself – as the creation of God – was constituted according to numerological principals. Thus the poet, in using a numerological structure, was both reflecting the divine order in the world and acting as a responsible creator.

Odysseus, according to Homer, King of Ithaca and husband of Penelope. In the *Iliad* he is one of the wisest and bravest of the Greeks. The *Odyssey* relates his ten years of troubles and adventures on his return voyage from Troy to Greece. See **Paris**.

Olives, Mount of, mountain outside Jerusalem on whose slopes is the Garden of Gethsemane. Christ taught and prayed there.

Olympus, Mt, highest mountain in Greece and home of the Olympian gods, such as Zeus and Hera.

Orpheus, famous figure in Greek myth, whose lineage is uncertain. He was a musician-poet of remarkable power, a power that was seen by the Renaissance to express the power of language.
    One of his adventures was the attempt to rescue his beloved Eurydice, a wood-nymph, from the underworld. With his music, he charmed Charon into letting him into the underworld, and pacified Cerberus. Persephone, the wife of Hades, pleaded on his behalf, and Hades allowed Eurydice to return with Orpheus, on condition that Orpheus did not look back at her until he returned to earth. Orpheus, tormented by doubt, glanced back and lost Eurydice for ever. Spenser varies the story, increasing Orpheus' power; Orpheus takes Eurydice without Hades' permission in *SC* 'Oct', and seems to succeed. (See also *FQ* 4.10.58.)

Ovid (Publius Ovidius Naso 43 BC–17 AD), Roman poet famous for his 15-book *Metamorphoses* (2 AD onwards). Corinna appears in his love elegies, the *Amores* (?20 BC).

Palinode, appears in SC 'May' and 'July'. A palinode is a recantation.

Pallas, see **Athene**.

Pan, Roman god of flocks and shepherds, mostly human down to the waist, and then goat to his hoofs. His favoured residence was Arcadia. Pastoral poets adopt him as a divine patron. As EK explains, he may also be taken to be Christ who 'calls himself the great and good shepherd . . . for Pan [derives from the Greek meaning] all or omnipotent, which is only the Lord Jesus'. EK also tells how Pan challenged Phoebus to a musical competition. Midas was the judge, who (because of personal bias) declared Pan the winner; Midas was rewarded with a pair of ass's ears by Phoebus. (See Ovid, *Meta* 11.146–93.)

Pandarus, character in Chaucer's *Troilus and Criseyde*, from whose actions the noun a 'pander' (that is a 'procurer') is derived.

Pandora, according to a Greek myth, Prometheus, a titan, tricked Zeus into accepting the fat and bones from sacrifices, leaving man to keep the good meat. To punish man (whom Prometheus had created), Zeus had Pandora (woman) fashioned. She was beautiful in every way: her name means 'all gifts'. Pandora was sent to Prometheus' brother, who foolishly accepted her. In curiosity, she opened the jar (or box) in which all of mankind's evils had until then been kept. These all flew out before she could close the jar, leaving only hope inside – which was then released.

Paris, son of Priam and Hecuba, the King and Queen of Troy. While Hecuba was pregnant, she dreamt she gave birth to a firebrand that burnt Troy to the ground. When Paris was born, he was exposed on Mt Ida to die. However, shepherds found and reared him.

Once while tending his flocks, three goddesses – Juno, Venus and Minerva – came and asked him to judge who was the fairest. Paris chose Venus. He eventually learnt who he was, and claimed his position as Prince. As Homer tells the story, Paris' seduction or rape of Helen (the wife of Menelaus, King of Sparta) led to the Trojan war, at the end of which Troy was burnt.

Parnass(us), mountain on the mainland of Greece. Delphi lies on the south-west spur; this was the pre-eminent shrine and oracle of Ancient Greece. To the north-east of Delphi is the Castalian spring, whose waters to the Romans signified poetic inspiration. Both mountain and spring were associated with Phoebus and the Muses. EK conflates Parnassus with Helicon, and the Hippocrene with the Castalian spring.

Peele, George (1556–1596), poet, playwright, pageant-writer and actor. Much of his writing celebrates the popular joys and patriotism of his period. He wrote a Spenserian eclogue, *An Eclogue Gratulatous* (1589).

Penelope, the wife of Odysseus. While he is away, Penelope is pressed to remarry by many suitors. She refuses. Finally, she puts the suitors off by declaring that, before she can remarry, she must weave a shroud for Odysseus' father. She weaves this during the day and then unravels it at night. After three years one of her maids betrays her secret.

Peneus, principal river in Thessaly which flows through the valley of Tempe.

Perionius (Joachim Périon, *c*. 1499–1559), Benedictine humanist.

Petrarch (Francesco Petrarca, 1304–74), Italian poet, classical scholar, and humanist who had a great influence on the English literary Renaissance. He wrote Latin eclogues (though his most famous poetry is in Italian), and was a friend of Boccaccio.

Petre, William (1575–1637), married to Katherine Somerset. (See **Guildford**).

Phillis, Cuddie's beloved, and, as EK notes, a common name in eclogues.

Philomela, in Roman myth, a woman who was turned into a nightingale after having been raped and mutilated by Tereus, the husband of her sister. (See Ovid, *Meta* 6.424–674.)

Phoebe, Spenser follows the (incorrect) tradition of using Phoebe as another name for Diana.

Phoebus (Phoebus Apollo), god of light, as well as archery, prophecy, poetry and music. Brother of Phoebe. In Virgil's *Ecl* he is patron of the Muses. Occasionally identified with the sun, and so with Helios.

Phoenicia, an ancient country, consisting of a narrow strip of land on the coast of what is now Syria.

Piers, appears in *SC* 'May' and 'Oct'. Recalls the Piers of *Piers Plowman*.

Piers Plowman, a poem of the alliterative revival written ? 1367–86 by William Langland in which Piers, a ploughman, has a series of visionary dreams. Containing some of the most intensely beautiful and moving poetry of the English language, the poem seeks to establish the proper life for the individual Christian and, in passing, offers a satirical portrait of the corrupt practices of the medieval Church.

Pindus, a mountain marking the north-west boundary of Thessaly. Used by Roman poets as a stock example of a high mountain.

Plato (427–347 BC), profoundly influential Greek philosopher, and friend of Socrates. His philosophy, mediated through Florentine and earlier neo-Platonists, was of immense influence in the Renaissance. Central to that philosophy was the notion of two worlds. Plato held that mankind's material world of the senses was a poor reflection or shadow of the unchanging world of Ideas or Forms. One's soul came from the Ideal world but was trapped in the material world by the body. One's aim should be to reascend to the Ideal world; in part this could be done through the attempt to attain knowledge of this Ideal world through study. The discipline of (Platonic) love was also thought to elevate the soul. See also **Cupid**.

Pluto, see **Hades**.

Ponsonby, William (c. 1547–1604), one of the most influential Elizabethan publishers with a reputation for radical Protestant literature. Published most of Spenser's (and Sidney's) works.

Proteus, a minor Greek sea-god who herds seals, knows all things, and has the power to change shape to avoid answering questions.

Psyche (Greek for 'soul' or 'butterfly'), the heroine of one of the tales in Lucius Apuleius' (fl. 155 AD) *Metamorphoses*. Venus, jealous of Psyche's beauty, sent Cupid to make her fall in love with someone ugly. However, Cupid fell in love with Psyche, and married her. Venus spitefully sought revenge, and subjected her daughter-in-law to much suffering before they were eventually reconciled.

The tale is often taken as an allegory of the soul's journey through the tribulations of life.

Ptolemaic cosmology, this pictured the cosmos as a series of concentric spheres (usually ten in the Renaissance), centred on the earth. The first seven spheres each contain a planet – the Moon, Mercury, Venus and so on; then comes the sphere of the fixed stars (the firmament), next the Crystalline sphere, and finally the Primum Mobile (which imparts motion to all of the inner spheres), beyond which God dwells in Empyrean Heaven.

Pythia, prophetess at Delphi; EK uses the name to describe a prophetess in Virgil's *Aeneid*.

Ralegh, Sir Walter (?1552–1618), a courtier who rose to a position of pre-eminence within Elizabeth's Court due to a combination of personal charm, literary ability, and military and naval service. (He waged a ruthless campaign in Ireland, where he became Captain of the Queen's guard in 1587.) At the height of his success, in 1592, he lost the Queen's favour by marrying one of her Ladies in Waiting, Elizabeth Throckmorton. Ralegh wrote 'The Ocean to Cynthia' (never completed) as part of his attempt to win back his position. This he never did, being accused of complicity in the Earl of Essex's rebellion of 1601. This also gained him the distrust of James I, who had him imprisoned and finally executed.

Reformation, diverse and influential religious movement (which cannot be divorced from its political inspirations and consequences) that came to fruition in the sixteenth century. Its central aim was to reform the Roman Catholic Church (in the areas of organization, worship and doctrine) by recovering and returning to the practices of the early Church. In particular, the reformers insisted that the source of authority for Christians was the Bible (not the Pope), and that justification was by faith alone (not through masses or penance). The movement led to the establishment of many Protestant Churches; in England this occurred in the 1530s, when Henry VIII (1491–1547) broke with Rome and established the Church of England. Elizabeth I re-established this Church after Mary (1553–8) had restored Roman Catholicism.

Renaissance ('rebirth'), a period of European history commonly held to have begun in Italy in the fourteenth century, to have reached England in the early sixteenth century, and to have ended by the mid-seventeenth century. During this time, there was a great flowering in the visual and literary arts. The Renaissance eludes a strict definition, but the following are often mentioned as distinguishing the period: the new learning of the humanists (based in part on the construction of a new relationship with the classical past); the arrival of the printing press; the new religion of the Reformation; the European discovery of the new world; new theories that placed the sun at the centre of the solar system; and new scientific methodologies. Renaissance literature shaped and was shaped by these movements, theories and discoveries.

Romulus, legendary founder, with his brother Remus, of Rome.

Rosalind, Colin Clout's beloved in *SC*, whose name, according to EK, conceals a real love of Spenser's. Mentioned in *SC* 'Jan', 'Apr', 'June', 'Aug', 'Nov', and 'Dec'.

Russell, Anne (1548– c. 1603), Countess of Warwick whose husband died in February *c.* 1589. Spenser also praises her in *RT*, ll.244–52, and dedicates *FH* to her and her sister, Margaret, the Countess of Cumberland (?1560–1616).

Sackville, Robert (1561–1609), Earl of Dorset, and third husband of Anne Spencer.

Sallust (Gaius Sallustius Crispus, 86–35 BC), Roman historian.

Sannazar (Jacopo Sannazzaro, 1456–1530), a Neapolitan author who wrote Latin eclogues, and a very popular prose and verse pastoral romance, the *Arcadia*.

Sheffield, Elizabeth (d. 1601), wife of the Earl of Ormonde, who owned land about 40 miles from Kilcolman.

Shure, the river Suir, which runs from north of Clonmel to Waterford.

Sidney, Sir Philip (1554–86), an influential literary patron, critic and writer of poetry and prose, as well as a courtier and soldier. By the late 1570s he was much concerned to advance the causes of Protestantism and English nationalism. As part of this support, he opposed the prospective match between Elizabeth I and the Duc d'Alençon. The dedication of *SC* to Sidney might signal a Protestant standpoint (see **Singleton, Leicester, & Harvey**).

Sidney died from wounds received while attacking a Spanish convoy in the Netherlands and was posthumously lionized as the perfect Protestant Renaissance man. Spenser supported this process, identifying Sidney with the lover in Sidney's sonnet sequence, *Astrophel and Stella*. (Spenser suggests 'Astrophel' as an alternative name for the plant 'Starlight'.)

Sinai, Mt, the mountain on which God gave Moses the ten commandments. See *Exodus* 19–20.

Singleton, Hugh (d. 1593), printer of 1st edn of *SC*, who had previously almost lost his right hand for publishing material critical of Elizabeth I's prospective marriage to the Duc d'Alençon. Depending on one's view of Singleton's bravery, this may point up or play down the Protestant bias of the poem: would Singleton have risked life or limb again?

Skelton, John (?1460–1529), distinguished English poet. His *Colin Clout* (1521–2) is the complaint of Colin against the misdeeds of ecclesiastics in general and Cardinal Wolsey in particular.

Smith, Sir Thomas (1513–77), statesman, great classical scholar (among other accomplishments), friend of Burghley and Leicester. He helped Harvey in his academic career, and Harvey claimed to be related to him.

Snackenborg, Helena (Swedish, d. 1631), Marchioness of Northampton, who married Gorges's uncle in 1591, 20 years after the death of her first husband. Spenser dedicated *Daph* to her (see **Gorges**).

Socrates (469–399 BC), profoundly influential Greek philosopher.

Spencers of Althorp, Spenser claimed kinship with the family of Sir John Spencer of Althorp, a claim that seems to have been acknowledged. The 2nd, 5th and 6th daughters (Elizabeth, Anne, and Alice) are celebrated in *Col* as Phyllis, Charillis and Amaryllis (see **Carey, Sackville & Stanley**). The manor-house of Althorp is in Northamptonshire, England.

Stanley, Ferdinando (?1559–94), Lord Strange, Earl of Derby. Patron of an acting company and of poets, and a poet himself. His wife, Alice or 'Amaryllis', was one of the Spencers of Althorp.

Stationers' Register, only members of the Stationers' Company were regularly allowed to print books for sale (others needed to have a special patent). Any member who wished to print a book had first to enter its name into this register.

Statius (Publius Papinus *c.* 45–96 AD), Latin poet, imitator of Virgil.

Stesichorus (Teisias, fl. 600–550 BC), Greek lyric poet.

Syrinx, beautiful nymph who followed Diana. Pan fell in love with her, and she escaped by being turned into a tuft of reeds in a river. Pan fashioned some of the reeds into a pipe. (See Ovid, *Meta* 1.689–712.)

Tempe, the valley between Mt Olympus and Mt Ossa in Thessaly.

Thenot, appears in *SC* 'Feb', 'Apr', and 'Nov'. As EK notes, Marot uses the name in his eclogues.

Theocritus (*c.* 300–260 BC), Greek poet whose *Idylls* established many of the formal characteristics of pastoral poetry.

Thessaly, an area in north-east Greece.

Thestylis Lodowick Bryskett (1547–?1612), Secretary of Munster Council in Ireland. Spenser was his deputy clerk *c.* 1584–9, and the two had been friends for some 20 years. In Ireland, Spenser involved him in a literary group; Bryskett wrote an elegy to Sidney called 'The Mourning Muse of Thestylis'.

Thomalin, appears in *SC* 'Mar' and 'July'.

Tiber, central Italy's greatest river.

Titans, pre-Olympian gods such as Atlas, Hyperion and Prometheus.

Tithones (properly Tithonus), the brother of Priam (see **Paris**), he became the lover of the goddess Eos (Dawn). She obtained immortality for him, but forgot to ask for eternal youth, with the result that he became old and shrivelled, little more than a voice.

Tityrus, Tityrus appears in Virgil's *Eclogues*, and is often taken to be Virgil's literary persona (cf. Colin Clout). In *SC*, Tityrus at times evokes Virgil and at others Chaucer. In this way, the figure of Tityrus is able to combine (as does Spenser's poem) both poets and their poetic traditions.

Triton, a Greek merman.

Tyrius, Maximus (*c.* 125–85 AD), sophist and itinerant lecturer.

Tully, English Renaissance name for Cicero.

Turberville, George (1540?–1610), sometime secretary to the ambassador to Russia, poet and author (in the 1560s and '70s). He produced popular translations of Ovid and Mantuan as well as his own poetry, and is credited with extending the capabilities of blank verse.

Valla, Laurentius (1407–57), Italian humanist, philosopher, and textual scholar who attacked medieval traditions and anticipated the views of Protestant reformers.

Venus, Roman goddess of love (through identification with the Greek goddess Aphrodite), born on the island of Cythera, off Greece. Also the morning and evening star. See **Cupid.**

Virgil (Publius Vergilius Maro, 70–19 BC), one of the greatest of Roman poets, famous for his *Eclogues* (*c.* 42–37 BC), *Georgics* (*c.* 37–1 BC), and his (almost finished) epic poem the *Aeneid* (?26–19 BC). Renaissance poetic theory held this progression through different genres to be the model for the aspiring poet.

Vulcan, Roman god of fire, often identified with the Greek god Hephaestus, god of fire and divine artificer. Being lame, his mother, Hera, threw him out of Olympus. He landed on Lemnos, an island in the Aegean, which became a centre of his worship.

Walsingham, Frances (1569–1632), Sidney's widow, whom Spenser conflates with the Stella ('Star') of Sidney's sonnet sequence, *Astrophel and Stella* (pubd 1591). She was the dedicatee of Spenser's elegy for Sidney, *As* (1595), by which time she had become by marriage the Countess of Essex.

Willye, appears in *SC* 'Mar' and 'Aug'.

Whitney, Geoffrey, Snr and Jnr (no dates & ?1548–?1601), Whitney Jnr dedicated his book of poems to Leicester.

Worcester, fourth Earl of (Edward Somerset, 1553–1628), the weddings of the first two of his seven daughters, Elizabeth and Katherine, are commemorated in *Prothalamion*. At one time a friend of the Earl of Essex, he was imprisoned by Essex during his attempted rebellion (for which imprisonment Essex apologized). He was one of the peers who found Essex guilty of treason and condemned him to death. He was a Roman Catholic and also the patron of a company of actors.

Wrenock, perhaps Richard Mulcaster (?1530–1611), Spenser's headmaster at Merchant Taylors', London.

Xenophon (*c.* 428–*c.* 354 BC), Athenian writer on many subjects, best known as a historian. He was a friend of Socrates.

Young, John (1534?–1605), Bishop of Rochester (Latin title: *episcopus Roffensis*) for whom Spenser was working in 1578. Young had been Master of Pembroke Hall while Spenser was an undergraduate, and was advanced within the Church by Grindal.

Zeus, King of the Greek gods; Spenser often conflates Zeus with Jove.

SPENSER AND HIS CRITICS[1]

Before John Hughes's 1715 edition of Spenser's works, criticism of
Spenser's poetry is piecemeal, as was the common practice of the
period. That criticism is overwhelmingly positive, if typically general.
The point of it is often simply that Spenser is a great poet who is
deservedly famous. That fame rests more securely on *The Shepherds'
Calendar*; for while the reputation of *The Faerie Queene* suffers in
the neo-classical period (for convenience, the period from
1660–1760), Spenser's mastery of pastoral is never doubted. Com-
ments on his other shorter poems are very slight.

The most significant single piece of criticism on Spenser's shorter
poetry before Hughes is EK's Dedicatory Epistle to *The Shepherds'
Calendar*. It gives the impression of defining the areas of debate that
others (mainly practising poets) would later address: Spenser is seen,
above all, as having extended the range and potential of English
poetry – 'By his toil we do nourish,/And by him are enlarged'
(Thomas Edwards, 1595).[2]

This achievement is seen in various terms: the formal complexity
and innovation of *The Shepherds' Calendar* is praised, and the poem
is often culled for examples; the work's relationship to classical and
European models of pastoral is valued highly, Spenser often being
seen as the English Virgil, sometimes as the English Theocritus;
similarly valued are the work's moral seriousness and didactic intents,
as well as its depiction of love; while the most frequent reservations
expressed are those concerning the archaic aspects of the language,
what Ben Jonson termed 'Chaucerisms' – 'Fie on the forged mint that
did create/New coin of words never articulate' (Joseph Hall, 1598).

Yet EK's Epistle only gives the impression of defining these areas
of debate: in fact the Epistle is positioning itself and *The Shepherds'
Calendar* in relation to an argument (which had been at its height in
the mid-sixteenth century) as to whether English was, as a language,
the equal of Latin, and how the language's deficiencies might be
remedied. The Epistle sets out to show how *The Shepherds' Calendar* an-
swers many literary prayers, and the subsequent, often nationalistic,

critical praise follows EK, since it too wishes to address that previous debate. Spenser becomes an *auctor*, alongside Chaucer, a name to be invoked to summon the authority and recognized achievements of English poetry, a name on which to fashion a tradition – Spenser becomes 'our Homer', whose 'ashes rest [...] by merry Chaucer's noble chest' (*Return from Parnassus: Part 2*, 1602).

By the time of Hughes's edition that tradition is seen to run from Chaucer to Spenser to Milton and finally on to Dryden; indeed, it is in the creative poetic responses to Spenser, an area which cannot be covered here, that the most valuable criticism of the shorter poems occurs.[3] Hughes, like most critics by this time, focuses his attention on *The Faerie Queene*, but he also begins to look in detail at particular shorter poems, and if he still stays mainly within the terms of Spenser's achievement established by EK, he moves beyond them in his detailed explication of what was previously only stated. Spenser, for Hughes, is the most influential English poet, the poet who had brought music to the language; and *The Shepherds' Calendar* is his most perfect work, 'a little country seat' of a poem, from which more true and natural pleasure may be derived than from the 'royal palace' of *The Faerie Queene*, magnificent but flawed in its reliance on the Italian model provided by Ariosto. For Hughes, as for John Dryden, *The Shepherds' Calendar* is perfect pastoral. Critic and poet are delighted with its formal perfection, its natural depiction of love and the simple pleasures of country life. Hughes sees *The Shepherds' Calendar* as primarily Theocritean, rather than Virgilian, on account of its low and rustic elements. He also recognizes that there are elements of satire, and that they are well worked, but wonders whether they are appropriate.

For pastoral is, at this time, generally given a rather narrow definition within literary criticism. Alexander Pope, in his 'A Discourse on Pastoral' (published 1717), argues – following the French neo-classicist Auguste Rapin – that pastoral should be 'an imitation of the action of a shepherd' which displays the qualities of 'simplicity, brevity and delicacy', the delicacy and delight consisting in showing 'the best side only of a shepherd's life, and in concealing its miseries'. From such a viewpoint, *The Shepherds' Calendar* has many imperfections in subject and form; Pope believes many of the poems to be over-long, their dialect too coarse, and the verse forms, as well as the allegory and satire, inappropriate. He also has reservations about Spenser's use of the calendar to structure *The Shepherds' Calendar*:

on the one hand, he thinks it 'very beautiful' because it gives the poems not only the general pastoral 'moral of innocence and simplicity' but also, by comparing 'human life to the several seasons' shows the interrelationship between the microcosm of man's life and the macrocosm of the living world; on the other hand, many of the months seem similar, as the year cannot be divided into twelve recognizable periods.

What definitions of pastoral such as Pope's and Hughes's both gave licence to was the simply nostalgic view of pastoral as a form of escapism. In 1750, Samuel Johnson is amazed at the insistence of 'modern critics' that pastoral be set in the 'golden age', a prescription for which he can find no authority in the classics (*Rambler*, 24 July). Along with Pope, he argues that pastoral poetry should represent rural nature, and also feels that its involvement with matters 'more rumbling than rural' (John Gay, *The Shepherd's Week*, 1714), such as theological controversy, is inappropriate. Moreover, rural is not rustic, and Spenser's 'obsolete terms and rustic words' are again condemned, here in particular for the lack of logic they display when combined with non-pastoral concerns: 'Surely, at the same time that a shepherd learns theology, he may gain some acquaintance with his native language.' For Johnson, pastoral has almost become a term of criticism: 'whatever images it can supply are long ago exhausted', he argues, and so the form is now 'easy, vulgar, and therefore disgusting' ('Life of Milton', 1781).

Elsewhere, however, Johnson praises Spenser alongside Shakespeare as the discoverer of the 'smoothness and harmony' that English was capable of (*Preface to Shakespeare*, 1765) and was, according to Hannah More, keen to include Spenser in his *Lives of the Poets* (1779–81). Similarly, Pope, for all his reservations, is willing to repeat Dryden's (and many others') valuation of Spenser as the third great pastoral poet, after Virgil and Theocritus. In Pope's own 'Pastorals', Spenser is a continued presence, and Pope declares himself, in his 'Summer', to be Spenser's true successor. Indeed, *The Shepherds' Calendar* is a constant presence in the poetry of the period, and is greatly valued, though the literary critical critera of the period make it hard to demonstrate this value convincingly.

Looking back, it can been seen that *The Shepherds' Calendar* is caught up in a redefinition of pastoral. The Renaissance and medieval sense of pastoral as providing an ethically charged landscape (in which to formulate moral, political and religious principles, and to examine the relationship which art might have with those principles), is lost in the eighteenth century. Pastoral becomes a far more prescribed, more purely imitative kind of literature, at its worst conventional and artificial in those words' pejorative senses. (Pastoral changes, one might say, from being a mode to a kind.) Nature poetry arises partly in response to this sense that pastoral is 'written out', and to an extent takes pastoral's place, exploring the relationships between art, man and nature in more naturalistic descriptions of the landscape and the countryside. Pastoral would re-emerge, for example in William Wordsworth's *Michael: A Pastoral Poem* (1802) or John Clare's *The Shepherds' Calendar* (1827), as a landscape expressive and constitutive of the individual's sense of him- or herself, in which nature itself was seen as an independent source of moral value.

Such a redefinition took the interest of the Romantic period (for convenience, the years 1790–1830) away from Spenser's *The Shepherds' Calendar*, a turning away reinforced by the period's high valuation of organic form and ambivalence towards allegory; *The Shepherds' Calendar* seemed an outdated pastoral, offering an uninteresting formal model, whose poetry (through its allegory) was too directly related to its times.

The Faerie Queene had always preoccupied critics; now that neo-classical criteria were in retreat and interest in romance intense, its critical reputation amongst Spenser's works became thoroughly dominant. Typically, allegory and narrative are left alone, and *The Faerie Queene* is praised for its beauties; Leigh Hunt is not unrepresentative when, in arguing that Spenser is the most pictorial of poets, he identifies particular passages with particular painters: Titian, Poussin, Correggio, Claude, Raphael, Rembrandt – Spenser contains them all ('A New Gallery of Pictures', 1833). Indeed, liking Spenser becomes for Hunt a test: 'not to like Spenser is not to like poetry for its own sake [. . .]. All the poets have liked him. There has not been a more genuine favourite among them, a writer beloved more as a matter of course, or more imitated'[4] ('The Wishing-Cap', 1833). Spenser has become the 'poets' poet' (Hunt attributes this to Charles Lamb in *Imagination and Fancy* (1844), but is probably misremembering Hazlitt's 'the most poetical of poets'). Spenser's melody is now linked with his sensuousness, and both are seen to make him the poet of another world: to Wordsworth he is 'Sweet Spenser, moving through his clouded heaven/With the moon's beauty and the moon's soft pace' (*The Prelude* (1850), 3.283–4); and to Hazlitt he is 'the poet of our waking dreams; and he has invented not only a language, but a music of his own for them' (*Lectures*, 1818).

The shorter poems and *The Shepherds' Calendar* were not forgotten in such criticism; indeed, to a degree it could be claimed about them that they were equal exemplars of Spenser's poetry, though they lacked the full trappings of *The Faerie Queene*'s romance world. So, for example, Hunt takes as his final picture Cupid jumping out of the ivy-bush in the 'March' eclogue of *The Shepherds' Calendar*. While Coleridge is more typical of the period in valuing *Epithalamion* and *Prothalamion*: 'Spenser's *Epithalamion* is truly sublime; and pray mark the swan-like movement of his exquisite *Prothalamion*. His attention to metre and rhythm is sometimes so extremely minute as to be painful even to my ear' (*Table Talk*, 24 June 1827). Detailed analysis, however, is usually restricted to single lines which illustrate a particular aspect of Spenser's music. That music is very often discussed in water imagery: Hazlitt, in the lecture quoted above, talks of the verse's infinite 'undulations [. . .] like those of the waves of the sea' (a reference to Florizel's description of Perdita's beauty in Shakespeare's *The Winter Tale*).

James Russell Lowell ('Spenser', 1875) culminates this line of Romantic thinking on Spenser. Often building on Hazlitt, Lowell attempts to site *The Shepherds' Calendar* more precisely in its literary context. He sees its publication not only as marking a new literary epoch (desperately needed after the previous dull century), but as doing so self-consciously: *The Shepherds' Calendar* represents 'a conscious and deliberate attempt at reform', the equivalent of Wordsworth's and Coleridge's *Lyrical Ballads* (1798). Like Wordsworth, Spenser is seen to be trying, laudably, to get 'back to nature and life', and is a great transformer of style and language; Spenser, however, is still seen to have wrongly chosen rusticity over simplicity, and sometimes tackles subjects that are inappropriate for pastoral. For Lowell sees the pastoral of *The Shepherds' Calendar* as Spenser's first attempt to escape from the realism of daily life into the 'dream world' triumphantly found in *The Faerie Queene*. This world is not that of 'unreality' but 'unrealism'; this is a fine distinction, and turns on Lowell's sense of the importance of imagination to the everyday business of being human, and in particular of imagination's role in revealing to us the transcendent aspects of our nature. This world, 'somewhere between mind and matter, between soul and sense, between the actual and the possible, is precisely the region which

Spenser assigns [. . .] to the poetic susceptibility of impression, – "To reign in the air from the earth to highest sky"'.

The quotation comes from *Muiopotmos*, and if *The Shepherds' Calendar* is finally mainly of historical interest to Lowell, *Muiopotmos* becomes a central statement of Spenser's poetic theory, his first mature poem. Lowell attractively reads the poem in general, and Clarion the butterfly in particular, as Spenser's meditation on the nature of poets and poetry: 'No German analyzer of aesthetics,' Lowell argues, 'has given us so convincing a definition of the artistic nature as these radiant verses.' The poet's imagination frees him (and later us) to float, like Clarion, 'between a blue sky and golden earth in imperishable sunshine' where he, 'lord of all the works of nature,' may 'reign in th'air from earth to highest sky' (*Muiopotmos*, ll.211–12). In this world, it is right and typically Spenserian that *birds* should become *brides* in *Prothalamion*. The poet is the person who senses the underlying harmonies in nature. 'What more felicity,' asks Lowell, 'can fall to creature' than to be a poet? (*Muiopotmos*, l.209.) So *Epithalamion* is seen as 'instinct with the same joyousness which must have been the familiar mood of Spenser [. . .] a profound delight in the beauty of the universe'. Lowell, in effect, makes Spenser the 'poets' poet' by making Spenser the archetype of (Romantic) poets and poetry.

Edward Dowden refutes what he sees as Lowell's picture of Spenser as an escapist dreamer; in its place he argues for Spenser as Milton described him – as 'our sage and serious Spenser, whom I dare to name a better teacher than Scotus or Aquinas' (*Areopagitica*, 1644). Dowden is everywhere keen to insist on the morality of Spenser's poetry, where Lowell had described coming across a moral as an 'unpleasant surprise [. . .] as when one's teeth close on a bit of gravel in a dish of strawberries and cream'. Without such morality, Spenser's sensuousness might easily become sensuality; Hazlitt had suggested as much. Milton's voluptuousness, he thought, was not lascivious; the poet appreciated beautiful things for their own sakes. Spenser, by contrast, 'has an eye to the consequences, and steeps everything in pleasure, often not of the purest kind' (*Examiner*, 1816). Yeats later suggested that Spenser had been made a poet by just such a sensuality, 'by what he had almost learnt to call his sins [. . .]. He is a poet of the delighted senses' (*Poems of Spenser*, 1902). Most others, however, were not willing to make a virtue of this: Cardinal Wiseman, England's Catholic primate, had condemned Spenser for his sensuous style in two lectures (1856 and 1857); and

John Palgrave, in *The Golden Treasury* (1861), an anthology that
reflected and helped define the taste of the mid-Victorian age, felt
that he had to leave out *Epithalamion* because it was 'too high-
kilted'. *Prothalamion*, which Palgrave thought less good, represented
Spenser instead; it showed 'The Renaissance impulse in England [. . .]
at its highest and purest'. (The omission of *Epithalamion* was
deplored by the editor of the 1906 edition of *The Golden Treasury*,
and the poem printed.)

To Dowden, Spenser is not only the poet who gives England her
Renaissance, but he is also the poet who is always pure. Like Lowell,
Dowden recognizes the historical importance of *The Shepherds'
Calendar*, but he goes on to explain this in far more detail, as part of
his sense of the work as personal autobiography. Dowden traces a
network of interrelationships between poet, poetry, Europe, Queen,
Church, Reformation, love of nature and love of a woman. *The
Shepherds' Calendar* is read as *The Faerie Queene* in embryo, and
Dowden's sense of its balance is impressive: 'it is now gay and
sportive, now staid and serious; sensuous ardour and moral wisdom
are united in it; the allegorical form in miniature is already employed;
it exhibits a mode of idealized treatment of contemporary public
affairs not dissimilar in essentials from that afterwards put to use in
his romantic epic' ('Spenser, The Poet and Teacher', 1984).

Dowden was Professor of English at Trinity College, Dublin. His
work marks the professionalization of Spenser studies; literary ama-
teurs would no longer be felt to have the requisite body of knowledge
from which to comment productively on the poems. Critical effort
was directed increasingly at gaining the best possible historically
informed understanding of Spenser's poetry – or rather of the virtues
of Spenser's poetry. As one survey of eighteenth-century Spenser
criticism noted: 'It requires as much courage to call Spenser a bore at
the present day as it then required to deny that he was barbarous'
(*Saturday Review*, 20 May 1876).

This attempt at historical understanding brought *The Shepherds'
Calendar* back as the focus of attention among the shorter poems.
Up to the end of the first quarter of the twentieth century much of
the criticism was local, intent on discovering sources and analogies
for the eclogues, tracing the poem's subsequent influence, exploring
the verse forms and language of the poem, explaining the contempor-
ary references, and from these analysing Spenser's religious, poetic
and political views. All of which would have delighted EK; clearly,

critics were still enjoying the poetry and the playful qualities of the commentary as they were originally invited to. Indeed, around the turn of the century, the identity of 'Immerito' was once more contested, a group of Baconians claiming *The Shepherds' Calendar* along with many other works. Criticism, as it sought to understand what Spenser was trying to do, and why he was trying to do it, and how these attempts were reflected in the particular forms of the poems, was once again within EK's and the sixteenth century's subject areas.

Overall, most effort was expended in understanding the allegory of the poem, and, as this area was pursued with increasing sophistication in the mid-twentieth century, in understanding the poem as allegory; it became clear that Spenser's allegory does not function (as the Romantics had tended to suggest) purely in terms of 'x' being 'y' – 'x' might be 'w' and 'z' as well. A single poem might have political and/or personal and/or religious meanings. Spenserian allegory is now seen as flexible, operating on different levels of meaning at the same time, and at different levels of meaning at different times. The culmination of this line of criticism is Paul McLane's full, sometimes tendentious, but very helpfully organized attempt 'to set forth as clearly as possible the complete allegory of the *Calender*' (1961).

At the same time, the place of *The Shepherds' Calendar* in relation to literary and philosophic traditions continued to be analysed (allegoric studies had tended to examine the poem's social and political positions). *Amoretti* was also of interest here, as critics attempted to analyse Spenser's concept of love. Until the 1930s, Spenser is seen mainly within a Petrarchan framework, and *Amoretti* is placed within the historical development of the sonnet. In the 1940s and 1950s, the neo-Platonic elements of *Amoretti* are examined more fully. This interest in Spenser's Platonism culminated in Ellrodt (1960). *Amoretti* was the only other shorter poem to receive substantial attention before the mid-century; around that time, *Epithalamion* emerged to greater prominence as critics began to trace the complex relationship between it and *Amoretti*, and to see *Amoretti and Epithalamion* as a single work.

Much of this often fragmentary critical effort was drawn together in the 10-volume *Variorum Edition* of Spenser (1932–57), which remains the standard edition. The *Variorum* bore testament to Spenser's academic prestige, and to the centre of Spenser studies having decisively shifted from England to America, where this edition was published. Yet, at the same time, there was a sense that Spenser was becoming a *forgotten* classic, acknowledgedly great but critically uninteresting. For while there was much Spenser criticism (the bibliography for 1900–1936 mentions some 1,400 items), Spenser, as B. E. C. Davis noted, had received 'less attention, apart from detached articles and cursory notices, than any other English poet of equal rank' (*Edmund Spenser*, 1933).

Not all the attention in this period (Davis talks of 'the last half-century') was 'detached articles'; W. L. Renwick's *Edmund Spenser* (1925) is the outstanding (though now outdated) exception. Offering what was in effect a far more detailed and convincing version of Dowden's essay, Renwick, where he treated *The Shepherds' Calendar*, paid particular attention to the poem's relationship to sixteenth-century poetics, and saw the poem's achievement not only in its naturalization of poetic forms, but in its creation of a new kind of poetic personality. In Renwick, *The Shepherds' Calendar* at last had its serious EK.

Yet Renwick is unusual and Davis's comment accurate enough. So, for example, Spenser failed to feature significantly in the 'revaluations' of the literary canon undertaken by T. S. Eliot, F. R. Leavis and the *Scrutiny* critics. Where mentioned at all he is typically devalued. D. A. Traversi recognizes in *The Shepherds' Calendar* 'the voice of a new sophistication', pleasing but dangerous, its language and conventions having lost contact with real life and so having lost the ability to convey real, healthy feeling. This loss is in part a product of Spenser's Puritanism, which 'is nothing else than the disembodied and destructive intellect preying on the body to kill the soul'. Spenser is seen, in fact, as a forerunner and accomplice of Milton, the other great Puritan poet; 'no two men have done more, by their very genius, to crush the true poetic tradition of England.' (*Scrutiny*, 1936)

Responding to this hostile dismissiveness, the critics of the second quarter of the century tend to have a defensive tone, a need to justify their subject matter. At times, the shorter poems seem to be sacrificed to redeem *The Faerie Queene*; C. S. Lewis, who defends *The Faerie Queene* so fervently (*The Allegory of Love*, 1936), is willing to dismiss the shorter poems as 'something of a digression' (*English Literature*, 1954). The one exception he makes is for *Epithalamion*, a near perfect poem of 'festal sublimity', which is, he notes, 'much rarer than tragic sublimity'. Elsewhere, however, and rather late in the critical day, American New Critical studies were shifting the academic effort away from historical scholarship and on to arguments for the organic unity and moral coherence of the shorter poems. Nelson (*The Poetry of Edmund Spenser*, 1963) is perhaps the most generally persuasive of these. A. C. Hamilton, in an influential article on *The Shepherds' Calendar*, argued that the poem's eclogues were ordered so as to develop an overall argument – for the rejection of the pastoral life in favour of an active life in the 'real' world ('The Argument of Spenser's *The Shepherds' Calendar*', 1956). In doing so he raised two questions to prominence: what relation did *The Shepherds' Calendar* have to pastoral; and what was Spenser's attitude to his art.

These were the related questions that were taken up in the early 1960s, by which time studies of Spenser no longer needed to apologize for their subject matter. Just as the critical understanding of the concept of allegory had grown more sophisticated, so pastoral now began to be seen less as a genre or kind, based upon a set of conventions, and more as a mode, which provides a set of terms and practices for thinking.

This renewed interest owed much to previous critical studies of pastoral. At the beginning of the century, Walter Greg had argued that pastoral was not amenable to formal definition, but was rather a 'philosophic conception' in which were articulated 'instincts and impulses deep-rooted in the nature of humanity' (*Pastoral Poetry and Pastoral Drama*, 1906). William Empson, while agreeing with Greg's sense of pastoral as a mode, saw pastoral not as an expression of deep-rooted instincts, but as in part creating the historically changing perception of humanity; he tried to show 'the ways in which the pastoral process of putting the complex into the simple [. . .] and the resulting social ideas have been used in English literature' (*Some Versions of Pastoral*, 1935). Bruno Snell, believing with Empson that pastoral played a part in constructing our reality, rather than simply in expressing it, shifted the focus from pastoral's effects in the political realm and onto its historical significance in creating the person's sense of self or soul. Snell argued that Virgil's Arcadia was a culminating moment in the discovery of the soul as an object distinct from the body and empirical reality, whose feelings were not divinely given but self-produced and personal, and which had, in its ability to be in tension with itself, a form of depth. Virgil's Arcadia, in effect, bequeathed to European thought an inner world or spiritual landscape. Snell argued this to be a place of becoming, not being, 'set half-way between myth and reality; it is also a no-man's land between two ages, an earthly beyond, a land of the soul yearning for its distant home in the past' (*The Discovery of the Mind*, 1946). Snell's phrasing is reminiscent of Hazlitt and Lowell; in effect Snell provides an academically persuasive and historically informed analysis of Spenser's 'waking dreams' (Hazlitt), and shows how 'unrealism' is not at all 'unreality' (Lowell).

This body of work bore fruit in many ways. Freed from the need for a single formal definition, critics began registering the different and shifting kinds of pastoral within *The Shepherds' Calendar*. Patrick Cullen saw this formal fluidity leading to a 'multiform ambivalence' of moral perspective that undermined the Dowdenesque desire to see Spenser as a teacher, and complicated Hamilton's sense of an overall argument. *The Shepherds' Calendar* was built around a system of tensions between opposites: regressive desires were matched by progressive desires, innocence was played off against naivety, the active was compared with the contemplative life. Spenser was valued for his moral balance, his unpartisan complexity. Or rather, he was so valued in his Arcadian eclogues. Cullen traced two traditions of pastoral: the Arcadian, summed up by the figure of the happy shepherd celebrating at ease beneath the shade of a tree; and the Mantuanesque, whose shepherd was the good pastor of his flock. In the Mantuanesque eclogues, for Cullen, the multivalence of experience of *The Shepherds' Calendar* 'is transmuted into a simplistic Christian conflict of good and evil' (*Spenser, Marvell, and Renaissance Pastoral*, 1970). Yet, within the whole, the tension between these two kinds functioned as a critique on pastoral itself; Spenser's pastoral was self-consciously examining its own forms of experience.

Cullen could be charged with a failure of critical sympathy in his response to the 'Mantuanesque' eclogues. Helen Cooper recovered the medieval, Latin and vernacular, literary context of Renaissance pastoral: *The Shepherds' Calendar* is seen 'as the high point of [these] two medieval traditions illuminated and transformed by Renaissance humanism' (*Pastoral: Medieval into Renaissance*, 1977). Within Cooper's more detailed picture of pastoral, Cullen's two-fold division becomes unproductive. Cooper also shows how the medieval, Christian tradition of figural shepherds (which Cullen registers as 'Mantuanesque'), when added to the Latin tradition of allegorical shepherds, greatly extends the capabilities of the pastoral mode. Far from being simplistic, such a figural aspect allows the pastoral of *The Shepherds' Calendar* greater access to the imaginative richness of symbolism; Spenser's pastoral ranged from the day to day, to the general, and on to the ineffable and divine.

Three hundred and sixty-five years after the publication of *Amoretti and Epithalamion*, A. Kent Hieatt argued that the poem was structured numerologically (*Short Time's Endless Monument*, 1960). *Epithalamion*'s 365 long lines represented the number of days in the year, its 23 stanzas and one tornata the hours in a day. The short lines measured the division of time within the stanza-hours; thus night fell in the poem after $16\frac{1}{4}$ hours, just as contemporary almanacs predicted for 11 June 1594 (Spenser's wedding day). The 23 stanzas contained 359 long lines, representing the 359 degrees travelled daily by the sun. There were 68 short lines as there are 4 seasons, 12 months and 52 weeks.

Hieatt's argument, still the most persuasive, led to other numerological analyses. Alexander Dunlop outlined a three-part structure within *Amoretti*, whose central section was formed by sonnets 22 to 69, which mark (and date) the passing of the days from Ash Wednesday to Easter Day in 1594 ('The unity of Spenser's *Amoretti*', 1970). What both Hieatt's and Dunlop's analysis showed was that Spenser had sited *Amoretti and Epithalamion* within both linear and cyclical times. The numerological structures of the poems place mortal human love alongside and within the timeless cycle of the endlessly repeated story of God's love for man. In this way, *Amoretti and Epithalamion* is a literary realization of the Christian understanding of the meaning of marriage. In this, Spenser was now seen to be quite un-Petrarchan; for Spenser's love, unlike Petrarch's, is consummated and yet still remains 'holy', in part divine. Spenser was radically reshaping literary tradition.

More recently, this sense of Spenser's difference has led to studies which insist on the complexities of tone and the dark tensions within *Amoretti and Epithalamion*. *Prothalamion*, a poem still to receive sustained critical attention, has been seen to be similarly anxious; though in its case this has led to discussions particularly of what kind of poem it may be, whether celebratory betrothal song or disaffected complaint. However, such moments of qualification or unease may well strengthen the overall celebratory nature of these poems; as with mature Shakespearean comedy, it is the recognition of '*et in Arcadia ego*' – one never escapes time and death – that convinces the reader that the joy and hope on offer are neither facile nor futile.

Discussion of Spenser's language, meanwhile, had continued at a low intensity. A rather different picture was emerging: in place of a Spenser creating an archaic poetic diction from nothing, his archaism (itself difficult to distinguish from dialect forms) was now seen to have perpetuated an already traditional poetic vocabulary. Often this was still seen as funtioning to suggest the rough simplicity of the shepherds in *The Shepherds' Calendar*. Martha Craig, however, placed Spenser's archaisms within a Cratylian view of language. In Plato's *Cratylus*, language was argued to be originally non-arbitrary; words (and so the etymology of words) revealed the nature of things. The primary purpose of Spenser's archaism, Craig argued, was to act 'as a sort of solvent of language', dissolving the reader's conventional expectations and drawing attention to the particular forms of the words ('The Secret Wit of Spenser's Language', 1967). This done, Spenser was free to use, or invent, the forms of words that were most revelatory of things or, in the case of rhyme for instance, of the connection between things. Spenser's archaism was not only 'a fancy language for a fanciful world', but also, 'a more fully significant language for a more fully significant world'. Craig was describing *The Faerie Queene*, but her argument is also productive when applied to the 'more fully significant world' of *The Shepherds' Calendar*.

Learning how to read that significance, and so how to read Spenser, can be seen as the chief, general goal of the criticism up to this time.

As the 1970s moved into the 1980s, the interest in pastoral shifted direction, becoming predominantly concerned with pastoral's relation to the structures of power. Representative of this shift, and some of the post-structuralist and post-modernist assumptions that underlay it, were a series of essays by Louis Montrose. Empson, in looking at the function of pastoral, had seen it working to mystify the workings of the social order by dissolving and transcending the distance between rich and poor; pastoral presented the simple poor as the noble and learned articulators of authentic values, and so worked to suggest that they had no need to envy the rich's wealth or status. Montrose, noting that pastoral was a particularly Elizabethan phenomenon, argued for a more complex and historically precise model of the ways in which it served to justify the Elizabethan monarchy. Tracing the interrelations between pastoral and the 'cults' of Elizabeth[5] (see the 'Glossary of Names'), he saw in *The Shepherds' Calendar* a developing recognition of the powerlessness of the poet ('"The perfecte paterne of a poete"', 1979). However much the poet might, Orpheus-like, claim to create Elizabeth as Eliza, Rosalind, or

Dido, the poet was eventually dependent on the actual personage for his social position; his pastoral could not but be 'a pastoral of power' – a relentlessly celebratory justification of the dominant power in his society. Pastoral became one more example of the Elizabethan state's (and power's) success at suppressing private opinion and thought.

In some ways, Montrose's (New Historicist) analysis was based on a historical picture that has since been shown to be inadequate. The Elizabethan state was often remarkably tolerant of social and religious diversity, and its power far from absolute. Montrose himself begins to recognize this in later essays, but this readjustment is taken further by John Bernard (*Ceremonies of Innocence*, 1989). Bernard, recovering the classical philosophical arguments that lie within the concepts of *otium* ('ease') and the *vita contemplativa* ('the contemplative life') – both seen in the shepherd's life – argues that pastoral has traditionally been a place in which the poet asserts and contructs his own moral authority in contradistinction to his society's. Far from being sycophantic to and constitutive of power, pastoral is innately and successfully oppositional.

Bernard, in keeping with recent work, proposes a two-stage development in Spenser's use of pastoral. The optimistic pastoral of *The Shepherds' Calendar* is closest to Montrose's 'pastoral of power', though even here the poet is seen as an agent, not an instrument. Spenser's pastoral gradually evolves to a 'pastoral of contemplation', seen fully in *Amoretti*, 'whose sources transcend the community altogether'. *Colin Clout's Come Home Again* is of particular importance as a bridge between the two kinds of Spenserian pastoral.

Colin Clout's Come Home Again had, in fact, emerged as a central text in the late 1970s, as a consideration of pastoral's and Spenser's relationship to the Elizabethan structures of power led to an examination of the colonial aspects of Spenser's poetry. For Spenser spent most of his adult life in Ireland, a land over which the English government was striving to establish its rule. Spenser's poetry, and particularly *The Faerie Queene*, may at times be read not so much as nationalistic celebration of that government but as colonial polemic justifying and encouraging that government. Yet, at the same time, Spenser was himself 'in exile' in Ireland, separated from the Court and Queen whose representation so preoccupied him.

Colin Clout's Come Home Again was particularly interesting in this context because of its direct yet ambivalent representation of the poet's distance from, journey to, and relationship with that Court and its Queen. Where was the home of the poem's title? In Ireland or

England? Richard McCabe, in an article tracing the extent to which Spenser is the product of an Irish environment, teases out these complexities concisely. He is also one of the few critics to develop Snell's analysis. He notes how Spenser exploits his creation of a persona, Colin, that both is and is not himself, and which already has an independent life in the public's consciousness. Spenser uses this 'I'/'him' quality of Colin 'to explore,' McCabe argues, 'increasingly problematic aspects of the relationship between fiction and reality, aesthetic ideals and practical necessities' ('Edmund Spenser', 1991). The particularity of this peculiarly political and Spenserian shadowland of 'waking dream' McCabe sums up in the suggestion that the poem, 'is more powerfully autobiographical in its "fiction" than its "fact"'.

Running parallel to the interest in pastoral's relationship to the structures of power, was an interest in the nature and construction of the role of poet, in the form of Spenser's self-fashioning. *The Shepherds' Calendar* was again the key text. Richard Helgerson analysed the way in which Spenser attempted to distinguish himself as a 'great poet' or laureate by attempting to maintain an 'ethically normative and unchanging self' in relation to the frivolity of the mass of amateur poets. This he did by becoming Immerito or Colin and so abandoning 'all social identity' except that of his socially beneficent vocation (*Self-Crowned Laureates*, 1983). For Helgerson, *The Shepherds' Calendar* is a laureate programme, putting itself forward through a critique of conventional, fruitless love poetry. Yet, even as Spenser puts himself forward as an 'eternal' laureate, by using a critique of contemporary poetry, he displays how historically specific his own construction of laureateship is. This produces an omnipresent tension within his poetry.

Richard Rambuss challenges the basically Virgilian pattern that underlies Helgerson's analysis by pointing out that Spenser had two careers; one as poet, and the other as successful secretary and bureaucrat. Rambuss looks at the way in which this other career informs and shapes Spenser's poetic career; pointing to 'the flagrance of its secrecy', he shows both how important the management of secrets and secrecy is to *The Shepherds' Calendar*, and how that poem is in part an advert for Spenser's qualities as a secretary (*Spenser's Secret Career*, 1993). Like Bernard, Rambuss traces a twofold division in Spenser's work; he sees *Complaints* as marking a turn away from poetry shaped by the keeping of secrets to a poetry and poetics which attempts to disclose secrets, joining this movement to Spenser's sense of disappointment with the Elizabethan Court.

The politics of pastoral and the nature of self-fashioning have, then, formed the dominant interests of the last decade and a half, and look to be continuing to do so, though with an increasing emphasis on the agency of the author and the personal and fragmented nature of power within the period. However, studies in other areas, themselves usually drawing on previous critical debates, have appeared. Anthea Hume has reopened the question of Spenser's Puritanism. Arguing against the notion, dominant from the middle of this century, of Spenser as a conservative Anglican, Hume portrays Spenser as a militant Protestant, whose anti-Catholic fervour in *The Shepherds' Calendar* qualifies him to be called a Puritan. Far from showing a balance or plurality of values, the eclogues are ordered to allow arguments couched in the idiom of Puritan propaganda to emerge as the imaginatively persuasive ones (*Edmund Spenser*, 1984).

Book-length studies of particular poems have also appeared. Perhaps the two that most deserve mention, and which, of course, show the influence of the contemporary criticism described above, are William C. Johnson's on *Amoretti* (*Spenser's Amoretti*, 1990) and Lynn Staley Johnson's on *The Shepherds' Calendar* (*The Shepherds' Calendar*, 1990). These are probably the best place to begin in studying those poems.

References

1. No full-scale survey of Spenser's critical reputation, let alone the critical reputation of his shorter poems, has yet been adequately undertaken; what follows must remain more an interpretative than a descriptive history.

2. This and other unlocated quotations are taken from Cummings (1971).

3. In terms of a school of Spenser (to put beside those of Ben Jonson and John Donne), Joan Grundy talks of two groups of Spenserians, both marked by a deep conservatism seen in their conscious and aggressive nostalgia. One group was based in London: Michael Drayton (1563–1631), William Browne (1591–1643), and George Wither

(1588–1667); and the other in Cambridge, constituted around Giles (1586–1623) and Phineas Fletcher (1582–1660). William Drummond (1585–1649), a Scot, may be added to this list and, as second-generation Cambridge pupils, Edward Benlowes (?1603–76) and Francis Quarles (1592–1644).

After 1660, Spenser's presence is usually traced in terms either of imitation or of creative engagement with his work, which engagement is usually referred to as 'influence'. Tradition, as Hughes and most others use the term, is in part a record of influence. The following is a highly selective and personal sample of poems which make up that record with reference to Spenser's shorter poems: John Milton's 'On the Morning of Christ's Nativity' (1645), A Masque Presented at Ludlow Castle, 1634 [Comus]; Andrew Marvell, 'The Garden' (1681); John Dryden, Fables Ancient and Modern (1700); Alexander Pope, 'Pastorals' (1709), The Dunciad (1745); John Gay, The Shepherd's Week (1714); George Crabbe, The Village (1783); Samuel Taylor Coleridge, 'The Rime of the Ancient Mariner' (1798); William Wordsworth, 'The World is too much with us' (1807); John Clare, The Shepherd's Calendar (1827); Percy Bysshe Shelley, The Witch of Atlas (1824); Alfred Tennyson, Maud: A Monodrama (1855); W. B. Yeats, 'The Song of the Happy Shepherd' (1889); T. S. Eliot, The Waste Land (1922).

There are about 250 known imitations and adaptations between 1660 and 1800. Most of these come after Matthew Prior's 1706 'Ode', which began a Spenserian vogue; this reached its height around the middle of the century, and probably explains to a degree Johnson's disgust at pastoral (see p. 254).

4. In 1805 Henry John Todd's eight-volume variorum edition of Spenser's works had established Spenser as a 'classic' author. It was the first edition since 1679 to print EK's introduction and notes to SC.

5. See 'Elizabeth' in the 'Glossary of Names'.

SUGGESTIONS FOR FURTHER READING

Reference Works

Brooks-Davies, Douglas ed., *Edmund Spenser: Selected Shorter Poems* (Harlow: Longmans, 1995) – very full notes and bibliographies.

Burrow, Colin, *Edmund Spenser* (Plymouth: Northcote House, 1996) – concise introduction.

Carpenter, Frederic Ives, *A Reference Guide to Edmund Spenser* (New York: Peter Smith, 1950; first pubd 1923) – for the nineteenth century.

Cory, Herbert E., *The Critics of Edmund Spenser* (New York: Haskell House, 1964; first pubd 1911) – out-of-date critical analysis, but useful guidance.

Cummings, R. M., ed., *Spenser: The Critical Heritage* (London: Routledge & Kegan Paul, 1971) – up to 1715.

Greenlaw, Edwin, *et al.*, eds, *The Works of Edmund Spenser: A Variorum Edition*, 10 vols (Baltimore: Johns Hopkins Press, 1943).

Hamilton, A. C., *et al.*, eds, *The Spenser Encyclopedia* (Toronto: University of London Press, 1990) – look here first.

Judson, Alexander, *The Life of Edmund Spenser* (Baltimore: Johns Hopkins Press, 1945) – the standard work.

Maley, Willy, *A Spenser Chronology* (Basingstoke: Macmillan, 1994).

McNeir, Waldo F. and Foster Provost, eds, *Edmund Spenser: An Annotated Bibliography, 1937–72* (New Jersey: Humanities Press, 1975).

Osgood, Charles Grovenor, *Concordance to the Poems of Edmund Spenser* (Washington: Carnegie Institution, 1915).

Periodicals – the following offer much of interest: *Spenser Studies: A Renaissance Poetry Annual*; *English Literary History*; *English Literary Renaissance*; *Studies in English Literature*.

Sipple, William L. with Bernard J. Vondersmith, *Edmund Spenser, 1900–1936: A Reference Guide* (Boston, Ma.: G. K. Hall, 1984)

Wells, W., *et al.*, 'Spenser Allusions in the Sixteenth and Seventeenth Centuries', *Studies in Philology* 68 (1971) & 69 (1972), 1–172 (1580–1625) & 173–351 (1626–1700) – fuller than Cummings.

Whitman, Charles Huntington, *A Subject Index to the Poems of Edmund Spenser* (New Haven: Yale University Press, 1918).

Criticism

Bernard, John D., *Ceremonies of Innocence: Pastoralism in the Poetry of Edmund Spenser* (Cambridge: Cambridge University Press, 1989).

Cooper, Helen, *Pastoral: Medieval into Renaissance* (Ipswich: D. S. Brewer, 1977).

Craig, Martha, 'The Secret Wit of Spenser's Language', in *Elizabethan Poetry: Modern Essays in Criticism*, ed. by Paul J. Alpers (London: Oxford University Press, 1967), pp. 447–72.

Cullen, Patrick, *Spenser, Marvell, and Renaissance Pastoral* (Cambridge, Ma.: Harvard University Press, 1970).

Dunlop, Alexander, 'The Unity of Spenser's *Amoretti*', in *Silent Poetry: Essays in Numerological Analysis*, ed. by Alastair Fowler (London: Routledge & Kegan Paul, 1970).

Ellrodt, Robert, *Neoplatonism in the Poetry of Spenser* (Geneva: Droz, 1960).

Grundy, Joan, *The Spenserian Poets: A Study in Elizabethan and Jacobean Poetry* (London: Edward Arnold, 1969).

Hamilton, A. C., 'The Argument of Spenser's *Shepheardes Calender*', *English Literary History* 23 (1956), 171–182.

Helgerson, Richard, *Self-Crowned Laureates: Spenser, Jonson, Milton and the Literary System* (Berkeley: University of California Press, 1983).

Hieatt, A. Kent, *Short Time's Endless Monument: The symbolism of the numbers in Edmund Spenser's 'Epithalamion'* (New York: Columbia University Press, 1960).

Hume, Anthea, *Edmund Spenser: Protestant Poet* (Cambridge: Cambridge University Press, 1960).

Johnson, Lynn Staley, *The Shepheardes Calender: An Introduction* (University Park: Pennsylvania State University Press, 1990).

Johnson, William C., *Spenser's Amoretti: Analogies of Love* (Lewisburg: Bucknell University Press, 1990).

Loades, D. M., *The Tudor Court* (London: Batsford, 1986).

McCabe, Richard A., 'Edmund Spenser, Poet of Exile', *Proceedings of the British Academy* 80 (1991; pubd 1993), 73–103.

McLane, Paul E., *Spenser's Shepheardes Calender: A Study in Elizabethan Allegory* (Notre Dame: University of Notre Dame Press, 1961).

Montrose, Louis Adrian, '"The perfecte paterne of a Poete": The Poetics of Courtship in *The Shepheardes Calender*', *Texas Studies in Literature and Language* 21 (1979), 34–67.

—— '"Eliza, Queene of shepheardes," and the Pastoral of Power', *English Literary Renaissance* 10 (1980), 153–82.

—— 'Of Gentlemen and Shepherds: The Politics of Elizabethan Pastoral Form', *English Literary History* 50 (1983), 415–59.

Nelson, William, *The Poetry of Edmund Spenser: A Study* (New York: Columbia University Press, 1963).

Rambuss, Richard, *Spenser's Secret Career* (Cambridge: Cambridge University Press, 1993).

Renwick, W. L., *Edmund Spenser: An Essay on Renaissance Poetry* (London: Edward Arnold, 1925).

Strong, Roy, *The Cult of Elizabeth: Elizabethan Portraiture and Pageantry* (London: Thames and Hudson, 1977).

Welch, Robert, *The Kilcolman Notebook* (Co. Kenny: Brandon, 1994) – a very fictitious and bizarre (New Historicist) account of Spenser's trip to London with Ralegh.

Other Criticism Referred to in 'Notes'

Cheney, Donald, 'Spenser's Fortieth Birthday and Related Fictions', *Spenser Studies* 4 (1983), 3–31.

Fowler, Alastair, *Triumphal Forms: Structural Patterns in Elizabethan Poetry* (London: Cambridge University Press, 1970).

Fukuda, Shohachi, 'The Numerological Patterning of *Amoretti and Epithalamion*', *Spenser Studies* 9 (1989), 33–48.

Hilliard, Nicholas, *A Treatise Concerning the Arte of Limning*, ed. by R. K. R. Thornton and T. G. S. Cain (Northumberland: Mid Northumberland Arts Group, 1981; unpubd previously, wr. 1589–1603).

Hutton, Ronald, *The Rise and Fall of Merry England: The Ritual Year 1400–1700* (Oxford: Oxford University Press, 1994).

Kerrigan, John, ed., *William Shakespeare: The Sonnets and A Lover's Complaint* (Harmondsworth: Penguin, 1986).

Mason, Tom, 'Abraham Cowley and the Wisdom of Anacreon', *The Cambridge Quarterly* 19 (1990), 103–37.

McCoy, Richard C., 'Lord of Liberty: Francis Davison and the cult of Elizabeth', in *The Reign of Elizabeth I: Court and Culture in the Last*

Decade, ed. by John Guy (Cambridge: Cambridge University Press, 1995), pp.212–28.

Prescott, A. L., 'Thirsty Deer and the Lord of Life: Some Contexts for *Amoretti* 67–70', *Spenser Studies* 6 (1986), 33–76.